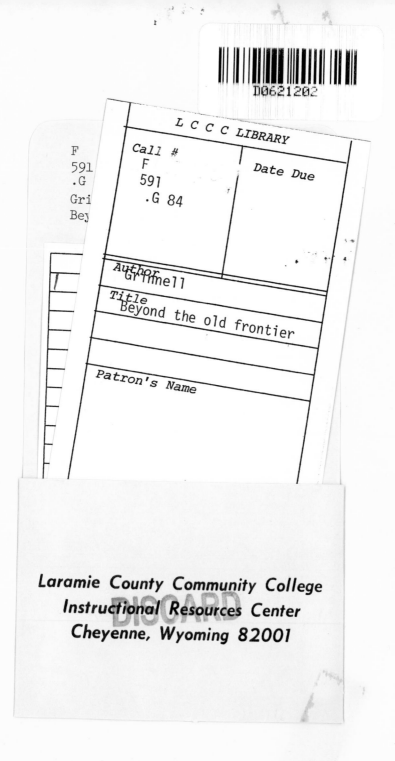

Corner House Publishers

SOCIAL SCIENCE REPRINTS

General Editor MAURICE FILLER

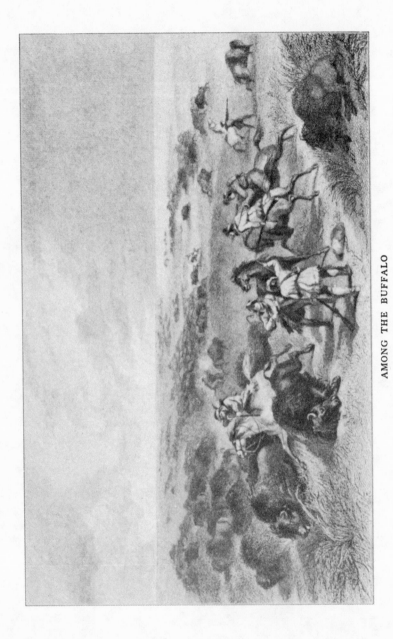

AMONG THE BUFFALO

BEYOND
THE OLD FRONTIER

ADVENTURES OF
INDIAN–FIGHTERS, HUNTERS, AND
FUR–TRADERS

BY

GEORGE BIRD GRINNELL

AUTHOR OF

"TRAILS OF THE PATHFINDERS," " BLACKFEET INDIAN STORIES," ETC.

ILLUSTRATED

CORNER HOUSE PUBLISHERS

WILLIAMSTOWN, MASSACHUSETTS 01267

1976

PREFACE

To-day the vast territory lying between the Mississippi River and the Pacific Ocean is occupied by many millions of people. Fifty years ago, except on the Pacific slope, it had few white inhabitants. Then it was the Far West, beyond the frontier, the Indian country—the unknown. A journey into it was believed to be full of peril. In the minds of the general public it was as far away as Central China is to-day.

Beyond the great river which bounded it on the east was a fringe of settlements. Scattered through the more distant country were the trading-posts to which the trapper brought his furs. Forts Garry, Benton, Union, Laramie, Bridger, and Bent were some of these. There were a few army posts, and as time went on others were established.

Gold had been discovered in California, and a wild rush of people anxious to better their condition had started across the plains, bound for the distant Eldorado. It was a curiously mixed population that set out on this long journey. Farmers from New England, business men and clerks from the Middle States, planters and younger sons from the South; on foot and on horseback, carrying their possessions, large or scanty, in vehicles drawn by horses, mules, oxen, and cows, they struggled westward. They endured enormous toils; perpetually in fear of attacks by Indians, meeting the dangers, delays, and perplexities of wild men, strange surroundings, rough travelling, swollen streams, and exhausted live-stock.

For many years the roads over which they had passed were marked by the skeletons of animals, by broken-down wagons, by furniture and household goods, thrown away to lighten the loads dragged by their feeble teams. Along these deep-worn roads were the graves of those who had perished on the way; sometimes mere mounds of earth, hardly showing on the level prairie, or perhaps marked by a bit of board thrust in the ground, bearing a pencilled name and date, which the winter's storms would soon obliterate.

Gold was discovered in the Rocky Mountains. The village of Denver was established, and along the mountain streams the prospector worked with pick and shovel and pan, and wore away his strength and his courage in hunting for the gold that often he did not find. Montana also began to yield gold, and Salmon River and Alder Gulch were at the beginnings of their fame. Steam-boat traffic on the upper Missouri River, at first established for the transportation of furs, gave easy access to the Montana mines. Stages were running across the continent, and the pony express had been established.

Between 1853 and 1863 the plains and mountains of the West began to receive a sedentary population and to prepare for that startling development which began about a generation later.

To most people who now inhabit the Western country the struggles of those early years are still unknown. Industrious, energetic, fertile in resources, they live their lives without a thought of the distant past, without considering the con-

ditions which made possible existence as it is to-day. They
are sturdy Americans absorbed in the diverse problems which
they have to meet, and, with astonishing success, devoting
themselves to the solution of those problems. This is as it
should be, yet it is worth while from time to time to take a
look backward, and to consider what those endured who went
before us. To most of us our own life is almost the only
struggle worth considering, and wrapped up in our personal
affairs, we do not remember the stupendous difficulties faced
by our forebears, who conquered this country and made possible its development, and the ease and luxury in which we
to-day have a part.

Not many years ago a change began to take place in
the view-point of many Americans. Far-sighted men and
women came to feel that the history made by their fathers
and mothers was worth preserving, and they began to write
and talk about this. What they said fell on sympathetic
ears, and interest was easily aroused, so that before long in
many of the Western States historical societies were established, and earnest men gave time and effort to the work of
inducing the early settlers to set down their recollections—
to describe the events in which they had taken part. Later
came the marking of historic spots and trails by monuments.

To-day the historical societies of many Western States
issue each year a volume filled with material of great interest
—matter that will be of enormous value to the historian who
shall set down the story of the development of the West.

Since the accounts which appear in the following pages
have to do with a country then unknown, the explorers who
penetrated it faced new conditions and met new and primitive peoples. To subsist in these unknown lands they were

forced to hunt its animals, and the purpose which led them so far afield was the trading for furs. The book thus deals with a number of cognate subjects, with exploration, hunting, the taking of fur, and Indians in peace and war; and in any or all of these there is excitement and interest enough.

Let us look back at some of the happenings in this forgotten West, which is now again being remembered.

CONTENTS

ILLUSTRATIONS

xi

AN EARLY FUR TRADER

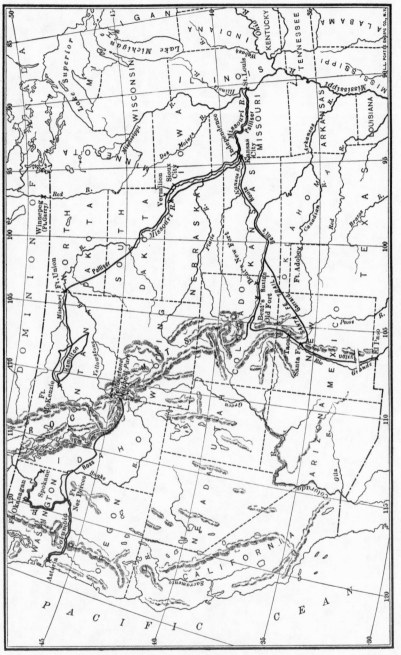

THE FRONTIER COUNTRY

AN EARLY FUR TRADER

ONE hundred years ago little more was known of the Pacific coast than that the land ended at the edge of the wide ocean, already furrowed by the keels of explorers, whalers, and traders.

On the north, Alexander McKenzie had reached the salt water, and a dozen years later Lewis and Clark had come to the mouth of the Columbia. A few years after that came the Astor settlement at Astoria, soon —in 1813—to be handed over to the British, to the Northwest Company, which remained in control there until its consolidation with the Hudson Bay Company in 1821.

One of the first commercial adventurers to the Columbia River, and one of the first men engaged by John Jacob Astor for his far western fur-trading expeditions, was Alexander Ross, a Scotchman, who came to Canada in early life, spent more than forty-four years in the fur trade, and finally died in the Red River settlement in 1856. Unlike most fur traders, he had the energy and the interest, in the later years of his life, to set down an account of what he had seen and done during those early years of anxiety, hard work, and success. His story "is not an arm-chair narrative derived from hearsay tales, but the result of practical experience on the spot." During most of the time while engaged in trading with the savage tribes west of the Rocky Mountains he was a leader; and the success or failure of his expeditions—often the lives of his men and himself—depended on what he thought, did, and said. He was a man of high courage, unfailing energy, and close observation. His was serious work, yet he possessed some sense of humor, which, however, he allows to appear only now and then in his books. As a close observer stationed in the midst of things and admirably acquainted with conditions, he saw the blunders made by Mr. Astor and criticised them freely; yet he was always loyal to his chief, and speaks with apparent contempt of those other men of the north, hired by Mr. Astor for their great experience in the fur trade, who, when the War of 1812 broke out and the Northwesters descended on Astoria, seemed glad to desert their employer and to renew their allegiance to the company that they had left for Astor's higher pay and greater privileges.

Ross wrote three books which are extraordinarily full of information, and most useful as accurate descriptions of early conditions in the country which is now the Northwestern United States. These are *Adventures on the Oregon or Columbia River*, *Fur Hunters of the Far West*, and, finally, an account of *The Red River Settlement*. These three books give us in more or less connected form a history of the Columbia River and the region about Old Fort Garry—now Winnipeg—a history far better than anything that has ever been set down.

The first book deals chiefly with the history of Mr. Astor's enterprise from its beginning in 1809 until the taking over of the trading-post by the Northwest Company, the change of name to Fort George, the sale of the property of the Astor Company, and the departure on April 3, 1814, of Mr. Hunt, Astor's representative, and the few men that went with him. After this, the Pacific Fur Company now being at an end, Ross, Cox, and McLellan entered the service of the Northwest Company.

The American Fur Company, established by Mr. Astor, began operations in 1809. One after another, other fur-trading companies were absorbed, until Astor saw himself at the head of all the fur trade south of Canada, with the possible hope of reaching out for the trade of the northern country east of the Rocky Mountains. West of that range was a vast field as yet almost untouched. True, the Russians had trading-posts in what was then Russian America, and sent the furs gathered there direct to China. True, also, that some American coasting vessels on the Pacific secured a few furs which they took to China, but this hardly touched the possibilities of half a continent. Astor clearly saw that, if systematized and carefully managed, this desultory traffic would be enormously profitable, and this led him to organize the Pacific Fur Company, the chief station of which was to be at the mouth of the Columbia River. That station might be connected with others on the Atlantic water-shed by a chain of trading-posts across the continent, and such a combination, he believed, would control the whole American fur trade. Furs could be shipped in either direction—down the Missouri, eastward; or to the west, down the Oregon, to go to China.

Understanding the wide experience of the northern fur traders, and with a view also to lessening the friction which might exist between the British and the American governments along the border, Astor engaged as field-workers for this far western service a number of the retired partners of the Northwest Company. Such men as McKay, McKenzie, McDougall, and Stuart were glad to become interested with him in the enterprise. Astor furnished the capital, amounting to two hundred thousand dollars; there were ten partners. The agreement was for a period of twenty years, with the proviso that if the project proved impractical or unprofitable after five years it might be dissolved. For these first five years, however, Astor was to bear all the expenses and losses, the other partners furnishing only their time and labor. The nine partners outside of Mr. Astor and Mr. Hunt each held four shares of the stock of two thousand dollars each, while Astor held fifty, and Hunt, as his representative and chief manager, five. The remaining shares were reserved for such clerks as might join the concern as adventurers, without other remuneration than their chances of success at the end of five years' trial. As was natural, Astor controlled the enterprise. His manager was Wilson Price Hunt, a man wholly without experience in the Indian trade, but energetic, active, and persevering.

Ross learned of the project from Mr. McKay, who asked him to go to Montreal to talk about the matter. Ross was asked to join the expedition, and was the first one to do so, and with Robert Stuart made so good a bargain that these two were promised their promotion at the end of three years. Soon after the arrangements were completed a party under Mr. Hunt started across the continent overland, while another party headed by McKay sailed, September 10, 1810, for the mouth of the Columbia River.

The sorrows of that voyage have often been described. Captain Thorn, in command of the "Tonquin," appears to have been a man impossible to get along with. They went around the Horn, touched at the Sandwich Islands, and at last reached the mouth of the Columbia River. There had been continual quarrels between the captain, his passengers, and the officers of the ship.

At last, however, the "Tonquin" was off the mouth of the Columbia River, a rough and stormy spot, of many sand-bars and high surf, and the weather was worse in spring than at any other time of the year. It was now March or April. Here there was constant mismanagement; boats were sent out to reconnoitre, and people were lost; the ship two or three times struck the bottom, became unmanageable, and was finally carried by the tide into Baker's Bay. There, sheltered from the sea, it was safe.

The fur traders got ashore and began to look for the missing boats and men. During this journey Ross learned something about the Indians' management of their canoes.

"We had on this occasion a specimen of Chinooke navigation. While crossing the river in an Indian canoe, on our way back to the ship, we were suddenly overtaken by a storm, and our craft was upset in the middle of the passage. The expertness of the natives in their favorite element was here put to the test. At this time we were upwards of two miles from the shore, while eight persons unable to swim were floating in every direction; coats, hats, and everything else adrift, and all depending on the fidelity of the four Indians who undertook to carry us over; yet, notwithstanding the roughness of the water, and the wind blowing a gale at the time, these poor fellows kept swimming about like so many fishes, righted the canoe, and got us all into her again, while they themselves staid in the water, with one hand on the canoe and the other paddling. In this manner they supported themselves, tossing to and fro, till we bailed the water out of our frail craft, and got under way again. Here it was that the Indians showed the skill and dexterity peculiar to them. The instant the canoe rose on the top of a wave, those on the windward side darted down their long paddles to the armpits in the water to prevent her from upsetting; while those on the leeside at the same moment pulled theirs up, but kept ready as soon as the wave had passed under her to thrust them down again in a similar manner, and thus by their alternate movements they kept the canoe steady, so that we got safe to shore without another upset, and with the loss of only a few articles of clothing; but we suffered severely from wet and cold.

"During this time the Indians from the village which we had left, seeing our critical situation, had manned and sent off two canoes to our assistance. One of the boats from the ship was also despatched for the same purpose; but all would have proved too late had we not been fortunate enough of ourselves to weather the storm."

A few days after this the long boat was swamped off Chinook Point, and ten persons were saved by these Chinooks.

The fur traders and their property being at last ashore, they began to look about for a place where their fort should be built. The site selected was a knoll about twelve miles from the mouth of the inlet, and between Point George on the west and Tonquin Point on the east. They went about their work with dogged energy, but not cheerfully. They were glad to be on shore and free from the tyranny of Captain Thorn, but saddened by the misfortunes they had met with—the loss of the men in landing.

Duncan McDougall, an old Northwester, was in command. He was a man of great experience, but Ross calls him a man of only ordinary capacity and unfit to command men. He became famous some years later by having the credit of conniving with the Northwest Company to swindle Mr. Astor out of most of his property at Astoria.

The little company that settled down in a new country amid wholly unaccustomed surroundings had before it a difficult—almost an impossible—task.

"The place thus selected for the emporium of the west, might challenge the whole continent to produce a spot of equal extent presenting more difficulties to the settler: studded with gigantic trees of almost incredible size, many of them measuring fifty feet in girth, and so close together, and intermingled with huge rocks, as to make it a work of no ordinary labour to level and clear the ground. With this task before us, every man, from the highest to the lowest, was armed with an axe in one hand and a gun in the other; the former for attacking the woods, the latter for defence against the savage hordes which were constantly prowling about. In the garb of labourers, and in the sweat of our brow, we now commenced earning our bread. In this manner we all kept toiling and tearing away, from sunrise till sunset—from Monday till Saturday; and during the nights we kept watch without intermission. . . .

"Many of the party had never handled an axe before, and but few of them knew how to use a gun, but necessity, the mother of invention, soon taught us both. After placing our guns in some secure place at hand, and viewing the height and the breadth of the tree to be cut down, the party, with some labour, would erect a scaffold round it; this done, four men—for that was the number appointed to each of those huge trees— would then mount the scaffold, and commence cutting, at the height of eight or ten feet from the ground, the handles of our axes varying, according to circumstances, from two and a half to five feet in length. At every other stroke, a look was cast round, to see that all was safe; but the least rustling among the bushes caused a general stop; more or less time was thus lost in anxious suspense. After listening and looking round, the party resumed their labour, cutting and looking about alternately. In this manner the day would be spent, and often to little purpose: as night often set in before the tree begun with in the morning was half cut down. Indeed, it sometimes required two days, or more, to fell one tree; but when nearly cut through, it would be viewed fifty different times, and from as many different positions, to ascertain where it was likely to fall, and to warn parties of the danger."

The labor that they had undertaken was hard and unceasing, the climate one of constant rains and fogs, the food was merely fish and wild roots; the Indians were so troublesome that in two months three of their men had been killed by them, others wounded by the fall of trees, and one had his hand blown off by gunpowder. All this produced discontent—four men deserted and were captured by the Indians, and a little later six more deserted, but were brought back by a friendly Indian.

Food and shelter were scanty and poor in quality. Heretofore all remonstrances to the man in command had received no attention, but at last even he realized the situation and distributed tents among the sick, and made some effort to improve the food.

As time passed and the white men began to learn something of the Chinook nature, it was discovered that these people, their immediate neighbors, had been telling the more distant Indians that the white men were enemies, just as they had been telling the white people that these distant tribes were enemies. The result of this was that the Chinooks were purchasing furs from the distant tribes and selling them to the traders at a handsome profit. As soon as this discovery was made, parties were sent out to learn something of these more distant tribes, to gain their confidence and to discover what they could about the country farther óff. These parties, though often in danger, finally succeeded in establishing friendly relations with those other tribes, but for a long time the impression given by the Chinooks did not wear off.

It was in May that they laid the foundation of their first building and named the establishment Astoria, in honor of the projector of the enterprise. The labor

ASTORIA

From an old print published in 1861

of building was extraordinary, for it was impossible for them to use the enormous trees close to the fort, and they were obliged to go back into the interior to find logs small enough for building. These logs were transported on their shoulders, or dragged along over the ground, and this last method was so effective that in six days eight men harnessed as a team brought to the site all the timber required for a building sixty feet long by twenty-six feet broad.

On the first of June the "Tonquin" left Astoria for a trading voyage to the north. She carried with her most of her cargo, only a little having been landed, the captain intending to complete the unloading on his return. A little later the ship was captured by the Indians and with all on board blown up, and the whole crew—among them McKay—were lost, and, of course, the cargo destroyed.

In mid-July the post received a visit from Mr. Thompson, a Northwester, who came down the Columbia in a light canoe with a crew of men, chiefly from Montreal. McDougall received him with great cordiality, somewhat to the astonishment of the former Northwesters, who, now in the service of the Pacific Fur Company, regarded the Northwesters as rivals, and so enemies. Toward the end of July a small expedition, fitted out with the view of establishing a trading-post in the interior, started up the Columbia River in company with the returning Mr. Thompson. Understanding very little about navigation and these new waters, and as little about the management of the Chinook canoe, the first day of their travel was one of constant toil, striving to avoid the dangers of running aground on sand-banks and of being thrown on the shore.   During the next few days they passed Bellevue Point and Point Vancouver, and at the foot of the Cascades they found a great body of Indians waiting for them to talk and to smoke.   The labor of the portage was extreme, and the Indians played all sorts of tricks on the white men, evidently trying to see just how far they would be allowed to go.   Here is an example:

"Not being accustomed myself to carry, I had of course, as well as some others, to stand sentinel; but seeing the rest almost wearied to death, I took hold of a roll of tobacco, and after adjusting it on my shoulder, and holding it fast with one hand, I moved on to ascend the first bank; at the top of which, however, I stood breathless, and could proceed no farther.   In this awkward plight, I met an Indian, and made signs to him to convey the tobacco across, and that I would give him all the buttons on my coat; but he shook his head and refused.   Thinking the fellow did not understand me, I threw the tobacco down, and pointing to the buttons one by one, at last he consented, and off he set at a full trot, and I after him; but just as we had reached his camp at the other end, he pitched it down a precipice of two hundred feet in height, and left me to recover it the best way I could.   Off I started after my tobacco; and if I was out of breath after getting up the first bank, I was ten times more so now. During my scrambling among the rocks to recover my tobacco, not only the wag that played me the trick, but fifty others, indulged in a hearty laugh at my expense; but the best of it was, the fellow came for his payment, and wished to get not only the buttons but the coat along with them. I was for giving him—what he richly deserved—buttons of another mould; but peace in our present situation was deemed the better policy: so the rogue got the buttons, and we saw him no more."

At the end of the month Thompson left them to hurry on eastward, and in the first days of August they reached a point on the river where they met horse Indians in considerable numbers. With these people they arranged to have the goods carried over the portage, and the Indians accepted the offer, and were so swift to do it that "in less than ten minutes after the whole cavalcade, goods and all, disappeared, leaving us standing in suspense and amazement." However, at the other end of the portage the property was found safe and the chiefs were guarding it. Nevertheless, that night was passed by the traders in some alarm, but the danger, whatever it was, was put off when they persuaded the chiefs of the Indians to come and sit within their circle, and to harangue to their people during the night.

This portage was nine miles long, and, although their goods had been transported, the canoes and the canoe tackle, boats, and cooking utensils remained to be carried over. Four times daily they had to make this journey, heavily loaded, under a burning sun.

The main camp of the Indians here was fully occupied only during the salmon season, at which time it held about three thousand people, but the constant inhabitants did not exceed one hundred persons, whom Ross called Wy-am-pams, a tribe of Shahaptin stock. These horse Indians were without doubt Nez-Percés or their representatives.

The traders had no choice of roads in getting into the country; and in following up the Columbia River they followed the course of the salmon, on which the Indians depended for food, and came to camp after camp of people, many of whom had never before seen white men. By August 8 they had trouble. The canoes, sailing with a fair wind, were overtaken by a squall, and everything was wet. Very incautiously they commenced to spread out these wet things to dry them, and were at once surrounded by covetous Indians. They lost no time in bundling their stuff together and putting it into the canoes, and, "in order to amuse for a moment, and to attract the attention of the crowd, I laid hold of an axe, and set it up at the distance of eighty yards, then taking up my rifle, drove a ball through it." This manœuvre was successful, and while the Indians were staring at the marvel the canoes got off. Near the mouth of the Walla Walla the traders discovered a large body of men coming toward them, all armed and painted and preceded by three chiefs, who made elaborate speeches and smoked with them. These were various tribes of Shahaptin stock, fine people, well dressed and possessed of many horses, four thousand being within sight of the camp. They were extremely friendly, and their chief, now and at later times, was helpful to the traders.

The next day they came to the point where the two main forks of the Columbia join—Clark's Fork on the north and Lewis Fork on the south—and there in the midst of the Indian camp stood a British flag, planted by Mr. Thompson, who had laid claim to the country north of the forks as British territory. He had left with the Indians a paper forbidding the subjects of other countries to trade north of this point, and the Indians seemed disposed to uphold this order. The Astorians wished to go up Clark's Fork, and in the afternoon the chiefs held a council, at which Ross and Stuart were present, and consent to go forward was gained. The people were friendly, and Tummatapam, the chief before alluded to, was a kindly man and seemed really to like the fur traders, who treated him very well.

Journeying up the North Fork, they were overtaken after a time by three mounted Walla Walla Indians, who gave them a bag of shot which they had left behind at their encampment of the night before; but on this day they saw only a few Indians and set no guard at night. The next day they were early afloat.

"On the 17th, we were paddling along at daylight. On putting on shore to breakfast, four Indians on horseback joined us. The moment they alighted, one set about hobbling their horses, another to gather small sticks, a third to make a fire, and the fourth to catch fish. For this purpose, the fisherman cut off a bit of his leathern shirt, about the size of a small bean; then pulling out two or three hairs from his horse's tail for a line, tied the bit of leather to one end of it, in place of a hook or fly. Thus prepared, he entered the river a little way, sat down on a stone and began throwing the small fish, three or four inches long, on shore, just as fast as he pleased; and while he was thus employed, another picked them up and threw them towards the fire while the third stuck them up round it in a circle, on small sticks; and they were no sooner up than roasted. The fellows then sitting down, swallowed them—heads, tails, bones, guts, fins, and all, in no time, just as one would swallow the yolk of an egg. Now all this was but the work of a few minutes; and before our man had his kettle ready for the fire, the Indians were already eating their breakfast. When the fish had hold of the bit of wet leather, or bait, their teeth got entangled in it, so as to give time to jerk them on shore, which was to us a new mode of angling; fire produced by the friction of two bits of wood was also a novelty; but what surprised us most of all, was the regularity with which they proceeded, and the quickness of the whole process, which actually took them less time to perform, than it has taken me to note it down."

A little later in the day came a pathetic example of the simplicity of the Indians and their extraordinary belief in the powers of the strange white people, when their parents brought to the fur-traders two dead children and asked that they restore them to life, for which favor a horse was to be given. At Priest Rapids the travellers were met by a large throng of Indians who were perfectly friendly, smoked with them, and performed the usual friendly acts of singing and dancing. The journey up the river continued to be strenuous, for the current was swift and the rapids many. Horses were plentiful here and the Indians were eager to sell them, but the traders, travelling by canoe, had no possible use for them and declined to purchase any more. A day or two after passing the Pisscow River, "the ibex, the white musk goat," is mentioned, one of the early references to this species, and speaking of one of its striking characters. Now soon they met with Indians who had in their possession a gun, tobacco, and some other articles which they said had been purchased from white people, no doubt a party of Northwesters. The first of September had come, and it was now time to look out for winter-quarters, if buildings were to be erected which could be occupied during the winter. The situation chosen was near the mouth of the Oakinacken—Okanagan—River at the end of a range of high, rocky, wooded hills. Here a small dwelling-house was begun, but before it was finished four men were sent back to Astoria, and four others set off for the head-waters of the Okanagan,[1] while Ross himself and one small dog called Weasel remained to hold the fort.

We may imagine that his situation was an uncomfortable one, and he fully appreciated its horrors, "alone in this unhallowed wilderness, without friend or white man within hundreds of miles of me, surrounded by savages who had never seen a white man, where every day seemed a week, every night a month. I pined, I languished, my head turned gray, and in a brief space ten years were added to my age. Yet man is born to endure, and my only consolation was in my Bible."

As soon as the others were gone Ross began to patch up the house and put the few goods left him into a kind of cellar which he made; then he set to work to learn the language of the Indians, and wrote vocabulary after vocabulary. The task was hard and wearisome, but his progress was encouraging.

A crowd of inquisitive Indians visited the place to see this lonely white man. Ross associated with them, traded with them, and at last began to talk to them and finally to comprehend their speech, but the evenings were long and the winter dreary. Each night he primed his gun and pistol and barricaded his door, and the kindly Indians always left the house at dusk. On the other hand, the Indians themselves feared attacks by enemies, and often gave him to understand that there was danger.

"One night I was suddenly awakened out my sleep

[1] Variously spelled to-day, Okanagan, Okinagan, and Okanogan.

by the unusual noise and continual barking of Weasel, running backwards and forwards through the house. Half asleep, half awake, I felt greatly agitated and alarmed. My faithful gun and pistol were at hand, for they lay always at my side in bed; but then all was dark, I could see nothing, could hear nothing but the barking of Weasel, which was continually growing louder and louder. I then thought there must be somebody in the house; for I was ready to put the worst construction on appearances. In this perplexing dilemma I got my hand, with as little noise as possible, to the muzzle of my gun, and gradually drawing out the ramrod, tried, with my right arm stretched out, to stir up the embers, so that I might see; but here again a new danger presented itself; I was exposing myself as a mark to a ball or an arrow, without the chance of defending myself, for the light would show me to the enemy before I could see my object; but there was no alternative, and something must be done. Between hope and despair I managed to stir up the ashes, so that I could see little Weasel running to and fro to the cellar-door. I concluded that the enemy must be skulking in the cellar. I then, but not without difficulty, got a candle lighted. Holding the candle in my left hand, I laid hold of my pistol. With the lynx-eye and wary step of a cat ready to pounce on its prey, I advanced rather obliquely, with my right arm stretched out at full length holding the cocked pistol, till I got to the cellar-door, the little dog all the while making a furious noise; when, lo! what was there but a skunk sitting on a roll of tobacco! The shot blew it almost to atoms, and so delicately perfumed everything in the house that I was scarcely able to live in it for days afterwards; but that was not all, the trivial incident was productive of very bad consequences. Several hundreds of Indians being encamped about the place at the time, no sooner did they see the light, or hear the shot, than they all rushed into the house, thinking something serious had happened. So far, however, there were no great harm; but when they beheld two rolls of tobacco and two small bales of goods, it appeared such wealth in their eyes that they could scarcely recover from the surprise. These tempting articles I had endeavored all along to keep as much as possible out of their sight, and dealt them out with a sparing hand, and as long as the Indians did not see them in bulk all went well; but after the overwhelming exhibition of so much property there was no satisfying them. They became importunate and troublesome for some time, and caused me much anxiety. The time fixed for Mr. Stuart's return had now arrived, and I most anxiously looked for him every hour. Often had I reason to curse the intrusion of the skunk into my house. After some time, however, things settled down again to their usual level, and good order and good feelings were again renewed between us."

Stuart did not come, and the Indians became more bold, and loitered about the place. Strange Indians were constantly arriving, and the Indians held frequent councils. Ross called a feast and gave the Indians a reason for Stuart's absence, suggesting that they should go to work and bring in furs, in order that when the goods came they might have something with which to buy them. Stuart was gone for 188 days, and finally returned March 22, 1812. During his absence Ross had secured 1,550 beaver, besides other furs, worth in the Canton market 2,250 pounds sterling and costing in the merchandise which had been exchanged for them only 35 pounds sterling—"a specimen of our trade among the Indians!"

Stuart had gone north to the head of the Okanagan and had crossed over to the south branch of the Fraser River and met "a powerful nation called the She Whaps." There he had been detained by snow and had wintered with these people, among whom he had arranged to establish a trading-post. From the post at the mouth of the river came bad news. The little schooner "Dolly," the frame of which had been sent out to Astoria in the "Tonquin," was too small to be of any particular service, and being manned by people without much knowledge of seamanship was unlucky from the beginning, and was finally abandoned as useless for the purpose of getting about. There was complaint also of the quality of the trade goods sent out by Mr. Astor, but of all the news that came to the people up the river the most important was the rumor that the "Tonquin" had been destroyed with

all on board. The story of this destruction, as told
by Ross Cox, was given in an earlier volume.[1] Not
many tears were shed over the death of Captain Thorn
at Astoria, we may feel sure, but that McKay should
have been lost was a real sorrow and a genuine misfortune, for McKay was a man of great experience
and of extraordinary force.

In the meantime, Wilson Price Hunt, Astor's chief
assistant, Donald McKenzie, and later Ramsay Crooks,
started from St. Louis to make the journey overland
to the coast. The original purpose was to strike the
upper reaches of the Columbia River and go down that
stream in canoes, but, as the courses and character of
the river were wholly unknown, all sorts of difficulties
were encountered, and the canoes were at last abandoned; the expedition split up into different parties,
and a number of men were lost. At last McKenzie
reached Astoria January 10, 1812, while Hunt's party
arrived in February.

At the end of March parties left Astoria, one under
Mr. Reed for New York overland, another under Mr.
Farnham to search for the goods left *en cache* by Hunt
on his journey, and a third under Robert Stuart to
Okanagan with supplies for that post. These all
started together under the command of Mr. Stuart.
At the Long Narrows they got into difficulties with
the Indians, and McLellan killed two Indians and the
others fled. Trouble was threatening, but peace was at

[1] *Trails of the Pathfinders*, p. 304.

last secured by the gift of six blankets and some other trifles. In the mêlée the despatches which Reed was taking to New York were lost, and when they were lost that expedition was at an end.

A little later they were hailed in English by some one asking them to come on shore, and when they reached the bank they found standing, "like two spectres," Crooks and John Day, who had been left among the Snake Indians by Mr. Hunt the preceding autumn. The story told by these two men was pathetic enough. They were starving most of the time, lived largely on roots, had been robbed of rifles, and would inevitably have perished had it not been for a good old man who treated them like a father—killed a horse to make dried meat for them, and was about to start them out on the journey to St. Louis that very day, when the canoes hove in sight.

Mr. Stuart rewarded the old man to whom these men owed their lives, took them along with him and returned to Astoria, where they found the company's ship "Beaver" just arriving with a supply of goods and reinforcements of men. It was now May, and a number of the partners being at Astoria it was determined that David Stuart should return to Okanagan, work to the north, and establish another post between that and New Caledonia, that McKenzie should winter on Snake River, that Clark should winter at Spokane, that Robert Stuart should go overland to St. Louis with despatches for Mr. Astor, and that Mr.

Hunt should go with the "Beaver" to the Russian settlements to the north. Sixty-two persons left Astoria for the interior on the 29th of June, it having been determined that all the land parties should travel together as far as the forks of the Columbia, where Lewis River and Clark River come together. These land parties were under the command of Mr. Clark. Nothing happened until they reached the Cascades, where a few arrows were shot at them, but at the Long Narrows the Indians were numerous and threatening. Mr. Clark, although usually a man of nerve, seems to have been frightened by this demonstration, and it required the determination of McKenzie and David Stuart to induce him to go forward. They got through the pass without molestation or loss.

In looking about through an Indian camp, McKenzie and Stuart saw in a lodge of one of the chiefs the rifle that had been taken away from Mr. Reed when he was wounded, and they were determined to have it. As soon as the Narrows had been safely passed, McKenzie took eight men and went direct to the chief's lodge. He put four men at the door and with the other four entered and asked for the stolen rifle. The chief denied that it was in his lodge. McKenzie asked for it again and said he was determined to have it, and when it was not given up, he took his knife and began to turn over and cut up everything that came in his way and at last discovered the rifle, and after scolding the chief returned to the canoes. No time was wasted, and the Indians, though gathering in crowds, did nothing. The next day they camped at a point where Crooks and John Day had been robbed of their arms. The Indians were friendly enough, and among those who flocked about the white men was the one who had taken John Day's rifle. He was at once captured and tied up, but a little later was set free.

At Walla Walla, Robert Stuart purchased ten horses from the Nez-Percés and set out for St. Louis with five men, including Messrs. Crooks and McLellan, who had resigned from the company. David Stuart went up the Okanagan, and Ross remained at the post at its mouth, a Scotchman and a French Canadian being with him. Later, Ross followed Robert Stuart's route of the previous winter, got to the She Whaps, and established a good trade. They paid five leaves of tobacco for a beaver skin, and at last when their goods were exhausted and Ross had only one yard of white cotton remaining, one of the chiefs gave him twenty prime beaver skins for it.

This trading station was at what Ross calls Come-loups—of course, the Kamloops of our day.

On his return from this trip, Ross was formally appointed to the post of Okanagan, although, as a matter of fact, he had been in charge of it since its establishment. In early December he went to Fort Spokane, where he met Mr. Clark, who was in charge of a post there, and an opposition post of the Northwest Company was close by. The politics and secret quarrels of the two companies, each striving to get the most fur, were constant—and, of course, were not hidden from the Indians, who in every way strove to play on the traders tricks similar to those played on them. Ross left Spokane Fort a few days later, and on his way home had one of those experiences that so often came to travellers in those old days and that have so often proved fatal.

"In the evening of the 13th, not far from home, as we were ascending a very steep hill, at the top of which is a vast plain, I and my man had to walk, leaving our horses to shift for themselves, and climb up as they could; and so steep and intricate were the windings that I had to throw off my coat, which, together with my gun, I laid on one of the pack-horses. The moment we reached the top, and before we could gather our horses or look about us, we were overtaken by a tremendous cold snow storm; the sun became instantly obscured, and the wind blew a hurricane. We were taken by surprise. I immediately called out to the men to shift for themselves, and let the horses do the same. Just at this moment I accidentally came in contact with one of the loaded horses, for such was the darkness that we could not see three feet ahead; but, unfortunately, it was not the horse on which I had laid my coat and gun. I instantly cut the tyings, threw off the load, and mounting on the pack-saddle, rode off at full speed through the deep snow, in the hopes of reaching a well-known place of shelter not far off; but in the darkness and confusion I missed the place, and at last got so benumbed with cold that I could ride no farther; and, besides, my horse was almost exhausted. In this plight I dismounted and took to walking, in order to warm myself. But no place of shelter was to be found. Night came on; the storm increased in violence; my horse gave up; and I myself was so exhausted, wandering through the deep snow, that I could go no further. Here I halted, unable to decide what to do. My situation appeared desperate: without my coat; without my gun; without even a fire-steel. In such a situation I must perish. At last I resolved on digging a hole in the snow; but in trying to do so, I was several times in danger of being suffocated with the drift and eddy. In this dilemma I unsaddled my horse, which stood motionless as a statue in the snow. I put the saddle under me, and the saddle-cloth, about the size of a handkerchief, round my shoulders, then squatted down in the dismal hole, more likely to prove my grave than a shelter. On entering the hole I said to myself, 'Keep awake and live; sleep and die.' I had not been long, however, in this dismal burrow before the cold, notwithstanding my utmost exertions to keep my feet warm, gained so fast upon me that I was obliged to take off my shoes, then pull my trousers, by little and little, over my feet, till at last I had the waistband round my toes; and all would not do. I was now reduced to the last shift, and tried to keep my feet warm at the risk of freezing my body. At last I had scarcely strength to move a limb; the cold was gaining fast upon me; and the inclination to sleep almost overcame me. In this condition I passed the whole night; nor did the morning promise me much relief; yet I thought it offered me a glimpse of hope, and that hope induced me to endeavour to break out of my snowy prison. I tried, but in vain, to put on my frozen shoes; I tried again and again before I could succeed. I then dug my saddle out of the snow, and after repeated efforts, reached the horse and put the saddle on; but could not myself get into the saddle. Ten o'clock next day came before there was any abatement of the storm, and when it did clear up a little I knew not where I was; still it was cheering to see the storm abate. I tried again to get into the saddle; and when I at last succeeded, my half frozen horse refused to carry me, for he could scarcely lift a leg. I then alighted and tried to walk; but the storm broke out again with redoubled violence. I saw no hope of saving myself but to kill the horse, open him, and get into his body, and I drew my hunting-knife for the purpose; but then it occurred to me that the body would freeze, and that I could not, in that case, extricate myself. I therefore abandoned the idea, laid my knife by, and tried again to walk, and again got into the saddle. The storm now abating a little, my horse began to move; and I kept wandering about through the snow till three o'clock in the afternoon, when the storm abated altogether; and the sun coming out, I recognized my position. I was then not two miles from my own house, where I arrived at dusk; and it was high time, for I could not have gone much farther; and after all it was my poor horse that saved me, for had I set out on foot, I should never, in my exhausted condition, have reached the house."

A little later he made another winter journey of great discomfort, suffering much from cold and hunger. His return to Okanagan was down what Ross calls the Sa-mick-a-meigh River,[1] a region which twenty-five or thirty years ago abounded in mountain sheep and was often visited by Eastern sportsmen.

In his account of the journey of Mr. Clarke and his party to Spokane, made the August previous, Ross gives an account of the loss and recovery of Ross Cox, which that author has himself told in detail in his book referred to in a previous volume.[2] Ross treats the adventure somewhat lightly, although he does remark that when he was at Spokane in the winter Cox had hardly recovered yet.

It was the next spring that Clarke, an old Northwester, who might have known better, committed the grave indiscretion of hanging an Indian who had stolen a silver goblet but afterward returned it. It was not until the deed had been done and the angry Indians had disappeared to carry the news in all directions and

---

[1] Similkameen.　　　　[2] *Trails of the Pathfinders*, p. 313.

to assemble surrounding tribes to take revenge on the white men that Clarke appreciated what he had done. Fortunately the people were all packed up ready to start, and they hastily loaded their canoes and went on down the stream.

McKenzie, in the meantime, had reached the middle of the Nez Percés country and was wintering there, but he soon found that he was not in a trapping country. The Nez Percés hunted buffalo for food and went to war for glory. They did not like beaver trapping and made a poor trade. Now, McKenzie while on a visit to Fort Spokane learned from McTavish, a North-wester, of the war between Great Britain and the United States. He hurried back to his post there, put his goods in cache, and set out for Astoria, which he reached in 1813. At Astoria things were not cheer-ful. The ship had not returned, and McDougall and McKenzie felt that they were likely to be pushed out of the country by the Northwesters. However, Mc-Kenzie turned about and started up the river. When he reached his post he found that his cache had been raised. The older Indians admitted the robbery, and said that it had been done by young men whom they could not control. McKenzie was a man of great courage, and when the chiefs would not assist him in recovering his property he determined to recover it himself.

"Accordingly next morning, after depositing in a safe place the few articles he had brought with him,

he and his little band, armed cap-a-pie, set out on foot
for the camp. On their approach, the Indians, sus-
pecting something, turned out in groups here and there,
also armed. But McKenzie, without a moment's hesitation, or giving them time to reflect, ordered Mr.
Seaton, who commanded the men, to surround the
first wigwam or lodge reached with charged bayonets,
while he himself and Mr. Reed entered the lodge, ran-
sacked it, turning everything topsy-turvy, and with
their drawn daggers cutting and ripping open everything that might be supposed to conceal the stolen
property. In this manner they went from one lodge
to another till they had searched five or six with various success, when the chiefs demanded a parley, and
gave McKenzie to understand that if he desisted they
would do the business themselves, and more effectually.
McKenzie, after some feigned reluctance, at last agreed
to the chiefs' proposition. They then asked him to
withdraw; but this he peremptorily refused, knowing
from experience that they were least exposed in the
camp; for Indians are always averse to hostilities taking place in their camp, in the midst of their women
and children. Had the Indians foreseen or been aware
of the intention of the whites, they would never have
allowed them within their camp. But they were taken
by surprise, and that circumstance saved the whites.
However, as soon as the chiefs undertook the business,
McKenzie and his men stood still and looked on. The
chiefs went from house to house, and after about three

hours time they returned, bringing with them a large portion of the property, and delivered it to McKenzie, when he and his men left the camp and returned home, bearing off in triumph the fruits of their valour; and well pleased with their hairbreadth adventure; an adventure not to be repeated. And under all circumstances, it was at the time considered the boldest step ever taken by the whites on Columbian ground."

However, the Indians determined to get even with McKenzie, and they did this by refusing to sell the horses which were absolutely necessary to the fur traders, since horses were the only food available, for they were not in a position to go out and run buffalo. McKenzie later got the best of them by this plan: When the whites had nothing to eat, the articles usually paid for a horse were tied up in a bundle; this done, McKenzie, with ten or twelve of his men, would sally forth with their rifles to the grazing ground of the horses, shoot the fattest they could find, and carry off the flesh to their camp, leaving the price stuck up on a pole alongside the head of the dead horse.

"This manœuvre succeeded several times, and annoyed the Indians very much; some of them lost their best horses by it. Then it was that they combined to attack the whites in their camp. This news was brought McKenzie by one of his hired spies, and was confirmed by the fact of an Indian offering to sell a horse for powder and ball only. From various other suspicious circumstances there remained but little doubt in the

ASSINIBOINE-PIEGAN BATTLE BEFORE THE WALLS OF FORT MACKENZIE

minds of the whites but that there was some dark de-
sign in agitation. In this critical conjuncture, Mc-
Kenzie again eluded their grasp by ensconcing himself
and his party in an island in the middle of the river.
There they remained, in a manner blockaded by the
Indians; but not so closely watched but that they appeared every now and then with their long rifles among
the Shahaptian horses; so that the Indians grew tired
of their predatory excursions, and therefore sent a messenger to McKenzie. A parley ensued between the
main land and the island; the result of which was, that
the Indians agreed to sell horses to the whites at the
usual price—the whites, on their part, to give up their
marauding practices."

The trade in horses now went on briskly, although
McKenzie regarded the Indians with much suspicion.
He procured food and bought eighty horses, which he
sent off to Spokane. It was about this time that news
came to them of Mr. Clark's ill-advised punishment
of the Indians. There was but one opinion among the
traders, and they pursued the only possible course:
took to their canoes, and went down the river to Astoria.

The journeyings of the party which had started overland to St. Louis the summer before were difficult
enough. They starved and travelled, and travelled
and starved; crossed the mountains, and wintered on
their eastern flanks, and finally reached St. Louis
April 30.

Mr. Hunt, after trading along the coast of Russian

America, went to the Sandwich Islands and then to Canton. On his return Mr. Hunt waited for a time at the Sandwich Islands, hoping that a ship from New York might come to the relief of Astoria. He waited in vain, and finally chartering the ship "Albatross" he reached Astoria in August.

The war between Great Britain and the United States had led the Northwest Fur Company to believe that before long they could get possession of Astoria, and thus hold the whole trade on the Pacific coast, except that of the Russians. The Northwesters McTavish and Stuart were on their way to the mouth of the Columbia to meet the ship "Isaac Tod," which was daily expected, and the Astorians had no means of defence. They could fight off the Northwesters, of course, but if a ship with guns came they would be helpless. McDougall seemed to have been quite willing to give up the post and to sell the furs to the Northwesters, and before long this took place. McDougall has generally been charged with secretly agreeing to swindle Mr. Astor by fixing absurdly low prices on the furs and goods. At all events, all of the goods on hand, wherever stationed, were delivered to the Northwest Company at ten per cent on cost and charges, while the furs were valued at so much per skin. Ross declared that the transaction was considered fair and equitable on both sides, but other men who were there speak of it in quite a different way. The Indians, who for the past year or two had declared themselves the firm friends of the fur traders, still wished to defend these friends from the attacks of their enemies. Old Come Comly even professed to be anxious to fight for them, but when the sloop-of-war "Raccoon" came into Baker's Bay the Indian chief wholly changed his attitude, and declared that he was glad that he had lived long enough to see a great ship of his brother King George enter the river. He received a drink of wine, a flag, coat, hat, and sword, and became wholly British.

Captain Black, of the "Raccoon," and his ship's company had hoped to capture Astoria with all its furs—a rich prize—and he was much disappointed when he found that all these things had been sold to the Northwest Company by amicable agreement.

In the spring of 1814 Mr. Hunt, accompanied by several members of the Astoria party, took their final departure from Fort George. A number of those who had been Astorians, when freed from their contracts or agreements by Mr. Hunt, again took service with the Northwest Company, most of them receiving such work as they were qualified to perform. Ross was put in charge of the post at Okanagan, as he had been under the Pacific Fur Company. Stationed here now for some time, he gives an excellent picture of the life, and especially good accounts of the manners, ways, and customs of the Indians, and, with an interesting Chinook vocabulary and a table of weather at the mouth of the Columbia, closes the volume.

As an account of the Astor project to control the fur trade of the Pacific coast and of the difficulties of establishing a trading post among the Indians of the Columbia River, the book is of extreme interest.

FUR HUNTERS OF THE FAR WEST

FUR HUNTERS OF THE FAR WEST

I

WITH THE NORTHWEST FUR COMPANY

AFTER the downfall of the Pacific Fur Company, the occupation of Astoria by the Northwesters, and the change of its name to Fort George, Ross took service with the Northwest Company. It is life as a fur trader with the Northwest Company that he describes in his book *The Fur Hunters of the Far West*. In point of time, these volumes precede most of the books on the far western fur trade, and they give faithful and interesting accounts of the conditions met with at the time. Ross's books, in fact, are foundation stones for any history of the settlement of the Northwest. Although the books were not written until long after the period of which they treat—for the preface of this work is dated June 1, 1854, while the book was published the next year— Ross must have kept full diaries of his goings and comings, for in most of his dates he is exact, and his narrative is full of details that would almost certainly have slipped from an unaided memory.

In his new service Ross discovered that matters were

now in charge of men who knew very little about the Indians of the Pacific coast, and who lightly regarded those persons who had been in the service of Mr. Astor, whom they called Yankees. The new-comers had much to learn.

One of the first acts of the Northwest Company was to despatch an expedition of twenty men, in charge of Messrs. Keith and Alexander Stuart, to report to Fort William, on Lake Superior, the news of the acquisition of Astoria by the Northwest Company. On reaching the Cascades of the Columbia they were attacked by a large number of Indians, and Mr. Stuart was wounded. Two Indians were killed, and the expedition returned to Fort George. The attack caused great indignation there, and an extraordinary expedition was fitted out to punish the Indians. Eighty-five picked men and two Chinook interpreters constituted the force; and besides the ordinary arms carried in the West they had "two great guns, six swivels, cutlasses, hand grenades, and hand knives."

As the expedition passed along up the river, it struck terror to the hearts of the Indians, while it is said that "the two Chinook interpreters could neither sleep nor eat, so grieved were they at the thoughts of the bloody scenes that were to be enacted."

The people who were to be punished, however—the Cath-le-yach-é-yach, a Chinookan tribe living below the Cascades—were not all frightened, and when they were required to deliver up the property taken from Keith and Stuart, they declared themselves ready to do so, but not until after the whites had delivered to them those who had killed two of their people. They sent off their women and children into the forest and prepared to fight. There were multitudinous parleys lasting for three or four days, at the end of which time the whites, regarding discretion as the better part of valor, "without recovering the property, firing a gun, or securing a single prisoner, sounded a retreat and returned home on the ninth day, having made matters ten times worse than they were before."

The expedition was much derided by the Indians, and the white people who took part in it were extremely mortified about it. The situation was really one of war, and when a short time afterward the Northwest brigade departed for the interior, the Indians at the Cascades did not come near to the camp nor in any degree interrupt their progress.

Consulted by McDonald, who was in charge of the Columbia trade, Ross had urged on him the importance of taking the "usual precautions" in travelling up the river. Nevertheless, no guard was set at night, and an alarm taking place, people jumped up and began to fire their guns at random and one of the men was shot dead. There seems no reason to suppose that there were actually any Indians in the camp.

At Fort Okanagan the expedition passed on, leaving Ross behind in charge of the post. He was now in a prairie country where horses were absolutely essential to travel, and no horses were to be had nearer than Eyakema valley, two hundred miles away, where the horse Indians, Cayuses, Nez Percés, and other warlike tribes encamped each spring, to collect the roots of the camas. Here horses were plenty, but, as it was a great camp occupied by many different tribes, to visit it was to incur some danger. However, Ross took a few trade goods and set out with three men, young McKay and two French Canadians, these last taking with them their Indian wives, to assist in the care of the horses.

It was an anxious time, and the perplexities of the journey were not lessened when, on the fourth night after leaving Okanagan, the chief of the Pisscows tribe, who had learned where Ross was going, sent two men to urge him to turn back, declaring that if they did not do so they were all dead men. However, Ross determined to go on; as he puts it, "I had risked my life there for the Americans, I could now do no less for the North-West Company; so with deep regret the friendly couriers left us and returned, and with no less reluctance we proceeded."

On the sixth day after leaving the fort they reached the valley, where they found a great camp, of which they could see the beginning, but not the end. It must have contained not less than 3,000 men, exclusive of women and children, and three times that number of horses. Everywhere was seen the active life of these primitive people. Councils were being held, women were gathering roots, men were hunting. Horse racing, games, singing, dancing, drumming, yelling, and a thousand other things were going on. The noise and confusion are hardly to be described; but the interest and the beauty of the scene could not have been appreciated by these men, who were carrying their lives in their hands and marching into danger.

"Our reception was cool, the chiefs were hostile and sullen, they saluted us in no very flattering accents. 'These are the men,' said they, 'who kill our relations, the people who have caused us to mourn.' And here, for the first time, I regretted we had not taken advice in time, and returned with the couriers, for the general aspect of things was against us. It was evident we stood on slippery ground; we felt our weakness. In all sudden and unexpected rencontres with hostile Indians, the first impulse is generally a tremor or sensation of fear, but that soon wears off; it was so with myself at this moment, for after a short interval I nerved myself to encounter the worst.

"The moment we dismounted, we were surrounded, and the savages, giving two or three war-whoops and yells, drove the animals we had ridden out of our sight; this of itself was a hostile movement. We had to judge from appearances, and be guided by circumstances. My first care was to try and direct their attention to something new, and to get rid of the temptation there was to dispose of my goods; so without a moment's delay, I commenced a trade in horses;

but every horse I bought during that and the following day, as well as those we had brought with us, were instantly driven out of sight, in the midst of yelling and jeering: nevertheless, I continued to trade while an article remained, putting the best face on things I could, and taking no notice of their conduct, as no insult or violence had as yet been offered to ourselves personally. Two days and nights had now elapsed since our arrival, without food or sleep; the Indians refused us the former, our own anxiety deprived us of the latter.

"During the third day I discovered that the two women were to have been either killed or taken from us and made slaves. So surrounded were we for miles on every side, that we could not stir unobserved; yet we had to devise some means for their escape, and to get them clear of the camp was a task of no ordinary difficulty and danger. In this critical conjuncture, however, something had to be done, and that without delay. One of them had a child at the breast, which increased the difficulty. To attempt sending them back by the road they came, would have been sacrificing them. To attempt an unknown path through the rugged mountains, however doubtful the issue, appeared the only prospect that held out a glimpse of hope; therefore, to this mode of escape I directed their attention. As soon as it was dark, they set out on their forlorn adventure without food, guide, or protection, to make their way home, under a kind Providence!

"'You are to proceed,' said I to them, 'due north, cross the mountains, and keep in that direction till you fall on the Pisscows River; take the first canoe you find, and proceed with all diligence down to the mouth of it and there await our arrival. But if we are not there on the fourth day, you may proceed to Oakanagan, and tell your story.' With these instructions we parted; and with but little hopes of our ever meeting again. I had no sooner set about getting the women off, than the husbands expressed a wish to accompany them; the desire was natural, yet I had to oppose it. This state of things distracted my attention: my eyes had now to be on my own people as well as on the Indians, as I was apprehensive they would desert. 'There is no hope for the women by going alone,' said the husbands, 'no hope for us by remaining here: we might as well be killed in the attempt to escape, as remain to be killed here.' 'No,' said I, 'by remaining here we do our duty; by going we should be deserting our duty.' To this remonstrance they made no reply. The Indians soon perceived that they had been outwitted. They turned over our baggage, and searched in every hole and corner. Disappointment creates ill humor: it was so with the Indians. They took the men's guns out of their hands, fired them off at their feet, and then, with savage laughter, laid them down again; took their hats off their heads, and after strutting about with these for some time, jeeringly gave them back to their owners: all this time, they never interfered with me, but I felt that every insult offered to my men was an indirect insult offered to myself.

"The day after the women went off, I ordered one of the men to try and cook something for us; for hitherto we had eaten nothing since our arrival, except a few raw roots which we managed to get unobserved. But the kettle was no sooner on the fire than five or six spears bore off, in savage triumph, the contents: they even emptied out the water, and threw the kettle on one side; and this was no sooner done than thirty or forty ill-favored wretches fired a volley in the embers before us, which caused a cloud of smoke and ashes to ascend, darkening the air around us: a strong hint not to put the kettle any more on the fire, and we took it.

"At this time the man who had put the kettle on the fire took the knife with which he had cut the venison to lay it by, when one of the Indians, called Eyacktana, a bold and turbulent chief, snatched it out of his hand; the man, in an angry tone, demanded his knife, saying to me, 'I'll have my knife from the villain, life or death.' 'No,' said I. The chief, seeing the man angry, threw down his robe, and grasping the knife in his fist, with the point downwards, raised his arm, making a motion in advance as if he intended using it. The crisis had now arrived! At this moment there was a dead silence. The Indians were flocking in from all quarters: a dense crowd surrounded us. Not a moment was to be lost; delay would be fatal, and nothing now seemed to remain for us but to sell our lives as dearly as possible. With this impression, grasping a pistol, I advanced a step towards the villain who held the knife, with the full determination of putting an end to his career before any of us should fall; but while in the act of lifting my foot and moving my arm, a second idea floated across my mind, admonishing me to soothe, and not provoke, the Indians, that Providence might yet make a way for us to escape: this thought saved the Indian's life, and ours too. Instead of drawing the pistol, as I intended, I took a knife from my belt, such as travellers generally use in this country, and presented it to him, saying, 'Here, my friend, is a chief's knife, I give it to you; that is not a chief's knife, give it back to the man.' Fortunately, he took mine in his hand; but, still sullen and savage, he said nothing. The moment was a critical one; our fate hung as by a thread: I shall never forget it! All the bystanders had their eyes now fixed on the chief, thoughtful and silent as he stood; we also stood motionless, not knowing what a moment might bring forth. At last the savage handed the man his knife, and turning mine round and round for some time in his hand, turned to his people, holding up the knife in his hand, exclaimed, 'She-augh Me-yokat Waltz'—Look, my friends, at the chief's knife: these words he repeated over and over again. He was delighted. The Indians flocked round him: all admired the toy, and in the excess of his joy he harangued the multitude in our favour. Fickle, indeed, are savages! They were now no longer enemies, but friends! Several others, following Eyacktana's example, harangued in turn, all in favour of the whites. This done, the great men squatted themselves down, the pipe of peace was called for, and while it was going round and round the smoking circle, I gave each of the six principal chiefs a small paper-cased looking-glass and a little vermilion, as a present; and in return, they presented me with two horses and twelve beavers, while the women soon brought us a variety of eatables.

"This sudden change regulated my movements. Indeed, I might say the battle was won. I now made a speech to them in turn, and, as many of them understood the language I spoke, I asked them what I should say to the great white chief when I got home, when he asks me where are all the horses I bought from you. What shall I say to him? At this question it was easy to see that their pride was touched. 'Tell him,' said Eyacktana, 'that we have but one mouth, and one word; all the horses you have bought from us are yours, they shall be delivered up.' This was just what I wanted. After a little counselling among themselves, Eyacktana was the first to speak, and he undertook to see them collected.

"By this time it was sun-down. The chief then mounted his horse, and desired me to mount mine and accompany him, telling one of his sons to take my men and property under his charge till our return. Being acquainted with Indian habits, I knew there would be repeated calls upon my purse, so I put some trinkets into my pocket, and we started on our nocturnal adventure; which I considered hazardous but not hopeless.

"Such a night we had! The chief harangued, travelled and harangued, the whole night, the people replied. We visited every street, alley, hole and corner of the camp, which we traversed lengthwise, crossway, east, west, south, and north, going from group to group, and the call was 'Deliver up the horses.' Here was gambling, there scalp-dancing; laughter in one place, mourning in another. Crowds were passing to and fro, whooping, yelling, dancing, drumming, singing. Men, women, and children were huddled together; flags flying, horses neighing, dogs howling, chained bears, tied wolves, grunting and growling, all pell-mell among the tents; and, to complete the confusion, the night was dark. At the end of each harangue the chief would approach me, and whisper in my ear, 'She-augh tamtay enim'—I have spoken well in your favour—a hint for me to reward his zeal by giving him something. This was repeated constantly, and I gave him each time a string of beads, or two buttons, or two rings. I often thought he repeated his harangues more frequently than necessary; but it answered his purpose, and I had no choice but to obey and pay.

"At daylight we got back; my people and property were safe; and in two hours after my eighty-five horses were delivered up, and in our possession. I was now convinced of the chief's influence, and had got so well into his good graces with my beads, buttons, and rings, that I hoped we were out of all our troubles. Our business being done, I ordered my men to tie up and prepare for home, which was glad tidings to them. With all this favourable change, we were much embarrassed and annoyed in our preparations to start. The savages interrupted us every moment. They jeered the men, frightened the horses, and kept handling, snapping, and firing off our guns; asking for this, that, and the other thing. The men's hats, pipes, belts, and knives were constantly in their hands. They wished to see everything, and everything they saw they wished to get, even to the buttons on their clothes. Their teasing curiosity had no bounds; and every delay increased our difficulties. Our patience was put to the test a thousand times; but at last we got ready, and my men started. To amuse the Indians, however, till they could get fairly off, I invited the chiefs to a parley, which I put a stop to as soon as I thought the men and horses had got clear of the camp. I then prepared to follow them, when a new difficulty arose. In the hurry and bustle of starting, my people had left a restive, awkward brute of a horse for me, wild as a deer, and as full of latent tricks as he was wild. I mounted and dismounted at least a dozen times; in vain I tried to make him advance. He reared, jumped and plunged; but refused to walk, trot, or gallop. Every trial to make him go was a failure. A young con-

ceited fop of an Indian, thinking he could make more
of him than I could, jumped on his back; the horse
reared and plunged as before, when, instead of slacken-
ing the bridle as he reared, he reined it tighter and
tighter, till the horse fell right over on his back, and
almost killed the fellow. Here Eyacktana, with a
frown, called out, 'Kap-sheesh she-eam'—the bad
horse—and gave me another; and for the generous
act I gave him my belt, the only article I had to spare.
But although the difficulties I had with the horse were
galling enough to me, they proved a source of great
amusement to the Indians, who enjoyed it with roars
of laughter."

When Ross got out of the camp he rode hard and
took a short cut in the effort to overtake his people,
but could not find them. Presently, however, from the
top of a ridge, he saw three horsemen coming toward
him at full tilt. He made preparation for defence, and
hiding behind a rock awaited the onslaught, but before
they got close to him he discovered that these were
the friendly Pisscows, who before had warned him to
turn back, and with them he went on. At last they
saw Ross's people, who were driving their horses as
fast as they could, but when they saw Ross and his
companions behind them they thought them enemies, and stopped to fight. All were glad enough to
get together, and at last, after various adventures, they
reached the fort at Okanagan.

II

WORK OF A FUR TRADER

A LITTLE later Ross went north to his own post at the She-Whaps, where he made a good trade. From here he decided to go west to the Pacific coast on foot, believing that the distance was not more than two hundred miles, but before he reached the coast a destructive hurricane passed so close to his party that his guide, altogether discouraged by fatigue and failure, deserted during the night, and Ross was obliged to return.

One winter, much alarm was caused among the Indians by the depredations of strange wolves, reported to be hundreds in number, and as big as buffalo, which were coming into the country, and on their march were killing all the horses. The Indians declared that all the horses would be killed, for men could not go near these wolves, nor would arrows or balls kill them. Shortly after the head chief of the Okanagan Indians had told this story to Ross, wolves killed five of the traders' horses. Ross took up those left alive, and then put out a dozen traps about the carcass of one that had been killed. The next morning four of the traps were sprung. "One of them held a large white wolf by the fore leg, a foot equally large was gnawed off and left in another, the third held a fox, and the fourth trap had disappeared altogether." Unable to get away, the captured wolf was quite ready to fight. It had gnawed the trap until its teeth were broken and its head was covered with blood. When killed it was found to weigh one hundred and twenty-seven pounds, an enormous animal. The one that had carried off the trap was at last discovered making the best of its way over the country, and pursuit resulted in its capture. The animal had dragged a trap and chain weighing eight and one-half pounds a distance of twenty-five miles, without appearing at all fatigued. Ross wanted the skin, but had left his knife behind him. However, it was not for nothing that he had been for years associated with Indians, and he took the flint out of his gun, skinned the animal, and went home with skin and trap.

The killing of these two wolves and the crippling of the third put an end to the destruction, and not another horse was killed in that part of the country during the season.

Ross comments interestingly on the methods used by wolves in decoying horses.

"If there is no snow, or but little, on the ground, two wolves approach in the most playful and caressing manner, lying, rolling, and frisking about, until the too credulous and unsuspecting victim is completely put off his guard by curiosity and familiarity. During this time the gang, squatted on their hind-quarters, look on at a distance. After some time spent in this way, the two assailants separate, when one approaches the horse's head, the other his tail, with a slyness and cunning peculiar to themselves. At this stage of the attack, their frolicsome approaches become very interesting—it is in right good earnest; the former is a mere decoy, the latter is the real assailant, and keeps his eyes steadily fixed on the ham-strings or flank of the horse. The critical moment is then watched, and the attack is simultaneous; both wolves spring at their victim the same instant, one to the throat, the other to the flank, and if successful, which they generally are, the hind one never lets go his hold till the horse is completely disabled. Instead of springing forward or kicking to disengage himself, the horse turns round and round without attempting a defence. The wolf before, then springs behind, to assist the other. The sinews are cut, and in half the time I have been describing it, the horse is on his side; his struggles are fruitless: the victory is won. At this signal, the lookers-on close in at a gallop, but the small fry of followers keep at a respectful distance, until their superiors are gorged, then they take their turn unmolested. The wolves, however, do not always kill to eat; like wasteful hunters, they often kill for the pleasure of killing, and leave the carcases untouched. The helplessness of the horse when attacked by wolves is not more singular than its timidity and want of action when in danger by fire. When assailed by fire, in the plains or elsewhere, their strength, swiftness, and sagacity, are of no avail; they never attempt to fly, but become bewildered in the smoke, turn round and round, stand and tremble, until they are burnt to death: which often happens in this country, in a conflagration of the plains."

It must be remembered, however, that Ross is speaking of wolves of the western mountains, animals which were not familiar with the buffalo, and which now, since horses had been brought into the country, had been supplied with a new food animal. Ross says also, and he is almost the only writer who speaks of anything of this kind, that wolves sometimes attacked men, and instances two men forced to take shelter for several hours in a tree by a band of seventeen wolves.

It was about this time that a change of heart began to take place among the authorities of the Northwest Company. Since Astoria had become Fort George few or no steps had been taken to make the most of the possibilities of the country, but those who were on the ground dwelt constantly on the poverty of the country, the hostility of the Indians, and the impracticability of trade. The people who came over the mountains to take the place of the Astorians brought with them their habits of the fur country of the east, and seemed unable to change them. The traders from the east preferred the birch-bark canoe, and spent much time in searching for bark. It was even provided—lest that of good quality should not be found on the waters of the Pacific slope—that a stock of bark should be shipped from Montreal to London, and thence around Cape Horn to Fort George, in order that canoes might be made.

In 1816 the Columbia River district was divided
by the authorities at Fort William into two separate
departments, each one with a bourgeois at the head.
Mr. Keith was chosen to preside at Fort George, while
Mr. McKenzie was given charge of the department of
the interior. There was much grumbling at this last
appointment. Ross was appointed as second in command to Mr. Keith. Shortly after this there were
various troubles at Fort George, one of the most important being the desertion of the blacksmith Jacob,
who fled to a hostile tribe, from which he was taken by
Ross, who went after him with thirty men. The enterprise was one which required that courage and endurance which Ross so often displayed in times of
difficulty. The west coast trade was further compli-
cated by the jealousy which Mr. Keith felt for Mr.
McKenzie. These difficulties were overcome, and Mc-
Kenzie again set out for his interior command, accompanied by a force of Iroquois, Abenakis, and Sandwich Islanders. Mr. Keith remained in command at
Fort George.

Many of the hunters and trappers at Fort George
lacked experience in dealing with the natives, and
before long there was trouble with the Indians. These
tried to exact tribute from the fur traders for trapping
on the tribal land, and the fur traders, far from showing
patience, were quite ready to quarrel. One or more of
the hunters were wounded on the Willamette and
some Indians were killed. Ross was sent out to try to

effect a reconciliation, but, as so often is the case where Indians have been killed, the people in the camps declined to smoke and to consider any other course than war. It was only by the exercise of great patience and forbearance, and finally by the gift of a flag to a chief, that the trouble was at last smoothed over, and the opposing parties smoked and made long speeches and then concluded a treaty—the whites having paid for the dead—which greatly pleased Mr. Keith.

McKenzie on his way up the Columbia did not get beyond the Cascades, for here he found the river frozen; so he camped and spent the winter among the Indians, showing, in his dealings with them, remarkable tact and judgment.

Ross describes with some humor the happenings at a feast, such as frequently took place in the camp where McKenzie now was:

"On the score of cheer, we will here gratify the curiosity of our readers with a brief description of one of their entertainments, called an Indian feast. The first thing that attracts the attention of a stranger, on being invited to a feast in these parts, is, to see seven or eight bustling squaws running to and fro with pieces of greasy bark, skins of animals, and old mats, to furnish the banqueting lodge, as receptacles for the delicate viands: at the door of the lodge is placed, on such occasions, a sturdy savage with a club in his hand, to keep the dogs at bay, while the preparations are going on.

"The banqueting hall is always of a size suitable to the occasion, large and roomy. A fire occupies the centre, round which, in circular order, are laid the eatables. The guests form a close ring round the whole. Every one approaches with a grave and solemn step. The party being all assembled, the reader may picture to himself our friend seated among the nobles of the place, his bark platter between his legs, filled top-heavy with the most delicious *mélange* of bear's grease, dog's flesh, wappatoes, obellies, amutes, and a profusion of other viands, roots and berries. Round the festive board, placed on *terra firma*, all the nabobs of the place are squatted down in a circle, each helping himself out of his platter with his fingers, observing every now and then to sleek down the hair by way of wiping the hands. Only one knife is used, and that is handed round from one to another in quick motion. Behind the banqueting circle sit, in anxious expectation, groups of the canine tribe, yawning, howling, and growling; these can only be kept in the rear by a stout cudgel, which each of the guests keeps by him, for the purpose of self-defence; yet it not unfrequently happens that some one of the more daring curs gets out of patience, breaks through the front rank, and carries off his booty; but when a trespass of this kind is committed, the unfortunate offender is well belaboured in his retreat, for the cudgels come down upon him with a terrible vengeance. The poor dog, however, has his revenge in turn, for the squabble and brawl that ensues disturbs all the dormant fleas of the domicile. This troop of black assailants jump about in all directions, so that a guest, by helping himself to the good things before him, keeping the dogs at bay behind him, and defending himself from the black squadrons that surround him, pays, perhaps, dearer for his entertainment at the Columbian Cascades than a foreign ambassador does in a London hotel!"

On leaving this place in the spring, the traders broke one of their boats while towing it up the Cascades, and there was no room in the other boats to load the cargo of the one that had been broken. There were sixty packages, of ninety pounds each, and this large and valuable cargo McKenzie turned over to a chief, to be kept for him until his return. When the brigade returned six months later the whole cargo was handed over safe and untouched to McKenzie. Such care for the property of their guests was often given by the old-time Indians.

The next summer when the inland brigade left Fort George for the interior, Ross accompanied it, for he was starting for his own post at She-Whaps. As usual, there were many annoyances—men deserted, others fell sick, some of the Iroquois were about to fire on the native Indians—and altogether the leaders of the party had their hands full in trying to keep peace.

Ross had with him a little dog which an Indian one morning got hold of and carried away. The dog, anxious to get back to his master, in its struggles to escape happened to scratch one of the children of his captor, and presently Ross saw the dog running to him, followed by two men with guns in their hands. The dog lay down by its master's feet, and one of the Indians cocked his gun to shoot the animal. Ross jumped up and took the gun from the Indian, who seemed very angry and demanded it again. After a time Ross handed it back to him, at the same time picking up his own gun and telling the Indian that if he attempted to kill the dog he himself would die. The man did not shoot the dog, but telling his trouble to the other Indians, they gathered about Ross and there was every prospect of a pretty quarrel. However, Ross and McKenzie, strong in their knowledge of Indian character, smoothed things over, made a little gift to the child that had been scratched, gave the chief some tobacco, and presently went on their way with the apparent good-will of the whole camp.

A day or two later another example was seen of the way in which Ross handled the Indians. The chiefs and the traders were smoking and talking.

"While thus engaged, and the crowd thronging around us, a fellow more like a baboon than a man, with a head full of feathers and a countenance of brass, having a fine gun in his hand, called out, 'How long are the whites to pass here, troubling our waters and scaring our fish, without paying us? Look at all these bales of goods going to our enemies,' said he; 'and look at our wives and children naked.' The fellow then made a pause, as if waiting an answer; but, as good fortune would have it, the rest of the Indians paid but little attention to him. No answer was made; nor was it a time to discuss the merits or demerits of such a question. Happening, however, to be near the fellow when he spoke, I turned briskly round, 'So long,' said I, 'as the Indians smoke our tobacco; just so long, and no longer, will the whites pass here.' Then I put some questions to him in turn. 'Who gave you that fine gun on your hand?' 'The whites,' answered he. 'And who gives you tobacco to smoke?' 'The whites,' he replied. Continuing the subject, 'Are you fond of your gun?' 'Yes.' 'And are you fond of tobacco to smoke?' To this question also the reply was 'Yes.' 'Then,' said I, 'you ought to be fond of the whites who supply all your wants.' 'Oh, yes!' rejoined he. The nature of the questions and answers set the bystanders laughing; and taking no further notice of the rascal, he sneaked off among the crowd, and we saw him no more. The question put by the feathered baboon amounted to nothing in itself; but it proved that the subject of tribute had been discussed among the Indians."

There was constant demand for readiness and quick-wittedness, for the whites were very few in number and the Indians numerous; moreover, these primitive people were altogether disposed to see how far the whites would permit them to go, and it was thus exceedingly easy to begin a quarrel about some trifling matter in which blood might be shed.

From his post in the She-Whaps Ross soon went east toward the Rocky Mountains, having been ordered to explore this country and see what it contained. He set out on foot with two of his best hands and two Indians. Each carried as baggage one-half dozen pairs of moccasins, a blanket, some ammunition, needles, thread, and tobacco, besides a small axe, a knife, a fire steel, and an awl. All they had besides was a kettle and a pint pot. For subsistence they depended on their guns, and for a further supply of shoes and clothing on the animals that they might kill by the way.

The country was extraordinarily rough. Fur-bearing animals were not plenty, but game was abundant, elk and deer being seen in great numbers, and so tame as to make it appear that they had never been disturbed.

In six days' travel down a stream, which Ross calls the Grisly-bear, they shot four elks, twenty-two deer, two otters, two beavers, and three black bears, without stepping out of the trail. A little later they saw moose, and still later is given a curious account of a battle between two large birds, both of which were captured. One of these was a white-headed eagle which weighed eight and three-quarter pounds, and the other "a wild-turkey cock, or what we call the Columbia grouse," which could only have been a sage grouse. This is said to have weighed eleven and one-quarter pounds!

During this same summer McKenzie had trouble with the Iroquois—seemingly most untrustworthy servants—who tried to kill McKenzie, perhaps with the idea of taking all the property of the expedition. However, McKenzie's quickness and readiness enabled him to put the Iroquois to flight.

Soon after his return from his Eastern exploration Ross was invited by the Indians to accompany them on a bear-hunt, which he describes:

"The party were all mounted on horseback, to the number of seventy-three, and exhibited a fine display of horsemanship. After some ten miles' travel, we commenced operations. Having reached the hunting-ground, the party separated into several divisions. We then perambulated the woods, crossed rivers, surrounded thickets, and scampered over hill and dale, with yell and song, for the greater part of two days; during which time we killed seven bears, nine wolves, and eleven small deer: one of the former I had the good luck to shoot myself. In the evening of the third day, however, our sport was checked by an accident. One of the great men, the chief Pacha of the hunting party, named Tu-tack-it, Is-tso-augh-an, or Short Legs, got severely wounded by a female bear.

"The only danger to be apprehended in these savage excursions is by following the wounded animal into a thicket, or hiding-place; but with the Indians the more danger the more honour, and some of them are foolhardy enough to run every hazard in order to strike the last fatal blow, (in which the honour lies,) sometimes with a lance, tomahawk, or knife, at the risk of their lives. No sooner is a bear wounded than it immediately flies for refuge to some hiding-place, unless too closely pursued; in which case, it turns round in savage fury on its pursuers, and woe awaits whoever is in the way.

"The bear in question had been wounded and took shelter in a small coppice. The bush was instantly surrounded by the horsemen, when the more bold and daring entered it on foot, armed with gun, knife, and tomahawk. Among the bushrangers on the present occasion was the chief, Short Legs, who, while scrambling over some fallen timber, happened to stumble near to where the wounded and enraged bear was concealed, but too close to be able to defend himself before the vicious animal got hold of him. At that moment I was not more than five or six paces from the chief, but could not get a chance of shooting, so I immediately called out for help, when several mustered round the spot. Availing ourselves of the doubtful alternative of killing her—even at the risk of killing the chief—we fired, and as good luck would have it, shot the animal and saved the man; then carrying the bear and wounded chief out of the bush, we laid both on the open ground. The sight of the chief was appalling: the scalp was torn from the crown of his head, down over the eyebrows! he was insensible, and for some time we all thought him dead; but after a short interval his pulse began to beat, and he gradually showed signs of returning animation.

"It was a curious and somewhat interesting scene to

see the party approach the spot where the accident happened. Not being able to get a chance of shooting, they threw their guns from them, and could scarcely be restrained from rushing on the fierce animal with their knives only. The bear all the time kept looking first at one, then at another, and casting her fierce and flaming eyes around the whole of us, as if ready to make a spring at each; yet she never let go her hold of the chief; but stood over him. Seeing herself surrounded by so many enemies, she moved her head from one position to another, and these movements gave us ultimately an opportunity of killing her.

"The misfortune produced a loud and clamorous scene of mourning among the chief's relations; we hastened home, carrying our dead bears along with us, and arrived at the camp early in the morning of the fourth day. The chief remained for three days speechless. In cutting off the scalp and dressing the wound, we found the skull, according to our imperfect knowledge of anatomy, fractured in two or three places; and at the end of eight days, I extracted a bone measuring two inches long, of an oblong form, and another of about an inch square, with several smaller pieces, all from the crown of the head! The wound, however, gradually closed up and healed, except a small spot about the size of an English shilling. In fifteen days, by the aid of Indian medicine, he was able to walk about, and at the end of six weeks from the time he got wounded, he was on horseback again at the chace."

More or less wolf-hunting was done through the winter, and Ross describes certain methods of catching and killing these animals.

The killing of wolves, foxes, and other wild animals by the whites was really only a recreation, and the traders preferred shooting them to any other mode of destruction. The wolves were usually afoot and searching for food at all hours of the day and night. They liked to get up on nearby hills or knolls, to sit and look about. It was the practice of the traders to scatter food about the places frequented by the wolves, and—when there were no wolves there—to practise shooting at a mark, watching where the balls hit and learning the elevation of the gun required to reach the spot, until finally many of them became very expert at this long-distance shooting.

"A band of Indians happening to come to the fort one day, and observing a wolf on one of the favourite places of resort, several of them prepared to take a circuitous turn to have a shot at the animal. Seeing them prepare—'Try,' said I, 'and kill it from where you are.' The Indians smiled at my ignorance. 'Can the whites,' said the chief, 'kill it at that distance?' 'The whites,' said I, 'do not live by hunting or shooting as do the Indians, or they might.' 'There is no gun,' continued the chief, 'that could kill at that distance.' By this time the wolf had laid hold of a bone, or piece of flesh, and was scampering off with it, at full speed, to the opposite woods. Taking hold of my gun

—'If we cannot kill it,' said I, 'we shall make it let go its prey.' 'My horse against your shot,' called out the chief, 'that you do not hit the wolf.' 'Done,' said I; but I certainly thought within myself that the chief ran no great risk of losing his horse, nor the wolf of losing his life. Taking an elevation of some fifteen or sixteen feet over it, by chance I shot the animal in his flight, to the astonishment of the chief, as well as all present, who, clapping their hands to their mouths in amazement, measured the distance by five arrow-shots: nothing but their wonder could exceed their admiration of this effect of fire-arms.

"When the ball struck the wolf, it was in the act of leaping; and we may judge of its speed at the time, from the fact that the distance from whence it took the last leap to where it was lying stretched, measured twenty-four feet! The ball struck the wolf in the left thigh, and passing through the body, neck and head, it lodged in the lower jaw; I cut it out with my pen-knife. The chief, on delivering up his horse, which he did cheerfully, asked me for the ball, and that ball was the favourite ornament of his neck for years after-wards. The horse I returned to its owner. The Indians then asked me for the skin of the dead wolf; and to each of the guns belonging to the party was appended a piece: the Indians fancying that the skin would enable them, in future, to kill animals at a great distance."

The following summer, McKenzie with Ross and

ninety-five men went up the river and encamped at
the site determined on for the new establishment of
Fort Nez Percés, about one-half mile from the mouth
of the Walla Walla. This country was occupied by
Indians of the Shahaptian stock—fierce, good warriors, and impulsive—easily moved in one direction or
the other. They seemed by no means favorable to
the coming whites; did not shake hands with them, and
in fact appeared disposed to boycott the new arrivals.

The situation was a difficult one, because the construction of a fort required a dividing of the party into
many small bands, and also because more Indians were
constantly coming in, and their actions caused much
uneasiness. They insisted on receiving pay for the
timber to be used in building the fort; they forbade
hunting and fishing; they set the price on all articles
of trade, and it was difficult to know what the outcome
of this might be.

The difficulties threatening the traders caused an
almost complete suspension of work. They stood on
their guard, ready for an attack at any time, while
for five days there was no intercourse between whites
and Indians; food was short, and one night the party
went to bed supperless. The Indians continued to
gather, and the traders thought that they were plot-
ting and planning—no one knew what.

A slight enclosure had been put up, behind which the
traders awaited whatever might happen. After a time,
the chiefs opened negotiations with the whites and

insisted that liberal presents should be made to all the Indians roundabout, in order to gain their favor. This was obviously impracticable, since all the property of the traders would not have sufficed to make a present to each Indian, and the demand was refused, with the result that the firmness of the white men caused the Indians to reduce their requests and finally to submit to the proposals of the whites, and as soon as this was agreed on a brisk trade went on.

The position chosen for the fort was noteworthy among the natives because it was the ground on which, some years before, Lewis and Clark had ratified a general peace between themselves and the tribes of the surrounding country. The situation was commanding. To the west was a spacious view of the great river, to the north and east were the wide expanses of the yellow plains, while to the south lay wild, rough hills on either side of the river, overlooked by two singular towering rocks on the east side of the stream, called by the natives "The Twins." In the distance lay the Blue Mountains.

Presently a large war-party returned to the camp with scalps and captives—a great triumph. Now came a demand from the Indians that the white traders should not give guns or balls to the enemies of these Indians, but after much negotiation and many speeches, the Indians agreed that peace should be made between themselves and the Snakes.

It was not long after this that a considerable party

was sent off to penetrate the country inhabited by the
Snakes and other tribes to the south. The traders
had secured two hundred and eighty horses, enough
for riding and packing, and the most of these were to
go off with the Snake expedition, which consisted of
fifty-five men, nearly two hundred horses, three hundred beaver-traps, and a considerable stock of trade
goods. Mr. McKenzie led the expedition, which left
Fort Nez Percés at the end of September. Ross, with
the remaining party, stayed at the Fort.

The neighboring Indians, of whom Ross speaks in
most cordial terms, treated the traders well and were
respectful and good-natured, but presently came rumors
of difficulties between the trading party to the Snakes
and that tribe, and one of these rumors was confirmed
by the arrival of a member of that expedition, an Iroquois, who had evidently had a hard time. According
to his account, the Iroquois after a time separated
from McKenzie to trap a small river which was well
stocked with beaver. The Iroquois, according to the
story, began to exchange their horses, guns, and traps
with a small party of Snakes, and presently had little
or nothing left. The returned Iroquois man got lost,
and finally, with great difficulty, without food, blanket,
or arms, got back to Fort Nez Percés. Other Iroquois returned and told various stories, and finally,
going back to Fort George, persuaded Mr. Keith to send
out a party to punish the Indians, who they said had
injured them. Such a party was sent out to the Cow-

litz River, and the Iroquois getting away from Mr.
Ogden killed twelve men, women, and children, and
scalped three of them.   This seemed fatal to further
friendly relations; nevertheless, at last peace was concluded between the traders and the Cowlitz Indians,
and was sealed by the marriage of the chief's daughter
to one of the fur traders.

There was more sporadic fighting and killing of
Indians and the murder of five people belonging to Fort
George, so that things got into a very bad condition,
which it took a long time to smooth over.

Late in the season Mr. McKenzie with six men on
snow-shoes returned from the interior and gave an
interesting account of the new country through which
he had passed—a country to him not wholly new, because he had been through it in 1811. He reported
that the Iroquois, instead of trapping and hunting,
had separated and were scattered all over the country
by twos and threes, living with the Indians, without
horses, without traps, without furs, and without clothing.   He left them as he found them.

Of the region traversed, Mr McKenzie reported:
"On our outward journey, the surface was moun-
tainous and rugged, and still more so on our way back.
Woods and valleys, rocks and plains, rivers and ravines, alternately met us; but altogether it is a delightful country.   There animals of every class rove about
undisturbed; wherever there was a little plain, the red
deer were seen grazing in herds about the rivers; round

every other point were clusters of poplar and elder, and where there was a sapling, the ingenious and industrious beaver was at work. Otters sported in the eddies; the wolf and the fox were seen sauntering in quest of prey; now and then a few cypresses or stunted pines were met with on the rocky parts, and in their spreading tops the raccoon sat secure. In the woods, the martin and black fox were numerous; the badger sat quietly looking from his mound; and in the numberless ravines, among bushes laden with fruits, the black, the brown, and the grisly bear were seen. The mountain sheep, and goat white as snow, browsed on the rocks, and ridges; and the big horn species ran among the lofty cliffs. Eagles and vultures, of uncommon size, flew about the rivers. When we approached, most of these animals stood motionless; they would then move off a little distance, but soon came anew to satisfy a curiosity that often proved fatal to them.

"The report of a gun did not alarm them: they would give a frisk at each shot, and stand again; but when the flag was unfurled, being of a reddish hue, it was with apparent reluctance they would retire beyond the pleasing sight. Hordes of wild horses were likewise seen on this occasion; and of all the animals seen on our journey they were the wildest, for none of them could be approached; their scent is exceedingly keen, their hearing also; and in their curiosity they were never known to come at any time within gun-shot. One band of these contained more than two hundred. Some of them were browsing on the face of the hills; others were running like deer up and down the steeps; and some were galloping backwards and forwards on the brows of the sloping mountains, with their flowing manes and bushy tails streaming in the wind."

Mr. McKenzie's successful trip commanded the admiration of all of the council of the head men at Fort George. Those who had formerly been opposed to him were now loud in his praises, and the establishment of Fort Nez Percés and the gaining of a foothold in the Snake country were warmly approved. He remained at Fort Nez Percés only seven days and then started back again. His report of the prospects in the Snake country was gratifying, but his people were giving great trouble.

III

INDIANS AND THEIR BATTLES

Fort Nez Percés was stockaded with an enclosure of pickets of sawn timber some twelve or fifteen feet high with four towers or bastions. The pickets were two and one-half feet broad by six inches thick. Near the top of the stockade was a balustrade four feet high, and a gallery five feet broad extended all around it, while the walls were loopholed. At each angle of the fort was a large reservoir holding two hundred gallons of water, and within the stockade were all the buildings, warehouses, stores, and dwelling-houses. These buildings were all loopholed and had sliding doors, and the trading-room was arranged with a small door in the wall, eighteen inches square, through which the Indians passed their furs, receiving from the traders on the inside the goods to which they were entitled. The outer gate was arranged to open and shut by a pulley, and besides this there were two double doors. Except on special occasions, the Indians were never invited into the fort. Nevertheless, at the gate there was a house for the accommodation of the Indians, with fire, tobacco, and a man to look after them at all times. The Indians, however, did not like this arrangement, because it seemed to show suspicion on the part of the white men; they themselves were suspicious of some plots. They asked whether the traders were afraid of them or afraid that they would steal, and while the traders denied that they were afraid of anything, they persisted in their plan, and at length the Indians accepted the situation. The traders were supplied with cannons, swivels, muskets, and bayonets, boarding-pikes and hand-grenades, while above the gate stood a small mortar. The position was a strong one, and Ross calls it the "Gibraltar of Columbia" and speaks of it as "a triumph of British energy and enterprise, of civilization over barbarism."

McKenzie, on his return to the interior, had promised to be at the river Skam-naugh about the 5th of June and had asked that an outfit with supplies for his party be sent to meet him there. For this reason Ross returned from his annual trip to Fort George nearly a month earlier than usual—by the 15th of May. A party of fifteen men under a clerk named Kittson was sent out to take McKenzie his supplies and reinforce him. Kittson was a new man in the service, and was full of confidence that he could handle and defeat all the Indians on the continent. He had good luck until the party got into the debatable land in the Snake territory, and here, first, a dozen of his horses were stolen, and then, a little later, all of them.

Meantime McKenzie had had the usual difficulties with his Iroquois trappers, who could not be trusted with goods to trade with the Snakes. When the people whom he expected to meet at the river were not there, he sent out ten men to look for them. Two days after starting, as they were passing through a canyon, they met, face to face, the Indians who had just taken all of Kittson's horses, and, recognizing the animals, charged the three horse-thieves. One was killed, another wounded and escaped, and a third was taken captive, and the traders turned the herd about and drove the horses back to Kittson's camp.

Kittson now had thirty-six men and joined Mc-Kenzie, on the way capturing two more Indian horse-thieves, caught at night while cutting loose the horses. Kittson handed over his supplies, received McKenzie's furs, and set out again for Fort Nez Percés.

When McKenzie and Kittson separated, the former
had only three men left with him, for his Iroquois did
not arrive, as expected. While waiting for them, a
threatening party of mountain Snakes appeared at his
camp, who were very importunate, so much so that
at last McKenzie took from his pile of goods a keg
of gunpowder and, lighting a match, threatened, if the
Indians continued to advance, to blow up the whole
party. Taken by surprise, they hesitated, and then
suddenly, without a word, took to flight, not from
fear of the threats of McKenzie, but because of the
sudden appearance of a large war-party of Shahaptians
on the other side of the river. Fortunately, these people could not cross the high and rushing stream, but
a little later they made an attack on Kittson's party
and killed two of his men. As soon as the war-party
had gone McKenzie and his men, with their property,
crossed the channel of the river to an island, where
they remained twenty-two days, until the return of
Kittson. McKenzie and Kittson were now in a situation not at all agreeable. On one side were the Nez
Percés, on the other the Blackfeet, and all about were
the Snakes. All these tribes were hostile to one another, and all of them more or less ill-disposed toward
the whites, so the summer was an anxious one, but Mc-
Kenzie purposed to winter in the upper country as
well as he might. Here Ross interjects an interesting
sketch of trappers' methods.

"A safe and secure spot, near wood and water, is first

selected for the camp. Here the chief of the party resides with the property. It is often exposed to danger, or sudden attack, in the absence of the trappers, and requires a vigilant eye to guard against the lurking savages. The camp is called head quarters. From hence all the trappers, some on foot, some on horseback, according to the distance they have to go, start every morning, in small parties, in all directions, ranging the distance of some twenty miles around. Six traps is the allowance for each hunter; but to guard against wear and tear, the complement is more frequently ten. These he sets every night, and visits again in the morning; sometimes oftener, according to distance, or other circumstances. The beaver taken in the traps are always conveyed to the camp, skinned, stretched, dried, folded up with the hair in the inside, laid by, and the flesh used for food. No sooner, therefore, has a hunter visited his traps, set them again, and looked out for some other place, than he returns to the camp, to feast, and enjoy the pleasures of an idle day.

"There is, however, much anxiety and danger in going through the ordinary routine of a trapper's duty. For as the enemy is generally lurking about among the rocks and hiding-places, watching an opportunity, the hunter has to keep a constant lookout; and the gun is often in one hand, while the trap is in the other. But when several are together, which is often the case in suspicious places, one-half set the traps, and the other half keep guard over them. Yet notwithstanding all their precautions, some of them fall victims to Indian treachery.

"The camp remains stationary while two-thirds of the trappers find beaver in the vicinity; but whenever the beaver becomes scarce, the camp is removed to some more favourable spot.   In this manner, the party keeps moving from place to place, during the whole season of hunting.   Whenever serious danger is apprehended, all the trappers make for the camp.   Were we, however, to calculate according to numbers, the prospects from such an expedition would be truly dazzling: say, seventy-five men, with each six traps, to be successfully employed during five months; that is, two in the spring, and three in the fall, equal to 131 working days, the result would be 58,950 beaver! Practically, however, the case is very different.   The apprehension of danger, at all times, is so great, that three-fourths of their time is lost in the necessary steps taken for their own safety.   There is also another serious drawback unavoidably accompanying every large party.   The beaver is a timid animal; the least noise, therefore, made about its haunt will keep it from coming out for nights together; and noise is unavoidable when the party is large.   But when the party is small, the hunter has a chance of being more or less successful.   Indeed, were the nature of the ground such as to admit of the trappers moving about in safety, at all times, and alone, six men, with six traps each, would, in the same space of time, and at the same rate, kill as many beavers—say 4,716—as the whole seventy-five could be expected to do! And yet the evil is without a remedy; for no small party can exist in these parts. Hence the reason why beavers are so numerous."

Ross points out also some of the troubles that the traders must meet with, which troubles were largely due, of course, to the absolute inability of the Indians to comprehend the conditions of this new life. The Indians asked for everything that they saw and berated the traders because their requests were not complied with. They were constantly playing jokes—or what they considered jokes—on the white men, which were irritating enough; and looked with contempt on the whites who were engaged in ordinary labor, which they, of course, did not in the least understand. The Indians, with all their freedom, were far from happy, because they were in a state of constant anxiety and alarm. People who felt themselves injured were likely to make war excursions and kill some one belonging to another tribe, which, of course, extended the field of the trouble.

When fighting took place, and people supposedly friendly to the whites were injured, the traders were blamed, because they sold guns, powder, and balls to any one who might wish to trade with them. The life of the trader was thus one of anxiety, and to handle the Indians successfully called for extraordinary self-control.

Not long before this time some Shahaptians had killed two of Kittson's men and several Snakes. The

Snakes followed them, but before overtaking them
came upon some Indians belonging to the Walla Walla,
camped not three miles from Fort Nez Percés, where
they killed a man, four women, and two children, and
captured two young women and a man. The next
day the whole Walla Walla camp moved down to the
fort, carrying the bodies of the dead. Ross saw the
disorderly procession coming on with shrieks and lam-
entations, and at first did not know what to make of
the advance, but presently the Indians reached the
gate of the fort, placed their dead upon the ground
there, and began to gash themselves with knives in
the oldtime way of mourning. They called to Ross
to come out to them, and he, while very reluctant,
had no choice—if he was to retain his influence with
them—but to obey.

"Turning round to the sentinel at the door, I told
him to lock the gate after me, and keep a sharp look
out. The moment I appeared outside the gate, so
horrible was the uproar, that it baffles all description.
Intoxicated with wrath and savage rage, they resembled
furies more than human beings; and their ghastly,
wild, and forbidding looks were all directed towards
me, as if I had been the cause of their calamity. Tam-
a-tap-um the chief then coming up to me, and pointing
to one of the dead bodies, said, 'You see my sister
there,' then uncovering the body to show the wounds,
added, 'That is a ball hole.' 'The whites', said he
again, 'have murdered our wives and our children.

They have given guns and balls to our enemies. Those very guns and balls have killed our relations.' These words were no sooner uttered than they were repeated over and over again by the whole frantic crowd; who, hearing the chief, believed them to be true. Excitement was now at its height. Their gestures, their passionate exclamations, showed what was working within, and I expected every moment to receive a ball or an arrow. One word of interruption spoken by me at the critical moment, in favour of the whites, might have proved fatal to myself. I therefore remained silent, watching a favourable opportunity, and also examining closely the holes in the garments of the dead bodies. The holes I was convinced were made by arrows, and not by balls as the chief had asserted; but it remained for me to convince others when an opportunity offered.

"Every violent fit of mourning was succeeded, as is generally the case among savages, by a momentary calm. As soon, therefore, as I perceived the rage of the crowd beginning to subside, and nature itself beginning to flag, I availed myself of the interval to speak in turn; for silence then would have been a tacit acknowledgment of our guilt. I therefore advanced, and taking the chief by the hand, said in a low tone of voice, as if overcome by grief, 'My friend, what is all this? Give me an explanation. You do not love the whites; you have told me nothing yet.' Tam-a-tap-um then turning to his people, beckoned to them with the hand to be silent; entire silence was not to be expected. He then went over the whole affair from beginning to end. When the chief ended, and the people were in a listening mood, I sympathized with their misfortunes, and observed that the whites had been undeservedly blamed. 'They are innocent,' said I, 'and that I can prove. Look at that,' said I, pointing to an arrow wound, which no one could mistake, 'the wounds are those of arrows, not balls. Nor were the Snakes themselves so much to blame; as we shall be able to show.'

"At these assertions the chief looked angry, and there was a buzz of disapprobation, among the crowd; but I told the chief to listen patiently until I had done. The chief then composed himself, and I proceeded. 'After your solemn acquiescence in a peace between yourselves and the Snakes, through the influence of the whites, the Shaw-ha-ap-tens violated the second pledge by going again to war, across the Blue Mountains; and not content with having killed their enemies, they killed their friends also. They killed two of the whites. The Snakes in the act of retaliation have therefore made you all to mourn this day; they have made the whites to mourn also. But your loss is less than ours; your relations have been killed; but still you have their bodies: that consolation is denied us. Our friends have been killed, but we know not where their bodies lie.' These facts neither the chief nor the crowd could gainsay. The chief, with a loud voice, explained what I had said to the listening multitude; when they with one voice exclaimed, 'It is true, it is true!' Leaving the chief, I then entered the fort, and taking some red cloth, laid six inches of it on each body, as a token of sympathy; then I told them to go and bury their dead. A loud fit of lamentation closed the scene. The bodies were then taken up, and the crowd moved off, in a quiet and orderly manner.

"But the satisfaction we enjoyed at the departure of the savages was of short duration, for they were scarcely out of sight, and I scarcely inside the door, when another band, related to those who had been killed, arrived at the fort gate, and the loud and clamorous scene of mourning was again renewed.

"Among this second crowd of visitors was a fellow dignified by the name of Prince, and brother to one of the young women who had been carried off by the Snakes. Prince encamped within fifty yards of the fort, and his tent was no sooner pitched than he began to chant the song of death. When an Indian resorts to this mode of mourning, it is a sure sign that, 'he has thrown his body away,' as the Indians term it, and meditates self-destruction. Being told of Prince's resolution, I went to his tent to see him, and found him standing, with his breast leaning upon the muzzle of his gun; his hair was dishevelled, and he was singing with great vehemence: he never raised his head to see who I was. I knew all was not right, and spoke to him; but receiving no answer, I went away, on my return to the fort. I had scarcely advanced twenty yards from his tent, before I heard the report of a gun behind me, and turning back again, I found the unfortunate fellow lying on the ground weltering in his blood, his gun partly under him. He was still breathing. The ball had entered his left breast, below the nipple, and came out near the backbone. The wound was bleeding freely, and he disgorged great quantities of blood. I went to the fort for some assistance, but on our return I expected that every moment would have been his last; however we dressed his wound, and did what we could to allay his suffering.

"The Indians now assembled in great numbers, and were noisy and violent. In the first instance, they threw all the blame of the unfortunate affair on the whites; but in their rage and violence, they quarrelled among themselves, and this new direction in their excitement removed the odium in some degree from the whites, and diverted the tide of popular fury into another channel. During the affair, one of those unfortunate wretches called medicine-men happened to be sitting at the fort gate, when a brother of the man who had just shot himself went up to him, saying, 'You dog! you have thrown your bad medicine on my brother, and he is dead; but you shall not live,' and in saying so, he shot him dead on the spot. The ball, after passing through the man's body, went more than three inches into one of the fort palisades. I was standing on the gallery at the moment he was shot, and had it been on any other occasion but in the midst of a quarrel between the Indians, we certainly should have avenged his death on the spot; for the murdered man was an excellent Indian, and a sincere friend of the whites.

"The scene now assumed a threatening aspect. Guns, bows, arrows, and every missile that could be laid hold of, came into requisition; and robes, feathers, bells, belts, and trinkets of every description, were rattling about in true savage style. The fellow who had just shot the medicine-man was shot in his turn, and before the chiefs arrived, or could get a hearing, three others were shot. The place appeared more like a field of battle than anything else; for besides the five bodies that lay lifeless on the ground, twice that number were desperately wounded.

"As soon as the deadly quarrel began, not knowing the intent of the Indians, nor how it might end, I shut the gates, and kept as clear of the quarrel as possible. In the midst of the confusion, the Indians poured in from all quarters, adding fuel to the flame; and some of them in approaching the place, thinking it was a quarrel between the whites and themselves, fired a shot or two at the fort before they were aware of the mistake. This made us take to our bastions: our matches were lighted, guns pointed, and we ourselves watched the maneuvres of the savages around us. One unguarded shot would have involved us in the quarrel, which it was our interest to avoid; as it would have put an end to all our prospects in the Snake as well as the Nez Percés quarter.

"As soon as the chiefs could get a hearing, peace was generally restored; and the five dead bodies were removed to the Indian camp, at a distance from the fort. Such a scene I should never wish to witness again. This affray, happening at our very door, gave us much uneasiness; as to keep the balance of good will at all times in our favour was a task of more than ordinary difficulty."

The next day more Indians came in, and soon several tribes were represented. The whites were indirectly taxed with all the troubles, and there was a vast deal of speech-making and many threats. At last, however, after a week of counselling, the matter quieted down, the different tribes all smoked together, and peace was made—to last for a time.

Ross has much to say about the different tribes of Shoshoni stock and their relations to each other. He was long with them and studied them carefully.

The Ban-at-tees, which we call Bannocks, seem to have been held by the Snake tribes to the south and west as chargeable with most of the disturbances between the whites and the Snakes, and after a time it developed that the Indians that murdered Mr. Reid and his party in the autumn of 1813 were Bannocks.

During the winter a hunter named Hodgens became separated from his party during a violent snow-storm and lost his way. A little later, in the same way,

he lost his horse; his gun became broken so that he
could not make a fire, and during two days and two
nights he was obliged to lie out without fire.

"On the fourteenth day, however, while scarcely
able to crawl, he had the good luck to fall on the main
camp of the War-are-ree-kas; where recognizing the
chief's tent, from the manner in which it was painted,
he advanced towards it, looking more like a ghost than
a living being. On his entering, Ama-ketsa, surprised
at his unexpected arrival, and still more surprised at
his emaciated appearance, stared him in the face for
some time, and could scarcely believe that it was a
white man; but as soon as he was convinced of the
reality, and made acquainted with the wanderer's forlorn state, he ordered one of his wives to put a new
pair of shoes on his feet, gave him something to eat,
and was extremely kind to him. Here Hodgens remained for eleven days in the chief's tent, nursed with
all the care and attention of a child of the family, until
his strength was recovered; and as soon as he was on
his legs again, Ama-ketsa furnished him with a horse,
some provisions, and sent one of his own sons to conduct him to the whites. Although Hodgens could give
the Indians no clue as to where the hunters were encamped, yet on the eighth day they arrived safe and
sound at their friends', and as straight as if they had
been led by a line to them; which convinced our
people that the Indians knew well the place of their
retreat. . . .

"A party of our people had been out a whole week in search of Hodgens, and found his dead horse, but despairing of finding him they returned to their camp; and all hope of ever finding Hodgens alive vanished: when he did come, their astonishment was equal to their delight. The friendly conduct of Ama-ketsa towards him was a strong proof of that chief's good-will towards our people. During our friends' stay in this place they had several surprises from the Indians, but they managed matters so well that no more of their horses were stolen."

There is distinct reference in this volume to the Yellowstone National Park, which may very well have been visited by Ross or some of his trappers. He speaks of "Pilot Knobs"—the Three Tetons—salt and sulphur springs and of boiling fountains, some of them so hot as to boil meat. These allusions do not, of course, necessarily refer to Yellowstone Park, for there are many other places in the Rocky Mountains where such things are found, but the references to the Three Tetons and to the source of the Lewis River are suggestive enough.

Ross speaks also of various foods of the country; of the use of horse flesh and dog flesh and also of the Snake tobacco, which, for a time at least, the Indians preferred to that imported by the whites. He credits the Snake Indians with extraordinary skill in wood-craft, shown especially by the methods they employ to avoid possible enemies.

IV

WITH THE HUDSON BAY COMPANY

THE time was now at hand when the Northwest Company should be merged into the Hudson Bay Company. This consolidation naturally cast a gloom over the retainers of the Northwest Company wherever they were situated. The people who had been employed by the Northwest Company were uncertain where they stood. Those who had been promoted prior to the "deed-poll"—March 26, 1821—were provided for by the Hudson Bay Company, whereas all others were excluded from these benefits. Some of them, however, received pecuniary compensation for their disappointment, and of these Ross was one, or he was told by an officer of the company that five hundred pounds sterling had been placed to his credit, but of this he never received a penny.

Ross now entered the service of the Hudson Bay Company. He had been for a short time with the Pacific Fur Company; had spent seven years with the Northwest Company and, except for his experience, was about where he had been when he started.

The servants of the Northwest Company had been in the habit of depositing their savings with the firm which was its head, and a few years after the consolidation of the two companies this concern failed and all these savings disappeared.

Toward the end of his first volume, after much information about Indians, half-breeds, trading, trappers, and travel, Ross draws an interesting picture of the manner in which the bourgeois—or proprietary partner—journeys through the fur country, and the absolute loyalty to him and to the company felt by the voyageurs, who were, indeed, the backbone of the northern fur trade. He says:

"The bourgeois is carried on board his canoe upon the back of some sturdy fellow generally appointed for this purpose. He seats himself on a convenient mattress, somewhat low in the centre of his canoe; his gun by his side, his little cherubs fondling around him, and his faithful spaniel lying at his feet. No sooner is he at his ease, than his pipe is presented by his attendant, and he then begins smoking, while his silken banner undulates over the stern of his painted vessel. Then the bending paddles are plied, and the fragile craft speeds through the currents with a degree of fleetness not to be surpassed;—yell upon yell from the hearty crew proclaiming their prowess and skill.

"A hundred miles performed, night arrives; the hands jump out quickly into the water, and their nabob and his companions are supported to terra firma. A roaring fire is kindled and supper is served; his honour then retires to enjoy his repose. At dawn of day they set out again; the men now and then relax their arms, and light their pipes; but no sooner does the headway of the canoe die away, than they renew their labours and their chorus: a particular voice being ever selected to lead the song. The guide conducts the march.

"At the hour of breakfast they put ashore on some green plot. The tea-kettle is boiling; a variegated mat is spread, and a cold collation set out. Twenty minutes—and they start anew. The dinner-hour arrives, they put aground again. The liquor-can accompanies the provision-basket; the contents are quickly set forth in simple style; and, after a refreshment of twenty minutes more, off they set again, until the twilight checks their progress.

"When it is practicable to make way in the dark, four hours is the voyageurs' allowance of rest; and at times, on boisterous lakes and bold shores, they keep for days and nights together on the water, without intermission, and without repose. They sing to keep time to their paddles; they sing to keep off drowsiness, caused by their fatigue; and they sing because the bourgeois likes it.

"Through hardships and dangers, wherever he leads, they are sure to follow with alacrity and cheerfulness— over mountains and hills, along valleys and dales, through woods and creeks, across lakes and rivers. They look not to the right, nor to the left; they make no halt in foul or fair weather. Such is their skill, that they venture to sail in the midst of waters like oceans, and, with amazing aptitude, they shoot down the most frightful rapids; and they generally come off safely.

"When about to arrive at the place of their destination, they dress with neatness, put on their plumes, and a chosen song is raised. They push up against the beach, as if they meant to dash the canoe into splinters; but most adroitly back their paddles at the right moment; whilst the foreman springs on shore, and, seizing the prow, arrests the vessel in its course. On this joyful occasion, every person advances to the waterside, and great guns are fired to announce the bourgeois' arrival. A general shaking of hands takes place, as it often happens that people have not met for years: even the bourgeois goes through this mode of salutation with the meanest. There is, perhaps, no country where the ties of affection are more binding than here. Each addresses his comrades as his brothers; and all address themselves to the bourgeois with reverence, as if he were their father."

About this time, Mr. McKenzie retired from the fur trade and went to live in northern New York. This left without occupation a number of hunters and trappers in the country, where Ross was stationed, and Ross made up his mind to leave the country and abandon the business which he had so long followed. He was still merely a clerk in the service of the great company. Finan McDonald, a Northwest veteran, now in the service of the Hudson Bay Company, was to be in charge of the people in the Snake country, and a little later John Warren Dease, a chief trader in the new company, reached Fort Nez Percés and told Ross that he had been named to take charge of the fort and the country immediately about it, while Ross was to succeed McKenzie in charge of the Snake country.

Nevertheless, Ross was determined to go back to the East and had started with his family, but on his way—when he reached the Rocky Mountains—he received a letter from Governor Simpson, offering him the management of the Snake country for three years at a liberal salary. Ross hesitated to accept, but finally did so, and went to Spokane House to make up his party. McDonald had recently come in there and with much grumbling; for he had had trouble with the Piegan Blackfeet, in which one of his men had been shot by treachery, and in a pitched battle afterward had with the same party he lost seven more of his men.

The account of this battle may properly be inserted here:

"One day, when they had travelled until dark in search of water, they found some at the bottom of a deep and rocky ravine, down which they went and encamped. They had seen no traces of enemies during the day, and being tired, they all went to sleep, without keeping watch. In the morning, however, just at the dawn of day, they were saluted from the top of the ravine before they got up, with a volley of balls about their ears; without, however, any being killed or wounded: one of them had the stock of his gun pierced through with a ball, and another of them his powder-horn shivered to pieces; but this was all the injury they sustained from the enemy's discharge. The alarm was instantly given, all hands in confusion sprang up and went out to see what was the matter; some with one shoe on and the other off, others naked, with a gun in one hand and their clothes in the other. When they perceived the Indians on the top of the rocks, yelling and flourishing their arms, the whites gave a loud huzza, and all hands were collected together in an instant; but the Indians instead of taking advantage of their position, wheeled about and marched off without firing another shot.

"McDonald, at the head of thirty men, set out to pursue them; but finding the ravine too steep and rocky to ascend, they were apprehensive that the sudden disappearance of the Indians was a stratagem to entrap them, when they might have been popped off by the enemy from behind stones and trees, without having an opportunity of defending themselves. Acting on this opinion, they returned, and taking a supply of powder and ball with them, they mounted their horses, to the number of forty-five, and then pursued the enemy, leaving twenty men behind to guard the camp. When our people got to the head of the ravine, the Indians were about a mile off, and all on foot, having no horses, with the exception of five for carrying their luggage; and our people, before they could get up with them, had to pass another ravine still deeper and broader than the one they were encamped in, so that before they got down on one side of it the enemy had got up on the other side. And here again the Indians did not avail themselves of their advantage, but allowed our people to follow without firing a shot at them, as if encouraging them on; and so bold and confident were they, that many of them bent themselves down in a posture of contempt, by way of bidding them defiance.

"As soon as our people had got over the second ravine, they took a sweep, wheeled about, and met the Indians in the teeth; then dismounting, the battle began, without a word being spoken on either side. As soon as the firing commenced, the Indians began their frantic gestures, and whooped and yelled with the view of intimidating; they fought like demons, one fellow all the time waving a scalp on the end of a pole: nor did they yield an inch of ground till more than twenty of them lay dead; at last, they threw down their guns, and held up their hands as a signal of peace. By this time our people had lost three men, and not thinking they had yet taken ample vengeance for their death, they made a rush on the Indians, killed the fellow who held the pole, and carried off the scalp and the five horses. The Indians then made a simultaneous dash on one side, and got into a small coppice of wood, leaving their dead on the spot where they fell. Our people supposed that they had first laid down their arms and next taken to the bush because they were short of ammunition, as many of the shots latterly were but mere puffs. Unfortunately for the Indians, the scalp taken proved to be none other than poor Anderson's, and this double proof of their guilt so enraged our people, that to the bush they followed them.

"McDonald sent to the camp for buck-shot, and then poured volleys into the bush among them, from the distance of some twenty or thirty yards, till they had expended fifty-six pounds weight; the Indians all this time only firing a single shot now and then when the folly and imprudence of our people led them too near; but they seldom missed their mark, and here three more of the whites fell. At this part of the conflict, two of our own people, an Iroquois and a Canadian, got into a high dispute which was the bravest man; when the former challenged the latter to go with him into the bush and scalp a Piegan. The Canadian accepted the challenge; taking each other by one hand, with a scalping knife in the other, savage like, they entered the bush, and advanced until they were within four or five feet of a Piegan, when the Iroquois said, 'I will scalp this one, you go and scalp another;' but just as the Iroquois was in the act of stretching out his hand to lay hold of his victim the Piegan shot him through the head, and so bespattered the Canadian with his brains that he was almost blind; the latter, however, got back again to his comrades, but deferred taking the scalp.

"M'Donald and his men being fatigued with firing, thought of another and more effectual plan of destroy-

ing the Piegans.   It blew a strong gale of wind at the
time, so they set fire to the bush of dry and decayed
wood; it burnt with the rapidity of straw, and the
devouring element laid the whole bush in ashes in a
very short time.   When it was first proposed, the question arose who should go and fire the bush, at the muzzle of the Piegans' guns.   'The oldest man in the
camp,' said M'Donald; 'and I'll guard him.'   The lot
fell upon Bastony, a superannuated hunter on the
wrong side of seventy; the poor and wrinkled old man
took the torch in his hand and advanced, trembling
every step with the fear of instant death before him;
while M'Donald and some others walked at his heels
with their guns cocked.   The bush was fired, the party
returned, and volleys of buck-shot were again poured
into the bush to aid the fire in the work of destruction.
   "About one hundred yards from the burning bush,
was another much larger bush, and while the fire was
consuming the one, our people advanced and stationed
themselves at the end of the other, to intercept any of
the Piegans who might attempt the doubtful alternative of saving themselves by taking refuge in it.   To
ensure success, our people left open the passage from
the one bush to the other, while they themselves stood
in two rows, one upon each side, with their guns cocked;
suddenly the half-roasted Piegans, after uttering a
scream of despair, burst through the flames and made a
last and expiring effort to gain the other bush; then
our people poured in upon each side of them a fatal

vólley of ball and buck-shot, which almost finished what the flames had spared. Yet, notwithstanding all these sanguinary precautions, a remnant escaped by getting into the bush. The wounded victims who fell under the last volley, the Iroquois dealt with in their own way—with the knife.

"After the massacre was ended, our people collected their dead and returned to the camp at sunset; not we should suppose to rejoice, but rather to mourn. We afterwards learned that only seven out of the seventy-five which formed the party of the unfortunate Piegans, returned home to relate the mournful tale. Although our people were drawn into this unfortunate affair with justice on their side, yet they persevered in it with folly and ended it with cruelty: no wonder, then, if they afterwards paid for their cruelty with their own blood."

After a short stay at Spokane House, Ross, who had been given—on paper—a force of eighty men, was able to get together only forty, a number of whom were quite unsatisfactory. At the Flathead River post, at the foot of the mountains, he picked up fourteen more, making the whole party fifty-five. It was a curious mixture of Americans, Canadian Frenchmen, half-breeds, Iroquois, natives of eastern Canada, Saulteaux, Crees, Spokanes, Kutenais, Flatheads, Kalispels, Palouse, and one Snake. Of the Canadians, five were more than sixty years of age, and two more than seventy. The Iroquois were good hunters, but untrustworthy, while the local Indians were useful chiefly in looking after the horses. Twenty-five of the people were married, so that in the company there were twenty-five women and sixty-four children. They carried with them a brass three-pounder cannon, more than two hundred beaver-traps, and about four hundred horses. It is understood, of course, that they carried no provisions, depending wholly on their guns for food, and Ross complains that on the day of starting they had killed but one deer, a slender repast for one hundred and thirty-seven hungry mouths.

Trouble with the Iroquois began almost at once. Having received their advances, they thought little about the debts that they owed for guns, horses, traps, clothing, and ammunition.

At a defile in Hell's Gate, where the Piegans and Blackfeet used to cross the mountains on their war journeys, they camped for some little time, and here the hunters, to their great satisfaction, killed four wild horses, besides twenty-seven elk and thirty-two small deer. The capture of the horses was a great triumph for the hunters, who were more delighted with their success in this little adventure than if they had killed a hundred buffalo.

Not long after this, two Iroquois deserted and turned back, and the leader, having previously lost another Iroquois by desertion, felt that this must be stopped. He therefore followed the deserters about sixteen miles back on the trail and captured them, but they refused to return, and it was necessary to threaten to tie one of them to a horse's tail before he would consent to go.

They were frequently meeting Indians; Piegans first and then Nez Percés, and whenever strangers were met with, the Iroquois traded off their property, even to their guns, receiving in return what Ross calls "trash."

The weather was now growing cold, partly, perhaps, because they were climbing all the time. Beaver were plenty and elk, deer, and mountain goats extremely abundant. They were now getting close to the head of the Flathead River and were fronting great mountains, largely snow-covered. Six men were sent out to try to find a way through the mountains, and at length returned reporting that it was quite impracticable to cross the mountains here, because after reaching the plateau above the timber the snow was five or six feet deep for about twelve long miles. Beyond the mountains, however, they said, was a large open plain where the snow was scarcely a foot deep. These scouts had killed buffalo and brought in backloads of it. To travel with horses for a dozen miles, through snow five or six feet deep and crusted, was quite impossible, and Ross was bitterly discouraged. Nevertheless, he determined that this was the best way to cross the mountains, and sent the men back to camp, with instructions to greatly modify their story for the ears of the people. The outcome of it was that, after much counselling and more or less quarrelling, the party started to break a way through this snow-covered plateau. It proved much more difficult than even Ross had supposed, but by working with horses and men and using wooden mallets to break the crust, and shovels to cut the way, they at length, thirty-three days from the time they reached that camp and after twenty-one days' extraordinary labor, got through the snow and came out on the other side, where there was feed for the horses and game for the men. Now, however, they were in the enemy's country, for it was here that the Blackfeet were constantly travelling about, and just beyond here that McDonald had lost seven of his men the year before.

Just after they came down out of the mountains, they crossed the trail made by Lewis and Clark up the middle fork of the Missouri, nearly twenty years before.

After they had passed beyond the snow, they found beaver extraordinarily abundant in certain localities. At one place they took ninety-five beaver in a single morning and sixty more during the same day. But, as they continued to go down the mountains, the beaver became more scarce, but the snow was less. The young grass had started, and buffalo were enormously abundant, though at this time not fat. Blackfeet and Piegan war roads were constantly crossed, and fresh tracks of men and horses often seen. These signs made Ross more and more vigilant, and presently he discovered that his Iroquois were turning out their horses to wander among the hills, and although he warned them against repeating this, they paid little attention to the warning. Under such carelessness it was evident that any war-party discovering the trappers would have no difficulty in running off the animals. These, though nominally belonging to the individuals who used them, had been obtained on credit from the company, and if they were stolen, the loss would be the company's. Only a day or two later, Martin, an Iroquois, was discovered to have turned loose six horses, whereupon Ross sent out for the horses, took them back into his own charge, gave Martin credit for the horses, and proceeded to move camp. Martin and his family remained sitting by the fire. However, the other Iroquois brought them along on some of their horses, and at night old men came to Ross to intercede with him, begging him to give back the horses to Martin. After much persuasion he did so, and the example was not forgotten either by the Iroquois or by others of the trappers.

The party proceeded eastward with disappointing results, for they found few beaver. Before long, therefore, they turned back, and, passing over the divide between the Salmon and Goddin Rivers, Ross sent off eight men to trap it downstream, but made them leave their horses behind, in order that they might more readily conceal themselves from the enemy, for Piegan Blackfeet were thought to be in the country. Meantime, the main party went off to John Day's Valley to supply themselves with buffalo meat, for recently game had been scarce and they had been wasteful of food when they had passed through a country of abundance.

From a camp in Day's Valley, two men were sent to Goddin River to bring back the eight who had been trapping there, and these messengers, carelessly advancing toward a smoke, which they took to be the fire of their own people, walked into the camp of a Piegan war-party. Their horses were captured, but the men threw themselves into the undergrowth and escaped by creeping along the margin of the river under its banks, which were overgrown with bushes. In the middle of the second night, they reached the camp in rags, with moccasins wholly worn out. A party of thirty-five started in pursuit of the Piegans. They did not overtake them, but found the eight trappers safe. They had slept within half a mile of the Piegan camp, neither party being aware of the presence of the other.

Passing over high, rough country, and pestered by the Iroquois, who spent most of their time in trying to get away from the main party, they reached the Rivière aux Malades. Ross now thought it best to let the Iroquois go off and hunt by themselves, but not all of them wished to go, and two of those who had given most trouble—Grey and Martin—preferred to remain with the main party. On the Malades River, there were good signs of beaver, and in one place they counted one hundred and forty-eight poplar trees cut down by that animal, in a space less than one hundred yards square. The first night they got fifty-two beaver, but were troubled by the rising and the falling of the water, caused, of course, by the melting of the snows on the mountains.

One afternoon a Piegan war-party, discovered approaching the camp, caused the greatest excitement. They did not attack, and presently Ross went out to meet them, gave them some tobacco, and told them to remain where they were. There were ninety-two Indians, and after a time Ross invited them to the camp, where they passed the night in smoking, dancing, and singing. Ross secured the Piegan arms, ordered forty of their horses hobbled and put in with the traders' horses, and thus provided against any hostile action. These Piegans claimed to be on a peace mission to the Shoshoni, and denied all knowledge of the horses taken from the two trappers only a few days before. Ross believed that they felt themselves too few to attack his party and planning to give them a fright, he seized two of their horses and four of their guns, to repay the loss of the horses and traps on Goddin River. The Piegans were humble and apologetic and denied everything, and finally Ross returned their property and gave them a little tobacco and ammunition. They went off in separate parties, but before they disappeared in the mountains all gathered together again.

A little later another Piegan war-party came to the camp in Ross's absence; but he returned before they had entered the camp. There were one hundred and ten of these, but they were badly armed, having only twenty-three guns and little or no ammunition. They professed to be friendly, and declared that they were not trying to take the property of the whites; for two nights before they had come into the camp and gone about among the horses, and had left evidences of their presence by moving a piece of meat which was roasting at the fire, and by rubbing two spots of red paint on a riding saddle at one of the tent doors. The chief who talked with Ross seemed so honest and frank that he was given some ammunition, tobacco, and a knife, and the two parties separated in a very friendly manner. Only a little later, they came across a Snake camp, to which also had come a number of Cayuse chiefs, and here were held ceremonial smokes and speeches, of a most friendly character.

Dropping down Reid's River and trapping constantly, the party at last reached another great Snake camp. By this time they had 1,855 beaver. In this neighborhood there was more or less trouble. The Indians practised all sorts of stratagems to secure the horses of the trappers, and did succeed in getting ten of them, eight of which were later returned. The natives also took a number of traps. Moreover, as they were not punished for what they did, their boldness grew, and at last an Indian picked up a bundle and when it was taken from him by force, he strung his bow and threatened to shoot the man. Ross gave his people much good advice, and pointed out that if they

would stick together they were perfectly able to cow
the Snakes; but they must act together. His plan
was to capture and hold ten of the Indians' horses as
security for property that had been taken. They went
out and caught the horses, and when they returned
with them to the camp, finding two Indians there,
they counted out one hundred bullets, and loaded their
cannon, letting the Indians see what was being done,
and sent a message to the camp that as soon as the
stolen traps had been delivered, they would give up
the horses.

"When the two Indians had returned with the message to their camp, I instructed my people to have their
arms in readiness, in such a position that each man could
have his eye upon his gun, and could lay hold of it at
a moment's warning; but to appear as careless as if
nothing was expected. That if the Indians did come,
as they certainly would, to claim their horses, and insisted on taking them, I would reason the matter with
them; and when that failed, I would give the most forward of them a blow with my pipe stem, which was
to be the signal for my people to act. The moment,
therefore, the signal was given, the men were to shout
according to Indian custom, seize, and make a demonstration with their arms; but were not to fire, until I
had first set the example. During this time there
was a great stir in the Indian camp; people were observed running to and fro, and we awaited the result
with anxiety.

"Not long after, we saw a procession of some fifty
or sixty persons, all on foot and unarmed, advancing
in a very orderly manner towards our camp; in front
of which was placed our big gun, well loaded, pointed,
and the match lit.   My men were in the rear, whistling,
singing, and apparently indifferent.   On the Indians
coming up to me and another man, who stood in front
to receive them near to where the horses were tied, I
drew a line of privilege, and made signs for them not
to pass it.   They, however, looked very angry, and
observed the line with reluctance, so that I had to
beckon to them several times before I was obeyed, or
could make them understand.   At last they made a
sort of irregular halt.

"I then made signs for the Indians to sit down; but
they shook their heads.   I asked where was Ama-
ketsa; but got no satisfactory reply.   One of the fellows immediately introduced the subject of the horses,
in very fierce and insolent language; I however, to
pacify him, and make friends, spoke kindly to them,
and began to reason the matter, and explain it to them
as well as I could; but the fellow already noticed, being
more forward and daring than the rest, sneered at my
argument, and at once laid hold of one of the horses
by the halter, and endeavoured to take it away without further ceremony.   I laid hold of the halter, in
order to prevent him, and the fellow every now and
then gave a tug to get the halter out of my hand; the
others kept urging him on, and they were the more

encouraged, seeing my people did not interfere; the latter were, however, on the alert, waiting impatiently for the signal, without the Indians being in the least aware of it.   Beginning to get a little out of humour, I made signs to the Indian, that if he did not let go, I would knock him down; but, prompted no doubt by the strong party that backed him, and seeing no one with me, he disregarded my threat by giving another tug at the halter.   I then struck him smartly on the side of the head with my pipe stem, and sent him reeling back among his companions; upon which my men sprang up, seized their arms, and gave a loud shout! The sudden act, with the terror conveyed by the cocking of so many guns, so surprised the Indians that they lost all presence of mind; throwing their robes, garments, and all from them, they plunged headlong into the river, and swam with the current till out of danger, every now and then popping up their heads and diving again, like so many wild fowl!   In less than a minute's time, there was not a soul of the embassy to be seen about our camp!   Never was anything more decisive.

"It may be satisfactory to the reader to know what kind of pipe stem it was that one could strike a heavy blow with.   The pipe-bowls generally used, both by Indians and Indian traders, are made of stone, and are large and heavy; the stems resemble a walking-stick more than anything else, and they are generally of ash, and from two-and-a-half to three feet long.

"We had intended removing camp the same day; but after what had happened, I thought it better to pass another day where we were, in order to give the Snakes as well as ourselves an opportunity of making up matters. Not a soul, however, came near us all that day afterwards, and we were at a loss to find out what was going on in the Snake camp. I therefore got about twenty of my men mounted on horseback, to take a turn round, in order to observe the movements of the Indians, but they having brought me word that the women were all employed in their usual duties, I felt satisfied.

"During the following day, ten persons were observed making for our camp, who, on arrival, spread out a buffalo robe, on which was laid all our stolen traps! some whole, some broken into several pieces, which they had been flattening for knives; the whole rendered almost useless to us. Ama-ketsa, who had not been present at the affray of the preceding day, accompanied this party, and made a long and apparently earnest apology for the loss of our traps, and the misunderstanding that ensued; but he did not forget to exculpate his own people from all blame, laying the odium of the whole affair on the Banatees. We knew the contrary: the War-are-ree-kas were the guilty parties, and perhaps Ama-ketsa himself was not altogether innocent; at least, some of his people said so. We, however, accepted the apology, and the traps, as they were; and delivering up all the horses, treated the chief with due honours, satisfied that the business ended so well.

"The chief had no sooner returned to his camp with the horses, than a brisk trade was opened; the Indians, men, women, and children, coming to us with as much confidence as if nothing had happened. On the next morning, while we were preparing to start, one of my men fell from his horse and broke his thigh; we, however, got it so set, as not to prevent our removal. Although everything wore the appearance of peace, yet I thought it necessary to take precautions, in order to avoid any trouble with the natives in passing their camp. I therefore appointed ten men mounted on horseback to go before, the camp followed in order after, while myself and twenty men brought up the rear; and all was peace and good order."

After a wide round from here they found themselves again on the Malades River, where thirty-seven of the people were poisoned, apparently .by beaver meat, and it was from this circumstance that the river got its name. Just beyond this, they captured a Bannock, by whom they were told that the beavers with the white flesh—supposedly poisonous—were always roasted by the Indians and never boiled; unless roasted the meat was bad.

At a point on the Bear River the travelling party observed two animals apparently playing in the water, and on approaching the place these were found to be black bears, one of which was shot. They found that the bears were apparently hunting a beaver which was found concealed in the shoal water, and the signs seemed to indicate that this was a hunting-place where the bears often came to kill beaver.

Returning to Canoe Point, they rested for a couple of days. Their horses, which, of course, were unshod, had become very tender-footed, and they provided moccasins—so to speak—for no less than twenty-seven head. This, of course, is an old Indian practice. Not far from here they found buffalo in great numbers, and began to kill and dry meat, and just here Ross gives interesting testimony with regard to some characteristics of the buffalo which is worth repeating in these days, when the buffalo are no longer with us:

"While on the subject of buffalo, we may notice that there is perhaps not an animal that roams in this, or in the wilds of any other country, more fierce and formidable, than a buffalo bull during the rutting season: neither the Polar bear, nor the Bengal tiger, surpass that animal in ferocity. When not mortally wounded, buffalo turn upon man or horse; but when mortally wounded, they stand fiercely eyeing their assailant, until life ebbs away.

"As we were travelling one day among a herd, we shot at a bull and wounded him severely—so much so, that he could neither run after us, nor from us; propping himself on his legs, therefore, he stood looking at us till we had fired ten balls through his body, now and then giving a shake of the head. Although he was apparently unable to stir, yet we kept at a respectful distance from him; for such is the agility of body and quickness of eye, and so hideous are the looks of buffalo, that we dared not for some time approach him: at last, one more bold than the rest went up and pushed the beast over;—he was dead! If not brought to the ground by the first or second shot, let the hunter be on his guard! The old bulls, when badly wounded and unable to pursue their assailant, prop themselves, as we have seen, and often stand in that position till dead; but the head of a wounded bull, while in an upright position, is invariably turned to his pursuer; so if the hunter be in doubt, let him change his position, to see if the bull changes his position also. The surest mark of his being mortally wounded and unable to stir, is, when he cannot turn his head round to his pursuer; in that case, you may safely walk up and throw him down.

"The wild cow calves generally at one period, and that period later by a month than our tame cattle; then they all, as if with one accord, withdraw themselves from the mountains and rocks, and resort in large families to the valleys, where there is open ground, with small clumps of wood affording shelter and preservation; as there they can see the approach of an enemy from afar. The cows herd together in the centre, and the bulls graze in the distance: all in sight of each other.

"The calving season is May, when the heat of the

sun is sufficiently strong for the preservation of their young in the open air; during which time the herd feeds round and round the place as if to defend the young calves from the approach of an enemy or from wolves. The resident Indian tribes seldom hunt or disturb the buffalo at this season, or before the first of July. The Indians often assured me, that, during the calving season, the bulls keep guard; and have been frequently known to assemble together, in order to keep at a distance any wolves, bears or other enemies, that might attempt to approach the cows."

A party sent after the Iroquois, who had gone off to trap by themselves, returned on the 14th of October, bringing with them not only the ten Iroquois but also seven American trappers. The Iroquois had had their usual success. They had no beaver, no traps, were naked and destitute of almost everything, and were in debt to the American trappers for having been brought to the Three Tetons. According to their story, they had been attacked by a war-party and robbed of nine hundred beaver, all their steel traps, and twenty-seven horses. Ross had the small satisfaction of saying to them, "I told you so," but this did not bring back the lost property. On the other hand, other stories were told by certain of the Iroquois, which suggested that perhaps the Iroquois had sold their beaver to the Americans.

It was not long before another war-party made its appearance, causing the usual excitement and alarm, but these proved to be Nez Percés who had started for the Blackfeet to steal horses. Before they got there, the Blackfeet discovered and ambushed them, killing six of the Nez Percés.

The newcomers warned Ross that enemies were about, and as the trapping party was just about to enter a narrow valley, Ross with thirty-five men set out to examine it before the main party entered. They had looked it partly over, when they saw distant Indians hurrying to cover, and pursued them. The strangers got into the timber. The trappers asked the Indians to come out of the woods and smoke, and the Indians invited them to come into the woods and smoke; but neither party accepted the invitation. The Indians claimed to be Crows, but Ross believed they were Blackfeet. The traders picked up some robes, arms, and moccasins, thrown away in flight, which they left near the hiding-place of the Indians, and were just about to return, when, as they were mounting, they saw what looked like a large party of people coming. They made preparations for a fight, and then discovered that the approaching body consisted of a large band of horses, driven by four men. Ross with fifteen men charged toward the horses, whose drivers fled, leaving the herd. Among the horses were forty-three which belonged in Ross's camp and one of those taken from the two trappers sent as messengers to the Goddin River party. The trappers overtook and captured three of the Indians and took them back to the camp.

There a court-martial was held and the three captives were condemned to die, but Ross the next morning succeeded in letting them escape.

The return to the Flathead House was devoid of any special events save those of ordinary prairie and mountain travel. On the way they had to pass through deep snows and across frozen rivers where the ice was not always safe, and at one such point they lost a horse, and two of the men came near sharing its fate. They reached there the last of November.

The results of the trip amounted to five thousand beaver, exclusive of other furs—a very successful summer.

In a note appended to a brief vocabulary of the Snake language given by Ross he makes the following interesting prophecy: "I can state with undiminished confidence, that the Snake country towards the Rocky Mountains is, and will be, rich in furs for some generations to come, and full of interest to men of enterprise. Indeed, the dangers by which it was then, and still is, in a more or less degree, surrounded, will always tend to preserve the furs in that inland quarter."

Little more than two generations have passed, and the fur in what used to be the Snake country has absolutely disappeared. The dangers from Indians have long been forgotten, though among the Indians toward the coast the tradition of the terrible Blackfeet yet persists, and they still speak of the Blackfeet as "bad people."

The following spring Governor Simpson wrote to

Ross, asking him to try and procure two Indian boys to be educated at the Red River Colony. Ross succeeded in getting a Kutenai and a Spokane boy, each ten or twelve years old. They were given up by the Indians with great regret. One of the fathers said: "We have given you our hearts—our children are our hearts; but bring them back again to us before they become white men—we wish to see them once more Indians—and after that, you can make them white men, if you like." The Kutenai boy died after two or three years at school, but some years later the Spokane boy returned to his people. He did not turn out very well.

The next spring Ross started to Spokane House to turn in his furs, and then finally to leave the fur trade. Here he met Governor Simpson, who promised him a situation in Red River Colony until such time as he should be able to establish himself. The governor started back with the party. The return journey was long and laborious. Isolated parties of Indians were met, in all of whom Ross took keen interest. He gives a graphic description of travel through mountains, and draws a picture which gives some idea of the difficulties of the journeys made by these early travellers, and of the hardihood and endurance of those who performed them.

Little does the traveller of the present day, hurrying along by train, or by steamboat, comprehend the constant labor of those early days.

They were journeying on foot up the course of a winding, rushing river:

"When the current proves too strong or the water too deep for one person to attempt [to cross] it alone, the whole join hands together, forming a chain, and thus cross in an oblique line, to break the strength of the current; the tallest always leading the van. By their united efforts, when a light person is swept off his feet, which not unfrequently happens, the party drag him along; and the first who reaches the shore always lays hold of the branches of some friendly tree or bush that may be in the way; the second does the same, and so on till all get out of the water. But often they are no sooner out than in again; and perhaps several traverses will have to be made within the space of a hundred yards, and sometimes within a few yards of each other; just as the rocks, or other impediments bar the way. After crossing several times, I regretted that I had not begun sooner to count the number; but before night, I had sixty-two traverses marked on my walking-stick, which served as my journal through-out the day.

"When not among ice and snow, or in the water, we had to walk on a stony beach, or on gravelly flats, being constantly in and out of the water: many had got their feet blistered, which was extremely painful. The cold made us advance at a quick pace, to keep ourselves warm; and despatch was the order of the day. The Governor himself, generally at the head, made the first plunge into the water, and was not the last to get out. His smile encouraged others, and his example checked murmuring. At a crossing-place there was seldom a moment's hesitation; all plunged in, and had to get out as they could. And we had to be lightly clad, so as to drag less water. Our general course to-day was north-east, but we had at times to follow every point of the compass, and might have travelled altogether twenty miles, although in a direct line we scarcely advanced eight. The ascent appeared to be gradual, yet the contrary was indicated by the rapidity of the current. After a day of excessive fatigue, we halted at dusk, cooked our suppers, dried our clothes, smoked our pipes, then, each spreading his blanket, we laid ourselves down to rest; and, perhaps, of all rest, that enjoyed on the voyage, after a hard day's labour, is the sweetest.

"To give a correct idea of this part of our journey, let the reader picture in his own mind a dark, narrow defile, skirted on one side by a chain of inaccessible mountains, rising to a great height, covered with snow, and slippery with ice from their tops down to the water's edge. And on the other side, a beach comparatively low, but studded in an irregular manner with standing and fallen trees, rocks, and ice, and full of drift-wood; over which the torrent everywhere rushes with such irresistible impetuosity, that very few would dare to adventure themselves in the stream. Let him again imagine a rapid river descending from some great height, filling up the whole channel between the rocky precipices on the south and the no less dangerous barrier on the north. And lastly, let him suppose that we were obliged to make our way on foot against such a torrent, by crossing and recrossing it in all its turns and windings from morning till night, up to the middle in water,—and he will understand that we have not exaggerated the difficulties to be overcome in crossing the Rocky Mountains."

At last the party reached the summit of the Rocky Mountains, and passing by the Rocky Mountain House, took canoes. Here they found Joseph Felix Larocque, and from here they went on down the Athabasca in canoes to Jasper House and to Fort Assiniboine; and there again changing to horses, at last reached Edmonton. This was then the centre of a great trade, and was under charge of Mr. Rowan, chief factor of the Hudson Bay Company, and earlier a partner in the Northwest Company.

The further journey back toward the Red River was marked by the meeting, near Lake Bourbon—Cedar Lake—with Captain Franklin and Dr. Richardson on their overland Arctic expedition.

At Norway House Governor Simpson stopped, while Ross was to keep on eastward. Governor Simpson, after again trying to persuade Ross to remain in the service of the company, made him a free grant of one hundred acres of land in the Red River Settlement, and paid him many compliments on his efficiency and success in the Snake country.

With a party of twenty-seven people, a motley crew

of incompetents, Ross started from Norway House
for Red River. He quotes an interestingly boastful
speech by an ancient French voyageur:

"'I have now,' said he, 'been forty-two years in this
country. For twenty-four I was a light canoe-man; I
required but little sleep, but sometimes got less than
I required. No portage was too long for me; all port-
ages were alike. My end of the canoe never touched
the ground till I saw the end of it. Fifty songs a
day were nothing to me. I could carry, paddle, walk,
and sing with any man I ever saw. During that
period, I saved the lives of ten bourgeois, and was
always the favourite, because when others stopped to
carry at a bad step, and lost time, I pushed on—over
rapids, over cascades, over chutes; all were the same
to me. No water, no weather, ever stopped the paddle
or the song. I have had twelve wives in the country;
and was once possessed of fifty horses, and six running
dogs, trimmed in the first style. I was then like a
bourgeois, rich and happy: no bourgeois had better-
dressed wives than I; no Indian chief finer horses; no
white man better-harnessed or swifter dogs. I beat
all Indians at the race, and no white man ever passed
me in the chase. I wanted for nothing; and I spent
all my earnings in the enjoyment of pleasure. Five
hundred pounds, twice told, have passed through my
hands; although now I have not a spare shirt to my
back, nor a penny to buy one. Yet, were I young again,
I should glory in commencing the same career again.

I would gladly spend another half-century in the same fields of enjoyment. There is no life so happy as a voyageur's life; none so independent; no place where a man enjoys so much variety and freedom as in the Indian country. Huzza! huzza! pour le pays sauvage!' After this *cri de joie*, he sat down in the boat, and we could not help admiring the wild enthusiasm of the old Frenchman. He had boasted and excited himself, till he was out of breath, and then sighed with regret that he could no longer enjoy the scenes of his past life."

On the journey there was excitement enough, storms and running aground—usual incidents of canoe travel —but at last they reached Red River, and Ross's fur trading journeys were over.

WHEN BEAVER SKINS WERE MONEY

WHEN BEAVER SKINS WERE MONEY

1

BENT'S FORT

WHENEVER the history of the Southwest shall be written, more than one long and interesting chapter must be devoted to the first permanent settlement on its plains and the first permanent settler there. In the accounts of that wide territory through which the old Santa Fé trail passed, William Bent and Bent's Old Fort have frequent mention.

Who were the Bents and whence did they come?

Silas Bent was born in the Colony of Massachusetts in 1768. His father is said to have been one of those who attended the famous "Boston Tea Party." Silas was educated for the bar, and came to St. Louis in 1804 at the time the government of Louisiana was turned over to the American authorities. Here he served as a judge of the Superior Court, and here he resided until his death, in 1827.

Of his seven sons, John was educated for the bar and became a well-known attorney of St. Louis. The youngest son, Silas, as flag-lieutenant of the flag-ship

"Mississippi," was with Perry in Japan, and wrote a report on the Japan current for an American scientific society. He delivered addresses on meteorology in St. Louis in 1879, and on climate as affecting cattle-breeding in the year 1884. Four other sons—Charles, William W., and later George and Robert—were prominent in the Indian trade on the upper Arkansas and elsewhere between 1820 and 1850, and remained trading in that region until they died.

The leading spirit in this family of Indian traders was William W. Bent. Early in life Charles and William Bent had been up on the Missouri River working for the American Fur Company. Colonel Bent stated to his son George that he went up there in the year 1816, when very young.[1] Very likely he was then a small boy only ten or twelve years old. It was there that Charles and William Bent became acquainted with Robert Campbell, of St. Louis, who remained a firm friend of the brothers throughout his life. William Bent could speak the Sioux language fluently and the Sioux had called him Wa-si′cha-chischī′-la, meaning Little White Man, a name which confirms the statement that he entered the trade very young, and seems to warrant the belief that his work for the fur company was at some post in the Sioux country.

In his testimony before the joint commission which inquired into Indian affairs on the plains in 1865,

[1] The history of *The Bent Family in America* gives the date of William Bent's birth as 1809, which can hardly be made to agree with this statement.

William Bent stated that he had first come to the upper Arkansas and settled near the Purgatoire, just below the present city of Pueblo, Colorado, in 1824; that is to say, two years before he and his brother began to erect their first trading establishment on the Arkansas. Previous to this time William Bent had been trapping in the mountains near there, and may very well have done some individual trading with the Indians.

William Bent was undoubtedly the first permanent white settler in what is now Colorado, and for a very long time he was not only its first settler, but remained its most important white citizen.

By his fair and open dealings, by his fearless conduct, and by his love of justice, William Bent soon won the respect and confidence of the Indians with whom he had to do. Among the rough fraternity of mountain trappers he was also very popular, his reputation for courage being remarkable even among that class of daring men. He was tirelessly active in prosecuting the aims of his trade, making frequent trips to the camps of the various tribes with which he, and later his company, had dealings, and to the Mexican settlements in the valley of Taos and to Santa Fé. Every year, probably from 1824 to 1864, he made at least one journey from the fort on the Arkansas, across the plains of Colorado, Kansas, and Missouri, to the settlements on the Missouri frontier.

About 1835 William Bent married Owl Woman, the

daughter of White Thunder, an important man among the Cheyennes, then the keeper of the medicine arrows. Bent's Fort was his home, and there his children were born, the oldest, Mary, about 1836, Robert in 1839— his own statement made in 1865 says 1841—George in July, 1843, and Julia in 1847. Owl Woman died at the fort in 1847 in giving birth to Julia, and her husband afterward married her sister, Yellow Woman. Charles Bent was the child of his second marriage.

William Bent appears to have been the first of the brothers to go into the Southwestern country to trade for fur, but Charles is said to have gone to Santa Fé as early as 1819, and a little later must have joined William. The two, with Ceran St. Vrain and one of the Chouteaus, established the early trading post near the Arkansas. After occupying this stockade for two years or more, they moved down below Pueblo and built another stockade on the Arkansas. Two years later they began to build the more ambitious post afterward known as Bent's, or Fort William, or Bent's Old Fort. George and Robert Bent apparently did not come out to the fort until after it was completed— perhaps after it had been for some time in operation. Benito Vasquez was at one time a partner in the company.

It was in 1828 that the Bent brothers, with St. Vrain, began this large fort, fifteen miles above the mouth of Purgatoire River. It was not completed until 1832. Four years seems a long time to be spent in the con-

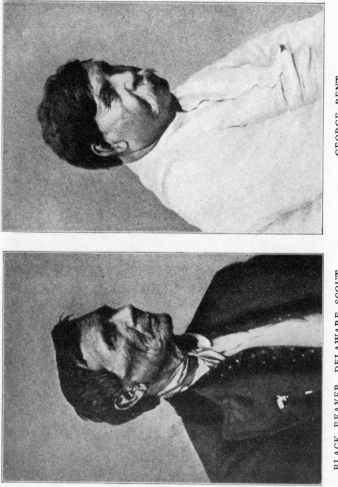

BLACK BEAVER, DELAWARE SCOUT

GEORGE BENT

struction of such a post, even though it was built of adobe brick, but there were reasons for the delay. Charles Bent was determined that the fort should be built of adobes in order to make it fireproof, so that under no circumstances could it be burned by the Indians. Besides that, adobes were much more durable and more comfortable—cool in summer, warm in winter—than logs would have been. When the question of how the fort should be built had been decided, Charles Bent went to New Mexico, and from Taos and Santa Fé sent over a number of Mexicans to make adobe brick. With them he sent some wagon-loads of Mexican wool to mix with the clay of the bricks, thus greatly lengthening the life of the adobes.

Only a short time, however, after the laborers had reached the intended site of the fort, smallpox broke out among them, and it was necessary to send away those not attacked. William Bent, St. Vrain, Kit Carson, and other white men who were there caught the small-pox from the Mexicans, and though none died they were so badly marked by it that some of the Indians who had known them well in the early years of the trading did not recognize them when they met again.

During the prevalence of the smallpox at the post William Bent sent a runner, Francisco, one of his Mexican herders, north, to warn the Cheyennes not to come near the post. Francisco set out for the Black Hills, and on his way encountered a large war-party of Cheyennes on their way to the fort. He told them of what had happened, and warned them to return north and not to come near the post until sent for. The Cheyennes obeyed, and it was not until some time later, when all at Fort William had recovered and when the temporary stockade with all the infected material that it contained had been burned, that Bent and St. Vrain, with a few pack-mules, started north for the Black Hills to find the Cheyennes and invite them to return to the post. The year of this journey has been given me as 1831. Perhaps it may have been a year earlier.

After the smallpox had ceased, more Mexican laborers were sent for, and work on the fort was resumed. Not long before his death, Kit Carson stated that at one time more than a hundred and fifty Mexicans were at work on the construction of the post.

Accounts of the dimensions of the fort differ, but on certain points all agree: that it was of adobes, set square with the points of the compass, and on the north bank of the Arkansas River. Garrard says that the post was a hundred feet square and the walls thirty feet in height. Another account says that the walls ran a hundred and fifty feet east and west and a hundred feet north and south, and that they were seventeen feet high. J. T. Hughes, however, in his *Doniphan's Expedition*, printed in Cincinnati in 1848, says:

"Fort Bent is situated on the north bank of the Arkansas, 650 miles west of Fort Leavenworth, in latitude 38° 2′ north, and longitude 103° 3′ west from

Greenwich.   The exterior walls of this fort, whose figure is that of an oblong square, are fifteen feet high
and four feet thick.   It is 180 feet long and 135 feet
wide and is divided into various compartments, the
whole built of adobes or sun-dried bricks."

At the southwest and northeast corners of these walls
were bastions, or round towers, thirty feet in height
and ten feet in diameter inside, with loopholes for
muskets and openings for cannon.   Garrard speaks of
the bastions as hexagonal in form.

Around the walls in the second stories of the bastions
hung sabres and great heavy lances with long, sharp
blades.   These were intended for use in case an attempt were made to take the fort by means of ladders
put up against the wall.   Besides these cutting and
piercing implements, the walls were hung with flint-lock
muskets and pistols.

In the east wall of the fort was a wide gateway
formed by two immense swinging doors made of heavy
planks.   These doors were studded with heavy nails
and plated with sheet-iron, so that they could never
be burned by the Indians.   The same was true of the
gateway which entered the corral, to be described
later.

Over the main gate of the fort was a square watch
tower surmounted by a belfry, from the top of which
rose a flagstaff.   The watch tower contained a single
room with windows on all sides, and in the room was
an old-fashioned long telescope, or spy-glass, mounted

on a pivot. Here certain members of the garrison, relieving each other at stated intervals, were constantly on the lookout. There was a chair for the watchman to sit in and a bed for his sleeping. If the watchman, through his glass, noticed anything unusual—for example, if he saw a great dust rising over the prairie—he notified the people below. If a suspicious-looking party of Indians was seen approaching, the watchman signalled to the herder to bring in the horses, for the stock was never turned loose, but was always on herd.

In the belfry, under a little roof which rose above the watch tower, hung the bell of the fort, which sounded the hours for meals. Two tame white-headed eagles kept at the fort were sometimes confined within this belfry, or at others were allowed to fly about free, returning of their own accord to sleep in the belfry. One of these eagles finally disappeared, and for a long time it was not known what had become of it. Then it was learned that it had been killed for its feathers by a young Indian at some distance from the fort.

At the back of the fort over the gate, which opened into the corral, was a second-story room rising high above the walls, as the watch tower did in front. This room—an extraordinary luxury for the time—was used as a billiard-room during the later years of the post. It was long enough to accommodate a large billiard-table, and across one end of the room ran a counter, or bar, over which drinkables were served. These luxuries were brought out by Robert and George

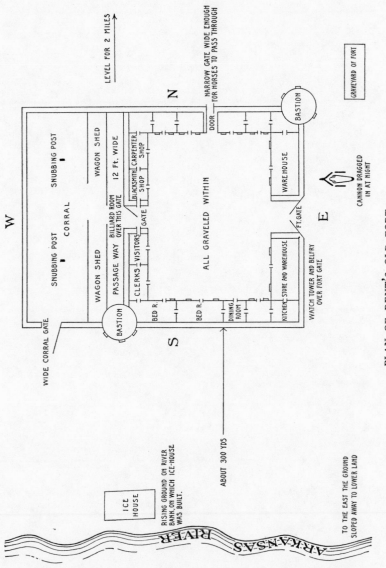

PLAN OF BENT'S OLD FORT

LEVEL FOR 2 MILES

NARROW GATE WIDE ENOUGH
FOR HORSES TO PASS THROUGH

W

N

WIDE CORRAL GATE

SNUBBING POST   SNUBBING POST

CORRAL

WAGON SHED   WAGON SHED

PASSAGE WAY   12 Ft. WIDE

BILLARD ROOM
OVER THIS GATE

BLACKSMITH CARPENTER
SHOP   SHOP

GATE

CLERKS   VISITORS

ALL GRAVELED WITHIN

DOOR

BASTION

BED R.

BED R.

DINING
ROOM

KITCHEN STORE AND WAREHOUSE

WAREHOUSE

FT. GATE

BASTION

S

E

WATCH TOWER AND BELFRY
OVER FORT GATE

CANNON DRAGGED
IN AT NIGHT

GRAVEYARD OF FORT

ICE
HOUSE

RISING GROUND ON RIVER
BANK, ON WHICH ICE-HOUSE
WAS BUILT.

ABOUT 300 YDS

ARKANSAS RIVER

TO THE EAST THE GROUND
SLOPED AWAY TO LOWER LAND

Bent, young men who did not come out to the fort until some time after it had been constructed, and who, being city-dwellers—for I have no record of their having any early experience of frontier life—no doubt felt that they required city amusements.

The watch tower and billiard-room were supported on heavy adobe walls running at right angles to the main enclosing walls of the fort, and these supporting walls formed the ends of the rooms on either side of the gates in the outer walls.

The stores, warehouses, and living-rooms of the post were ranged around the walls, and opened into the patio, or courtyard—the hollow square within. In some of the books dealing with these old times it is said that when the Indians entered the fort to trade, cannon were loaded and sentries patrolled the walls with loaded guns. This may have been true of the early days of the fort, but it was not true of the latter part of the decade between 1840 and 1850. At that time the Indians, or at least the Cheyenne Indians, had free run of the post and were allowed to go upstairs, on the walls, and into the watch tower. The various rooms about the courtyard received light and air from the doors and windows opening out into this courtyard, which was gravelled. The floors of the rooms were of beaten clay, as was commonly the case in Mexican houses, and the roofs were built in the same fashion that long prevailed in the West. Poles were laid from the front wall to the rear, slightly inclined toward the front. Over these poles twigs or brush were laid, and over the brush clay was spread, tramped hard, and gravel thrown over this. These roofs were used as a promenade by the men of the fort and their families in the evenings. The top of the fort walls reached about four feet above these roofs, or breast-high of a man, and these walls were pierced with loop-holes through which to shoot in case of attack.

Hughes in his *Doniphan's Expedition* says: "The march upon Santa Fé was resumed Aug. 2, 1846, after a respite of three days in the neighborhood of Fort Bent. As we passed the fort the American flag was raised in compliment to our troops and in concert with our own streamed most animatingly on the gale that swept from the desert, while the tops of the houses were crowded with Mexican girls and Indian squaws, beholding the American Army."

On the west side of the fort and outside the walls was the horse corral. It was as wide as the fort and deep enough to contain a large herd. The walls were about eight feet high and three feet thick at the top. The gate was on the south side of the corral, and so faced the river. It was of wood, but was completely plated with sheet-iron. More than that, to prevent any one from climbing in by night, the tops of the walls had been thickly planted with cactus—a large variety which grows about a foot high and has great fleshy leaves closely covered with many and sharp thorns. This grew so luxuriantly that in some places the leaves hung down over the walls, both within and without, and gave most efficient protection against any living thing that might wish to surmount the wall.

Through the west wall of the fort a door was cut, leading from the stockade into the corral, permitting people to go through and get horses without going outside the fort and opening the main gate of the corral. This door was wide and arched at the top. It was made large enough, so that in case of necessity— if by chance an attacking party seemed likely to capture the horses and mules in the corral—the door could be opened and the herd run inside the main stockade.

About two hundred yards to the south of the fort, and so toward the river bank, on a little mound, stood a large ice-house built of adobes or sun-dried bricks. In winter when the river was frozen this ice-house was filled, and in it during the summer was kept all the surplus fresh meat—buffalo tongues, antelope, dried meat and tongues—and also all the bacon. At times the ice-house was hung thick with flesh food.

On hot days, with the other little children, young George Bent used to go down to the ice-house and get in it to cool off, and his father's negro cook used to come down and send them away, warning them not to go in there from the hot sun, as it was too cold and they might get sick. This negro cook, Andrew Green by name, a slave owned by Governor Charles Bent, was with him when he was killed in Taos, and afterward came to the fort and was there for many

years, but was at last taken back to St. Louis and
there set free. He had a brother "Dick," often
mentioned in the old books.

Besides Bent's Fort, Bent and St. Vrain owned
Fort St. Vrain, on the South Platte, opposite the
mouth of St. Vrain's Fork, and Fort Adobe, on the
Canadian. Both these posts were built of adobe
brick. Fort St. Vrain was built to trade with the
Northern Indians; that is, with the Sioux and Northern Cheyennes, who seldom got down south as far
as the Arkansas River, and so would not often come
to Fort William. The Fort Adobe on the Canadian
was built by request of the chiefs of the Kiowa, Comanche, and Apache to trade with these people. The
chiefs who made this request were To'hau sen (Little
Mountain) and Eagle-Tail Feathers, speaking for
the Kiowa, Shaved Head for the Comanche, and
Poor (Lean) Bear for the Apache.

These in their day were men of importance. Shaved
Head was a great friend of the whites and a man of
much influence with his own people and with neighboring tribes. He wore the left side of his head shaved
close, while the hair on the right side was long, hanging down to his waist or below. His left ear was
perforated with many holes made by a blunt awl
heated red-hot, and was adorned with many little
brass rings. Before peace was made between the
Kiowas, Comanches, and Apaches in the year 1840, the
last three tribes were more or less afraid to visit Fort

William, lest they should there meet a large camp of their enemies, and Colonel Bent and the traders were also especially anxious to avoid any collision at the fort. Each tribe would expect the trader to take its part, and this he could not do without incurring the enmity of the other tribes. The wish of the trader was to be on good terms with all tribes, and this William Bent accomplished with singular discretion. Although he had a Cheyenne wife, he was on excellent terms, and always remained so, with the enemies of the Cheyennes.

Both Fort St. Vrain and Fort Adobe, being built of adobes, lasted for a long time, and their ruins have been seen until quite recently. Near the ruins of Fort Adobe two important fights have taken place, to be referred to later.

In the business of the fort William Bent had the direction of the trade with the Indians, while his brother Charles seems to have had more to do with affairs in the Mexican settlements, until his death there, at the hands of the Mexicans and Pueblos, in the year 1847. It is not certain when St. Vrain, Lee, and Benito Vasquez became partners in the business, nor how long they were interested in it. George and Robert Bent, who came out from St. Louis, certainly later than the two elder brothers, may have been partners, but there is nothing to show that they were so. Robert died in 1847.

Some time before this George Bent went to Mexico

and there married a Mexican girl, by whom he had two children, a son and a daughter. The son, Robert, went to school in St. Louis. He died at Dodge City, Kan., in 1875. George Bent was a great friend of Frank P. Blair, whom he appointed guardian for his children. He died at the fort about 1848 of consumption, and was buried near his brother Robert in the graveyard which lay a short distance northeast of the northeast bastion of the fort. The old tailor, a Frenchman, afterward planted cactus over George Bent's grave to protect it from the wolves and coyotes. Their remains were later removed to St. Louis.

After the death of Charles Bent, in 1847, William Bent continued his work. Perhaps St. Vrain may have remained a partner for a time. Fitzpatrick speaks of "Messrs. Bent and St. Vrain's post" in 1850. Bent was an active man and interested in many other projects besides the fort and trade with the Indians. He bought sheep and mules in New Mexico and drove them across the plains to the Missouri market. In the forties, in company with several other men, he secured a large land grant from the Mexican government in the Arkansas valley above the fort and attempted to found a colony there. Mexican settlers were established on the lands. The colonists were inert, the Indians were hostile, and from these and other causes the project proved a failure. In 1847 William Bent and St. Vrain drove a large herd of Mexican cattle to the Arkansas and wintered them in the valley near the fort, thus making the first step toward establishing the cattle industry, which many years later so flourished on the plains.

Besides his lands near the fort, Bent had a fine farm at Westport (now Kansas City), in Missouri, and a ranch south of the Arkansas in the Mexican territory. In 1846 he guided Colonel Price's Missouri regiment across the plains to New Mexico, and was so popular among the volunteer officers that they gave him the brevet of colonel, a title which stuck to him until the day of his death.

II

GOVERNOR CHARLES BENT

CHARLES BENT was a close rival to his brother William in the esteem of his fellow traders and the trappers and Indians of the Arkansas. He seems from the first, however, to have taken the most active part in the Santa Fé trade of the company, leaving the Indian trade to the other partners. Among the traders and teamsters of the Santa Fé caravans he was as much liked as William Bent was among the trappers and Indians; indeed, on more than one occasion, he was elected captain of the caravan and conducted it safely to Santa Fé. These caravans of Missouri traders were richly laden for those days. The outfit of 1832 brought back from New Mexico $100,000 in specie and $90,000 in other property, including large numbers of Mexican mules. In 1833 the caravan with Bent as captain assembled at Diamond Springs, on the Missouri frontier. There were 184 men, with ninety-three large wagons loaded with goods. They brought back $100,000 in money and much other property.

Charles Bent married a Mexican woman and made his home at San Fernando,[1] a small town in the valley of Taos. He was popular among his Mexican and Pueblo neighbors until he was appointed governor of the territory by General Kearny, who marched into New Mexico with his little army in the fall. Having put Governor Bent and his civil government in control of affairs, the general left a few troops in and about Santa Fé, and with the rest of his forces marched for California. Hardly had he gone when rumors of a revolt of the Mexican and Indian population against American rule began to be heard, and late in December evidence of such a plot was unearthed. These events are set forth in the following letter from Governor Bent to the Hon. James Buchanan, secretary of state:

"Santa Fé, N. M., Dec. 26, 1846.—Sir: I have been informed indirectly that Col. A. W. Doniphan, who, in October last, marched with his regiment against the Navajo Indians, has made treaty of peace with them. Not having been officially notified of this treaty, I am not able to state the terms upon which

[1] This name is spelled in various ways even by Mexicans.

it has been concluded; but, so far as I am able to learn, I have but little ground to hope that it will be permanent.

"On the 17th inst. I received information from a Mexican friendly to our Government that a conspiracy was on foot among the native Mexicans, having for its object the expulsion of the United States troops and the civil authorities from the territory. I immediately brought into requisition every means in my power to ascertain who were the movers in the rebellion, and have succeeded in securing seven of the secondary conspirators. The military and civil officers are now both in pursuit of the two leaders and prime movers of the rebellion; but as several days have elapsed, I am apprehensive that they will have made their escape from the territory.

"So far as I am informed this conspiracy is confined to the four northern counties of the territory, and the men considered as leaders in the affair cannot be said to be men of much standing.

"After obtaining the necessary information to designate and secure the persons of the participators in the conspiracy, I thought it advisable to turn them over to the military authorities in order that these persons might be dealt with more summarily and expeditiously than they could have been by the civil authorities.

"The occurrence of this conspiracy at this early period of the occupation of the territory will, I think,

conclusively convince our Government of the necessity of maintaining here, for several years to come,
an efficient military force."

Having taken measures for the arrest of the leaders
of the conspiracy, Governor Bent set out from Santa
Fé early in January for a few days' visit to his family
at San Fernando, near the pueblo of Taos, inhabited
by civilized Pueblo Indians. Three Pueblo thieves
had been arrested and locked up in the calabozo at
San Fernando some time before Governor Bent's
arrival. On the 19th of January a mob of Pueblos
entered the town and attempted to force the American
sheriff, Lee, to give up these three prisoners. Lee,
being helpless to resist the Indians' demands, was
on the point of releasing his prisoners when the prefect
of the town, Vigil, a Mexican who had taken office
under the American Government, appeared among
the Indians and, calling out to them in a fury that
they were all thieves and scoundrels, ordered Lee
to hold the three prisoners. Enraged at the prefect's
harsh words, the Pueblos rushed upon him, killed
him, cut his body into small pieces, and then, being
joined by a number of Mexicans, set out to kill every
American in the settlement.

Governor Bent's house was the first they visited.
He was still in bed when aroused by his wife on the
approach of the mob, and he at once sprang up and
ran to a window, through which he called to a Mexican
neighbor to help him get through into his house and

conceal him.   The Mexican refused his aid and replied
that he must die.   Seeing that all ways of escape
were blocked, the governor quietly left the window
and returned to his family.   "He withdrew into his
room," writes Mr. Dunn, "and the Indians began
tearing up the roof.   With all the calmness of a noble
soul he stood awaiting his doom.   His wife brought
him his pistols and told him to fight, to avenge himself, even if he must die.   The Indians were exposed
to his aim, but he replied, 'No, I will not kill any
one of them; for the sake of you, my wife, and you,
my children.   At present my death is all these people
wish.'   As the savages poured into the room he ap-
pealed to their manhood and honor, but in vain.
They laughed at his plea.   They told him they were
about to kill every American in New Mexico and
would begin with him.   An arrow followed the word,
another and another, but the mode was not swift
enough.   One, more impatient, sent a bullet through
his heart.   As he fell, Tomas, a chief, stepped forward, snatched one of his pistols, and shot him in
the face.   They took his scalp, stretched it on a board
with brass nails, and carried it through the streets
in triumph."

Garrard, who was at Taos in the days immediately
following the massacre, tells of Governor Bent's death
in the following words:

"While here in Fernandez (San Fernandez) with
his family he was one morning early aroused from sleep

by the populace, who, with the aid of the Pueblos de Taos, were collected in front of his dwelling, striving to gain admittance. While they were effecting an entrance, he, with an axe, cut through an adobe wall into another house. The wife of the occupant, a clever, though thriftless, Canadian, heard him, and with all her strength rendered him assistance, though she was a Mexican. He retreated to a room, but seeing no way of escaping from the infuriated assailants who fired upon him through a window, he spoke to his weeping wife and trembling children clinging to him with all the tenacity of love and despair, and taking a paper from his pocket endeavored to write, but fast losing strength he commended them to God and his brothers, and fell pierced by a Pueblo's ball. Rushing in and tearing off the gray-haired scalp, the Indians bore it away in triumph.''

Among the people killed were Stephen Lee, Narcisse Beaubien, and others.

When the news of Governor Bent's death reached the plains it created great excitement, for Charles Bent was exceedingly popular with white people and Indians alike. The Cheyennes proposed to send a war-party to Taos and to kill all the Mexicans, but William Bent would not permit it. A party from Bent's Fort set out for Taos, but on the road were met by messengers announcing that Colonel Price had marched into Taos at the head of two hundred and fifty men and had had a fight with Mexicans and

Indians in which two hundred were killed, and had then bombarded the town and knocked down its walls. A neighboring town was razed and a large amount of property destroyed.

The killing of the people at Turley's Ranch, on the Arroyo Hondo, was a costly triumph to the Pueblos. Here were shut up men who fought well for their lives.

Ruxton tells of the battle in graphic language:

"The massacre of Turley and his people, and the destruction of his mill, were not consummated without considerable loss to the barbarous and cowardly assailants.   There were in the house, at the time of the attack, eight white men, including Americans, French-Canadians, and one or two Englishmen, with plenty of arms and ammunition.   Turley had been warned of the intended insurrection, but had treated the report with indifference and neglect, until one morning a man named Otterbees, in the employ of Turley, and who had been dispatched to Santa Fé with several mule-loads of whiskey a few days before, made his appearance at the gate on horseback, and hastily informing the inmates of the mill that the New Mexicans had risen and massacred Governor Bent and other Americans, galloped off.   Even then Turley felt assured that he would not be molested, but, at the solicitations of his men, agreed to close the gate of the yard round which were the buildings of a mill and distillery, and make preparations for defence.

"A few hours after, a large crowd of Mexicans

and Pueblo Indians made their appearance, all armed with guns and bows and arrows, and advancing with a white flag summoned Turley to surrender his house and the Americans in it, guaranteeing that his own life should be saved, but that every other American in the valley of Taos had to be destroyed; that the Governor and all the Americans at Fernandez and the rancho had been killed, and that not one was to be left alive in all New Mexico.

"To this summons Turley answered that he would never surrender his house nor his men, and that, if they wanted it or them, 'they must take them.'

"The enemy then drew off, and, after a short consultation, commenced the attack. The first day they numbered about 500, but the crowd was hourly augmented by the arrival of parties of Indians from the more distant pueblos, and of New Mexicans from Fernandez, La Cañada, and other places.

"The building lay at the foot of a gradual slope in the sierra, which was covered with cedar-bushes. In front ran the stream of the Arroyo Hondo, about twenty yards from one side of the square, and on the other side was broken ground, which rose abruptly and formed the bank of the ravine. In rear and behind the still-house was some garden-ground, inclosed by a small fence, and into which a small wicket-gate opened from the corral.

"As soon as the attack was determined upon, the assailants broke, and, scattering, concealed themselves under the cover of the rocks and bushes that surrounded the house.

"From these they kept up an incessant fire upon every exposed portion of the building where they saw the Americans preparing for defence.

"They, on their parts, were not idle; not a man but was an old mountaineer, and each had his trusty rifle with good store of ammunition. Wherever one of the assailants exposed a hand's breadth of his person there whistled a ball from an unerring barrel. The windows had been blockaded, loop-holes being left to fire through, and through these a lively fire was maintained. Already several of the enemy had bitten the dust, and parties were constantly seen bearing off the wounded up the banks of the Cañada. Darkness came on, and during the night a continual fire was kept up on the mill, while its defenders, reserving their ammunition, kept their posts with stern and silent determination. The night was spent in running balls, cutting patches, and completing the defences of the building. In the morning the fight was renewed, and it was found that the Mexicans had effected a lodgment in a part of the stables, which were separated from the other portions of the building, and between which was an open space of a few feet. The assailants, during the night, had sought to break down the wall, and thus enter the main building, but the strength of the adobes and logs of which it was composed resisted effectually all their attempts.

"Those in the stable seemed anxious to regain the outside, for their position was unavailable as a means of annoyance to the besieged, and several had darted across the narrow space which divided it from the other part of the building, and which slightly projected, and behind which they were out of the line of fire. As soon, however, as the attention of the defenders was called to this point, the first man who attempted to cross, and who happened to be a Pueblo chief, was dropped on the instant and fell dead in the center of the intervening space. It appeared an object to recover the body, for an Indian immediately dashed out to the fallen chief and attempted to drag him within the cover of the wall. The rifle which covered the spot again poured forth its deadly contents, and the Indian, springing into the air, fell over the body of his chief, struck to the heart. Another and another met with a similar fate, and at last three rushed at once to the spot, and, seizing the body by the legs and head, had already lifted it from the ground, when three puffs of smoke blew from the barricaded window, followed by the sharp cracks of as many rifles, and the three daring Indians added their number to the pile of corses which now covered the body of the dead chief.

"As yet the besieged had met with no casualties; but after the fall of the seven Indians, in the manner above described, the whole body of assailants, with a shout of rage, poured in a rattling volley, and two of the defenders of the mill fell mortally wounded.

One, shot through the loins, suffered great agony, and was removed to the still-house, where he was laid upon a large pile of grain, as being the softest bed to be found.

"In the middle of the day the assailants renewed the attack more fiercely than before, their baffled attempts adding to their furious rage. The little garrison bravely stood to the defence of the mill, never throwing away a shot, but firing coolly, and only when a fair mark was presented to their unerring aim. Their ammunition, however, was fast failing, and to add to the danger of their situation the enemy set fire to the mill, which blazed fiercely and threatened destruction to the whole building. Twice they succeeded in overcoming the flames, and, taking advantage of their being thus occupied, the Mexicans and Indians charged into the corral, which was full of hogs and sheep, and vented their cowardly rage upon the animals, spearing and shooting all that came in their way. No sooner, however, were the flames extinguished in one place, than they broke out more fiercely in another; and as a successful defence was perfectly hopeless, and the numbers of the assailants increased every moment, a council of war was held by the survivors of the little garrison, when it was determined, as soon as night approached, that everyone should attempt to escape as best he might, and in the meantime the defence of the mill was to be continued.

"Just at dusk, Albert and another man ran to the wicket-gate, which opened into a kind of inclosed space, and in which was a number of armed Mexicans. They both rushed out at the same moment, discharging their rifles full in the faces of the crowd. Albert in the confusion threw himself under the fence, whence he saw his companion shot down immediately, and heard his cries for mercy, mingled with shrieks of pain and anguish, as the cowards pierced him with knives and lances. Lying without motion under the fence, as soon as it was quite dark he crept over the logs and ran up the mountain, traveled day and night, and, scarcely stopping or resting, reached the Greenhorn, almost dead with hunger and fatigue. Turley himself succeeded in escaping from the mill and in reaching the mountain unseen. Here he met a Mexican, mounted on a horse, who had been a most intimate friend of the unfortunate man for many years. To this man Turley offered his watch (which was treble its worth) for the use of his horse, but was refused. The inhuman wretch, however, affected pity and commiseration for the fugitive, and advised him to go to a certain place where he would bring or send him assistance; but on reaching the mill, which was now a mass of fire, he immediately informed the Mexicans of his place of concealment, whither a large party instantly proceeded and shot him to death.

"Two others escaped and reached Santa Fé in safety. The mill and Turley's house were sacked and gutted, and all his hard-earned savings, which were considerable, and concealed in gold about the house, were discovered, and of course, seized upon, by the victorious Mexicans.

"The Indians, however, met a few days after with a severe retribution. The troops marched out of Santa Fé, attacked their pueblo, and levelled it to the ground, killing many hundreds of its defenders, and taking many prisoners, most of whom were hanged."

The death of Charles Bent, of his brother Robert later in the same year, and of George Bent in 1848, left only Colonel William Bent to carry on the business of Bent's Fort, and the trade with Mexico, together with all the other operations in which he was engaged. From this time forth William Bent worked alone.

Charles Bent had one son and two daughters. Alfred, the son, died some years ago. One of the daughters is said to be still living (1909) in Mexico, very old. Tom Boggs married the other daughter. She had one son, Charles Boggs. He and his mother are both believed to be dead.

III

FORT ST. VRAIN AND FORT ADOBE

IN its best days Bent's Fort did a business surpassed in volume by only one company in the United States —John Jacob Astor's great American Fur Company. As already stated, besides Bent's Fort the Bent partners had a post on the South Platte at the mouth of St. Vrain's Fork, and one on the Canadian River, called the Fort Adobe, for trade with tribes of Indians hostile to the Cheyennes—trade which Colonel Bent, of course, wished to hold.

St. Vrain's Fork runs into the South Platte from the north and west, a few miles south or southwest of Greeley, Colo.

The site of the fort, known later and now as Adobe Walls, was the scene of two hard battles between white men and Indians. The first of these took place in 1864, and was fought between the Kiowas, Apaches, and Comanches, with a few Cheyennes and Arapahoes, who were present chiefly as onlookers, and a detachment of troops under the command of Kit Carson, who then bore a commission in the United States army. Carson had with him a number of Ute scouts. The fight was a severe one, and Carson, after burning one of the Kiowa villages, was obliged to retreat. In that battle the Indians fought bravely, and one of them possessed a cavalry bugle and knew the various calls. Carson and his officers generally acknowledged that they were beaten by the Indians, and Carson finally withdrew, the Indians saving most of their property, though they lost a number of men. Among the Kiowas killed was a young man who wore a coat of mail.

At this fight a spring-wagon was found in the possession of the Indians, and its presence in the Kiowa camp has often been wondered at. At that time wagons were never used by plains Indians, whose only vehicle was the travois, which consisted of two long poles tied together over the horses' withers, and dragging on the ground behind. Across these poles, behind the horses' hocks, was lashed a platform, on which a considerable burden might be transported.

The late Robert M. Peck, of Los Angeles, Cal., who was a soldier, serving under Major Sedgwick, then in command of troops along the Arkansas, not long before his death told the story of an ambulance presented to one of the Kiowa chiefs by the quartermaster of the troops under Major Sedgwick, which may have been this one.   Mr. Peck said:

"That was before the Kiowa war broke out in 1859. To' hau sen was always friendly to the whites, and tried to keep the Kiowas peaceable.   A small party of them, his immediate following, kept out of that war.   These were mostly the old warriors, but the younger men, who constituted a majority of the tribe, went on the warpath after Lieut. George D. Bayard, of our regiment killed one of the Kiowa chiefs, called Pawnee, near Peacock's ranch, on Walnut Creek.

"That summer (1859) we had been camping along the Arkansas River, moving camp occasionally up or down the river, trying to keep Satank and his turbulent followers from beginning another outbreak.   Old To' hau sen used frequently to come to our camp.   Lieut. McIntyre wanted to get rid of this old ambulance, which he had long had on his hands and which in some of its parts was nearly worn out. After inducing Major Sedgwick to have it condemned as unfit for service, Lieut. McIntyre had his blacksmith fix it up a little and presented it to the old chief. McIntyre fitted a couple of sets of old harness to a pair of To' hau sen's ponies and had some of the soldiers break the animals to work in the ambulance. But when To' hau sen tried to drive the team, he could not learn to handle the lines. He took the reins off the harness and had a couple of Indian boys ride the horses, and they generally went at a gallop. The old chief seemed very proud of the ambulance."

The second battle of the Adobe Walls took place in June, 1874, when the Kiowas, Comanches, and Cheyennes made an attack on some buffalo-hunters, who had built themselves houses in the shelter of the Adobe Walls. The attack on the buffalo-hunters was made in the endeavor to drive these hide-hunters out of the buffalo country, in order to save the buffalo for themselves. The hunters finally drove off the Indians with much loss, but soon afterward abandoned their camp.

St. Vrain's Fort and the Adobe Fort were abandoned between 1840 and 1850, when the fur business began to decline. By this time the beaver had begun to get scarce, having been pretty thoroughly trapped out of many of the mountain streams, and besides that the silk hat had been invented, and was rapidly taking the place of the old beaver hat, and the demand for beaver skins was greatly reduced.   Now, the mountains were full of idle trappers, and a colony of these settled some miles above Bent's Fort, on the site of the present city of Pueblo, Col., where they did a little farming and a great deal of smuggling of liquor from Mexico to the plains country.   The stagnation in the beaver trade, of course, affected the business of William Bent, who, since the death of his brother Charles, had not lessened his activities in trading.   At this time his chief business was in buffalo robes and in horses.   The establishment at the fort was now reduced, and in the early fifties Bent tried to sell it to the government for a military post, but failing to receive what he considered a fair price for his property, in 1852 he laid large charges of gunpowder in the buildings and blew the old fort into the air.

In the winter of 1852–53 he had two trading houses of logs among the Cheyennes at the Big Timbers, and in the autumn of 1853 began to build his new fort of stone on the north side of the Arkansas River, about thirty-eight miles below old Fort William, and finished it the same year.   This was the winter camp of the Cheyennes.   At that time the Big Timbers extended up the river beyond the fort, and within three miles of the mouth of Purgatoire River, but by 1865 practically all the timber had been cut down, leaving the fort in the midst of a treeless prairie.

In 1858 gold was discovered in the country northwest of the new fort.   There was a rush of gold-seekers to the country the following year, and for some reason William Bent decided to lease his post to the War Department. This he did. A garrison was sent there. It was at first intended to call the new fort Fort Fauntleroy, after the colonel of the old Second Dragoons, but finally the place was rechristened Fort Wise, in honor of the Governor of Virginia. The following summer, 1860, the troops built a stockade half a mile above Bent's old stone buildings. When the Civil War began in 1861 and Governor Wise joined the Confederates, the post was again renamed; this time Fort Lyon, in honor of General Lyon, who had been killed not long before at Wilson's Creek, Mo. In 1866 the river threatened to carry away the post, and it was moved twenty miles up the river.

Meanwhile William Bent had built a new stockade on the north side of the river, in the valley of Purgatoire Creek, and lived there, continuing to trade with the Indians. Kit Carson lived on the same side of the river, and not far from the Bent stockade. Carson died at Fort Lyon, May 23, 1868, and his friend William Bent, at his home, May 19, 1869. Ceran St. Vrain died October 29, 1870. The last year of his life was spent at Taos, N. M., but he died at the home of his son Felix, in Mora, N. M.

In 1839 Mr. Farnham visited Bent's Fort, and met two of the Bent brothers, whose names he does not give. They were clad like trappers, in splendid deerskin hunting-shirts and leggings, with long fringes on the outer seams of the arms and legs, the shirts decorated with designs worked in colored porcupine quills, and on their feet moccasins covered with quill work and beading.

This great establishment, standing alone in the midst of a wilderness, much impressed the traveller, who not long before had left a region where men, if not crowded together, were at least seen frequently, for he had recently come from Peoria, Ill. He spoke of it as a solitary abode of men seeking wealth in the face of hardship and danger, and declared that it reared "its towers over the uncultivated wastes of nature like an old baronial castle that has withstood the wars and desolations of centuries." To him the Indian women, walking swiftly about the courtyard and on the roofs of the houses, clad in long deerskin dresses and bright moccasins, were full of interest; while the naked children, with perfect forms and the red of the Saxon blood showing through the darker hue of the mother race, excited his enthusiasm. He wondered at the novel manners and customs that he saw, at the grave bourgeois and their clerks and traders, who, in time of leisure, sat cross-legged under a shade, smoking the long-stemmed Indian stone pipe, which they deliberately passed from hand to hand, until it was smoked out; at the simple food—dried buffalo meat and bread made from the unbolted wheaten meal from Taos, repasts which lacked sweets and condiments.

Here, as it seemed to him, were gathered people from

the ends of the earth: old trappers whose faces were lined and leathery from long exposure to the snows of winter and the burning heats of summer; Indians, some of whom were clad in civilized clothing, but retained the reserve and silence of their race; Mexican servants, hardly more civilized than the Indians; and all these seated on the ground, gathered around a great dish of dried meat, which constituted their only food. The prairie men who talked narrated their adventures in the North, the West, the South, and among the mountains, while others, less given to conversation, nodded or grunted in assent or comment. The talk was of where the buffalo had been, or would be; of the danger from hostile tribes; of past fights, when men had been wounded and killed; and of attacks by Indians on hunters or traders who were passing through the country.

He describes the opening of the gates on the winter's morning, the cautious sliding in and out of the Indians, whose tents stood around the fort, till the court was full of people with long, hanging black locks and dark, flashing watchful eyes; the traders and clerks busy at their work; the patrols walking the battlements with loaded muskets; the guards in the bastion, standing with burning matches by the carronades; and when the sun set, the Indians retiring again to their camp outside, to talk over their newly purchased blankets and beads, and to sing and drink and dance; and finally the night sentinel on the fort that treads his weary watch away. "This," he says, "presents a tolerable view of this post in the season of business."

Soon after the construction of the fort a brass cannon had been purchased in St. Louis and brought out for the purpose of impressing the Indians. It was used there for many years, but in 1846, when General Kearny passed by, some enthusiastic employee charged it with too great a load of powder, and in saluting the General it burst. Some time after that an iron cannon was brought from Santa Fé, and during the day always stood outside the big gate of the fort, and was often fired in honor of some great Indian chief when he came into the post with his camp. The old brass cannon lay about the post for some time, and is mentioned by Garrard.

The passage of General Kearny's little army on its march into Mexico made a gala day at Bent's Fort. The army had encamped nine miles below the post to complete its organization, for it had come straggling across the plains from Missouri in small detachments. On the morning of August 2 the fort was filled to overflowing with people: soldiers and officers, white trappers, Indian trappers, Mexicans, Cheyennes, Arapahoes, Kiowas, and Indian women, the wives of trappers from the far away Columbia and St. Lawrence. Every one was busy talking—a babel of tongues and jargons. The employees, with their wives and children, had gathered on the flat roofs to witness the wonderful spectacle, while in a securely hidden nook Charles Bent was rejoicing the souls of a few of his army friends with the icy contents of "a pitcher covered with the dew of promise."

A cloud of dust moving up the valley "at the rate of a horse walking fast" at length announced the approach of the troops. At the head of the column rode General Kearny, behind him a company of the old First United States Dragoons, behind the dragoons a regiment of Missouri volunteer cavalry and two batteries of volunteer artillery, and of infantry but two companies. It was an army of 1,700 men, and yet to the Indians assembled at the fort it must have seemed indeed an army, for perhaps few of them had ever dreamed that there were half as many men in the whole "white tribe." The column drew near the fort, swinging to the left, forded the river to the Mexican bank, turned again up the valley, and went on its way, a part to the city of Mexico, a part to California, and a part only to Santa Fé, whence but a few months later they would march to avenge the murder of Charles Bent, now doling out mint-juleps to the loitering officers in the little room upstairs in the fort.

IV

KIT CARSON, HUNTER

THERE were two or three employees at the fort whose labors never ceased. These were the hunters who were obliged constantly to provide meat for

GENERAL S. W. KEARNY

From an original daguerreotype

the employees. Though the number of these varied, there might be from sixty to a hundred men employed at the fort, and many of these had families, so that the population was considerable.

For a number of years the principal hunter for the fort was Kit Carson, who was often assisted by a Mexican or two, though in times when work was slack many of the traders, trappers, employees, and teamsters devoted themselves to hunting. Often game could be killed within sight of the post, but at other times it was necessary for the hunter to take with him a wagon or pack-animals, for he might be obliged to go several days' journey before securing the necessary food. It was the duty of Carson and his assistants to provide meat for the whole post. It was here that in 1843 Carson was married to a Mexican girl.

Though, as already suggested, difficulties sometimes occurred with the Indians, these troubles were very rare; yet the vigilance of the garrison, drilled into them from earliest times by William Bent, never relaxed.

The animals belonging to the fort were a constant temptation to the Indians. The fort stood on the open plain by the riverside, and there was an abundance of good grass close at hand, so that the herd could be grazed within sight of the walls. Even so, however, the Indians occasionally swept off the stock, as in 1839, when a party of Comanches hid in the bushes on the river-bank, ran off every hoof of stock belonging to the post, and killed the Mexican herder.

Farnham while there heard this account of the event:
"About the middle of June, 1839, a band of sixty of
them [Comanches] under cover of night crossed the
river and concealed themselves among the bushes that
grow thickly on the bank near the place where the
animals of the establishment feed during the day. No
sentinel being on duty at the time, their presence was
unobserved: and when morning came the Mexican
horse guard mounted his horse, and with the noise
and shouting usual with that class of servants when so
employed, rushed his charge out of the fort; and riding
rapidly from side to side of the rear of the band, urged
them on and soon had them nibbling the short dry
grass in a little vale within grape shot distance of the
guns of the bastion. It is customary for a guard of
animals about these trading-posts to take his station
beyond his charge; and if they stray from each other,
or attempt to stroll too far, he drives them together,
and thus keeps them in the best possible situation to be
driven hastily to the corral, should the Indians, or other
evil persons, swoop down upon them. And as there is
constant danger of this, his horse is held by a long rope,
and grazes around him, that he may be mounted quickly
at the first alarm for a retreat within the walls. The
faithful guard at Bent's, on the morning of the disaster
I am relating, had dismounted after driving out his
animals, and sat upon the ground, watching with the
greatest fidelity for every call of duty; when these 50
or 60 Indians sprang from their hiding places, ran

KIT CARSON

From the painting in the Capitol at Denver, Colorado

upon the animals, yelling horribly, and attempted to drive them across the river. The guard, however, nothing daunted, mounted quickly, and drove his horse at full speed among them. The mules and horses hearing his voice amidst the frightening yells of the savages, immediately started at a lively pace for the fort; but the Indians were on all sides, and bewildered them. The guard still pressed them onward, and called for help; and on they rushed, despite the efforts of the Indians to the contrary. The battlements were covered with men. They shouted encouragement to the brave guard—'Onward, onward,' and the injunction was obeyed. He spurred his horse to his greatest speed from side to side and whipped the hindermost of the band with his leading rope. He had saved every animal: he was within 20 yards of the open gate: he fell: three arrows from the bows of the Cumanches had cloven his heart, and, relieved of him, the lords of the quiver gathered their prey, and drove them to the borders of Texas, without injury to life or limb. I saw this faithful guard's grave: He had been buried a few days. The wolves had been digging into it. Thus 40 or 50 mules and horses and their best servant's life were lost to the Messrs. Bents in a single day."

Long before this, in 1831, when the fort was still unfinished, Carson with twelve white employees went down the river to the Big Timbers to cut logs for use in the construction work. He had all the horses and mules belonging to the post with him, and while he

and his men were at work, a party of sixty Crows crept
up close to them, and coming out of the brush and
timber drove off the herd.   Carson and his men, all
on foot, followed the Crows across the open prairie.
With them were two mounted Cheyenne warriors, who
had been visiting the camp when the Crows made their
attack, but who luckily had both their ponies by them,
and thus saved them.   The Crows had not gone many
miles before they halted, and camped in a thicket on the
margin of a little stream, thinking that a party of
twelve men would not dare to follow them on foot;
therefore, when they beheld Carson and his men coming on their trail they were greatly astonished.   They
left the stolen animals behind them, and came boldly
out on the open prairie to annihilate the venturesome
white men, but all of Carson's party had excellent
rifles and one or two pistols apiece.   Carson used to
tell how surprised those Crows were when they charged
down upon his men and were met by a stunning volley.
They turned and made for the thicket, the whites following them at a run.   Into the thicket went the Crows
and in after them tumbled Carson and his men.   Some
spirited bushwhacking ensued, then out at the far edge
of the thicket came the Crows, with Carson and his
men still after them.   Meantime, when the Crows had
come out to charge the whites, the two mounted Cheyennes had quietly slipped round in the rear and run
off all the captured horses, so now Carson's men
mounted and rode exultingly back to their camp, while

the discomfited Crows plodded on homeward, nursing their wounds.

In the years before the great peace was made between the Kiowas and Comanches, and the Cheyennes and Arapahoes, the home country of the Southern Cheyennes lay chiefly between the Arkansas and the South Platte Rivers. In August many of them used to go east as far as the valley of the Republican, for the purpose of gathering winter supplies of choke-cherries and plums. In the autumn the Suhtai and the Hill people—His'sĭ-o-mē'ta-nē—went up west into the foothills of the mountains to kill mule-deer, which were plenty there, and at that season fat. All the different bands of Cheyennes used to make annual trips to the mountains for the purpose of securing lodge-poles. A cedar which grew there was also much employed in the manufacture of bows.

At this time the range of the Kiowas was from the Cimarron south to the Red River of Texas, on the ridge of the Staked Plains. They kept south in order to avoid, so far as possible, the raiding parties of Cheyennes and Arapahoes, who were constantly trying to take horses from them. In those days—and still earlier—the Kiowas used to make frequent trips north to visit their old friends and neighbors, the Crows, but when they did this they kept away to the westward, close to the mountains, in order to avoid the camps of the Cheyennes. Nevertheless, such travelling parties were occasionally met by the Cheyennes or Arapahoes, and fights occurred. It was in such a fight that an old woman, now (1912) known as White Cow Woman, or the Kiowa Woman, was captured. She was a white child, taken from the whites by the Kiowas when two or three years of age, and a year or two later captured from the Kiowas as stated by the Cheyennes. She is now supposed to be seventy-six or seventy-seven years old. The fight when she was captured took place in 1835, or three years before the great fight on Wolf Creek.

Before the Mexican War the Arkansas was the boundary between the United States and Mexico, and Bent's Fort was, therefore, on the extreme border of the United States. In those days the Indians used to make raids into Mexican territory, sweeping off great herds of horses and mules. They also captured many Mexicans, and many a Comanche and Kiowa warrior owned two or three peons, whom he kept to herd his horses for him.

These peons were often badly treated by their Mexican masters, and after they had been for a short time with the Indians, they liked the new life so well that they would not return to their old masters, even if they had the opportunity. Many of these men led the warriors in raids into Mexico. They kept in communication with peons in the Mexican settlements, and from them learned just which places were unguarded, where the best herds and most plunder were to be secured, and where the Mexican troops were stationed. The peon then led his war-party to the locality selected, and they ran off the herds, burned ranches, and carried off plunder and peon women and men. Some of the peons captured became chiefs in the tribes that had taken them. In the old days, Colonel Bent sometimes purchased these Mexican peons from the Kiowas. In 1908 one of these peons was still living at the Kiowa Agency, eighty-two years old.

Carson was employed by the Bents as hunter for many years. Sometimes he remained at the fort, supplying the table with meat, at other times he went with the wagon-train to Missouri, acting as hunter for the outfit. The following advertisement from the Missouri *Intelligencer* marked Carson's first appearance on the page of history:

"NOTICE: To whom it may concern: That Christopher Carson, a boy about sixteen years, small of his age, but thickset, light hair, ran away from the subscriber, living in Franklin, Howard Co., Mo., to whom he had been bound to learn the saddler's trade, on or about the first day of September last. He is supposed to have made his way toward the upper part of the State. All persons are notified not to harbor, support or subsist said boy under penalty of the law. One cent reward will be given to any person who will bring back said boy.

"DAVID WORKMAN.

"Franklin, Oct. 6, 1826."

This runaway boy joined the Santa Fé caravan of
Charles Bent, and from that time on for a number of
years was employed by Bent and St. Vrain. From
1834 to 1842, he was constantly at the fort. He married a daughter of Charles Beaubien, of Taos, who,
with his son, Narcisse Beaubien, was killed at the time
of the Pueblo massacre in January, 1847.

During the Civil War, Carson received a commission
in the militia of New Mexico or Colorado, and rose to
the rank of colonel and brevet brigadier-general.

V

LIFE AT BENT'S FORT

BENT'S OLD FORT was a stopping-place for all
travellers on the Santa Fé trail, and visitors often
remained there for weeks at a time, for Colonel
Bent kept open house. On holidays, such as Christmas and the Fourth of July, if any number of people
were there, they often had balls or dances, in which
trappers, travellers, Indians, Indian women, and Mexican women all took part. Employed about the post
there was always a Frenchman or two who could
play the violin and guitar. On one occasion Frank P.
Blair,[1] then twenty-three years old, afterward a general in the Union army, and at one time a vice-presi-
dential candidate, played the banjo all night at a ball
at the fort.

[1] Appointed Attorney-general of New Mexico by General Kearny in
1846. Took an active part on the side of the Union in Missouri in 1860-1.

Just before each Fourth of July, a party was always sent up into the mountains on the Purgatoire River to gather wild mint for mint-juleps to be drunk in honor of the day. For the brewing of these, ice from the ice-house was used. In those days this drink was called "hail storm."

The employees at the fort were divided into classes, to each of which special duties were assigned. Certain men remained always at the post guarding it, trading with Indians and trappers, and keeping the books. These we may call clerks, or store-keepers, and mechanics. Another group took care of the live-stock, herding and caring for the horses and mules, while still others had charge of the wagon-train that hauled the furs to the States, and brought back new goods to the fort. Other men, led by veteran traders, went to trade in the Indian camps at a distance.

Excepting in summer, when the trains were absent on their way to St. Louis, the population of the fort was large. There were traders, clerks, trappers, hunters, teamsters, herders, and laborers, and these were of as many races as there were trades. The clerks, traders, and trappers were chiefly Americans, the hunters and laborers might be white men, Mexicans, or Frenchmen. Some of the Delawares and Shawnees— of whom Black Beaver was one of the most famous— were hunters and trappers, while others of their race were teamsters, and went back and forth with the trains between Westport and Fort William. The herders were chiefly Mexicans, as were also some of the laborers, while the cook of the bourgeois was a negro. Almost all these people had taken Indian wives from one tribe or another, and the fort was plentifully peopled with women and children, as well as with men.

During the summer season matters were often very quiet about the fort. In April, just about the time that the Indians set out on their summer buffalo-hunt, the train started for St. Louis. It was under the personal conduct of Colonel Bent, but in charge of a wagon-master, who was responsible for everything. It was loaded with robes. With the train went most of the teamsters and herders, together with some of the laborers. The journey was to last nearly six months. Each heavy wagon was drawn by six yoke of oxen, driven by a teamster, who might be a white man or a Delaware or a Shawnee. With the train went great herds of horses to be sold when the settlements were reached. Agent Fitzpatrick says that the Cheyennes moved with the train as far as Pawnee Fork, and then scattered on their hunt.

Travel was slow, for the teams made but ten or twelve miles a day. On each trip they camped at about the same places, and to the men who accompanied the train the route was as well known as is the main street to the people of a small town. When camp was reached at night the wagons were corralled, the bulls freed from their yokes, and, in charge of the night herders, who during the day had been sleeping in the wagons, were driven off to the best grass and there fed and rested until morning, when they were driven back to the corral to be turned over to the teamsters. The horse herd was taken off in another direction, and held during the night by the horse night herders. Within the great corral of wagons the fires were kindled, and the mess cooks prepared the simple meal of bread, already cooked, and coffee.

At daylight in the morning the oxen were brought in and yoked, the blankets tied up and thrown into the wagons, and long before the sun appeared the train was in motion. Travel was kept up until ten or eleven o'clock, depending on the weather. If it was hot they stopped earlier; if cool, they travelled longer. Then camp was made, the wagons were again corralled, the herds turned out, and the principal meal of the day, which might be called breakfast or dinner, was prepared. Perhaps during the morning the hunters had killed buffalo or antelope, and this with bread satisfied the keen appetites of the men. If fresh meat had not been killed, there was always an abundance of dried meat, which every one liked. At two or three o'clock the herds were again brought in, and the train was set in motion, the journey continuing until dark or after. So the quiet routine of the march was kept up until the settlements were reached.

The whole train was in charge of the wagon-master, who was its absolute governing head. He fixed the length of the march, the time for starting and halting.

If a difficult stream was to be crossed, he rode ahead of the train and directed the crossing of the first team, and then of all the others, not leaving the place until the difficulty had been wholly overcome. Besides looking after a multitude of details, such as the shoeing of the oxen, the greasing of the wagons, which took place every two or three days, and the condition of the animals in the yokes, he also issued rations to the men, and was, in fact, the fountain of all authority. With the cavalyard [1] were always driven a number of loose work-oxen, and if an animal in the yoke was injured, or became lame or footsore, it was turned into the herd and replaced by a fresh ox.

When the axles of the wagons were to be greased, the wheels were lifted from the ground by a very long lever, on the end of which several men threw themselves to raise the wagon, so that the wheel could be taken off. If one of the teamsters became sick or disabled, it was customary for the wagon-master to drive the leading team.

The train often consisted of from twenty to thirty wagons, most of them—in later years—laden with bales of buffalo robes on the way to the settlements, and returned full of goods. The front end of the wagon inclined somewhat forward, and about half-way down the front was a box, secured by a lock, in which the teamster kept the spare keys for his ox-bows, various

---

[1] Sp. *caballada:* literally, a herd of horses; more broadly, a herd of horses and work-cattle. Also pronounced cávaya, and spelled in a variety of ways.

other tools, and some of his own small personal be-
longings.

Two hunters, one a white man, and the other a Mexican, or Indian, accompanied the train, and each morning, as soon as it was ready to start, they set out to kill
game, and usually when the train came to the appointed
camping-place, they were found there resting in the
shade, with a load of meat. Sometimes, if they killed
an animal close to the road, they loaded it on a horse
and brought it back to the trail, so that it could be
thrown into a wagon when the train passed.

The Shawnees and Delawares were great hunters,
and almost always when the train stopped for noon,
and their cattle had been turned out and the meal
eaten, these men would be seen striding off over the
prairie, each with a long rifle over his shoulder.

In the train there were several messes. Colonel Bent
and any member of his family, or visitor, messed together, the white teamsters and the Mexicans also
messed together, while the Delawares and Shawnees, by
preference, messed by themselves. Each man had his
own quart cup and plate, and carried his own knife in
its sheath. Forks or spoons were not known. Each
man marked his own plate and cup, usually by rudely
scratching his initials or mark on it, and when he had
finished using it, he washed or cleansed it himself.
Each mess chose its cook from among its members.
The food eaten by these travellers, though simple, was
wholesome and abundant. Meat was the staple; but

they also had bread and abundant coffee, and occasionally boiled dried apples and rice. Usually there was sugar, though sometimes they had to depend on the old-fashioned "long sweetening"; that is, New Orleans molasses, which was imported in hogsheads for trade with the Indians.

The train was occasionally attacked by Indians, but they were always beaten off. In 1847 the Comanches attacked the wagons at Pawnee Fork, but they were repulsed, and Red Sleeves, their chief, was killed. The fork is called by the Indians Red Sleeves' Creek, in remembrance of this affair. Charles Hallock, who made the journey with one of these trains, wrote an account of an attack by Comanches, which was printed in *Harper's Magazine*, in 1859.

After the return to the post in autumn, the cattle were turned out into the herd, wagons ranged around outside of the corral, while the yokes and chains for each bull team were cared for by the driver of the team. Usually they were carried into the fort and piled up in some shady place. The keys for the bows were tied to the yokes, and the chains lay close to them.

Rarely a few ox-bows were lost by being taken away by the Indians, who greatly coveted the hickory wood for the manufacture of bows. There was no hickory nearer than Council Grove, and if an Indian could get hold of an ox-bow, he steamed and straightened it, and from it made a useful bow.

Back at the fort only a few men were left; the clerks, a trader or two, and a few laborers and herders. There were frequent calls there by Indians, chiefly war-parties stopping to secure supplies of arms and ammunition. Hunting parties occasionally called to procure ordinary goods. Parties of white travellers came and stayed for a little while, and then went on again. During this time especial precautions were taken against trouble with the Indians. At night, the fort was closed early, and conditions sometimes arose under which admission to the fort might be refused by the trader. This watchfulness, which was never relaxed, was not caused by any special fear of Indian attacks, but was merely the carrying out of those measures of prudence which Colonel Bent had always practised, and which he had so thoroughly inculcated in his men that they had become fixed habits.

Usually the Cheyenne Indians were freely admitted to the fort, and were allowed to wander through it, more or less at will. They might go up on the roof and into the watch-tower, but were warned by the chiefs not to touch anything. They might go about and look, and, if they wished to, ask questions, but they were not to take things in their hands. Toward the close of the day, as the sun got low, a chief or principal man went through the fort, and said to the young men who were lounging here and there: "Now, soon these people will wish to close the gates of this house, and you had better now go out and return to your camps." When this was said the young men always obeyed, for in those days the chiefs had control over their young men; they listened to what was said to them and obeyed.

On one occasion a war-party of Shoshoni came down from the mountains and visited Bent's Fort, and insisted on coming in. The trader in charge, probably Murray, declined to let them in, and when they endeavored to force their way into the post, he killed one of them, when the others went away. The Indian's body was buried at some little distance from the fort, and his scalp was afterward given to a war-party of Cheyennes and Arapahoes.

In winter the scenes at the fort were very different. Now it harbored a much larger population. All the employees were there, except a few traders and teamsters and laborers, who might be out visiting the different camps, and who were constantly going and returning. The greater part of the laborers and teamsters had little or nothing to do, and spent most of the winter in idleness, lounging about the fort, or occasionally going out hunting. Besides the regular inhabitants there were many visitors, some of whom spent a long time at the fort. Hunters and trappers from the mountains, often with their families, came in to purchase goods for the next summer's journey, or to visit, and then, having supplied their wants, returned to their mountain camps. All visitors were welcome to stay as long as they pleased.

Though the fort was full of idle men, nevertheless time did not hang heavy on their hands. There were amusements of various sorts, hunting parties, games, and not infrequent dances, in which the moccasined trappers, in their fringed, beaded, or porcupine-quilled buckskin garments swung merry-faced, laughing Indian women in the rough but hearty dances of the frontier. To the employees of the fort liquor was ever dealt out with a sparing hand, and there is no memory of any trouble among the people who belonged at the post. It was a contented and cheerful family that dwelt within these four adobe walls.

Perhaps the most important persons at the fort, after the directing head who governed the whole organization, were the traders, who dealt out goods to the Indians in the post, receiving their furs in payment, and who were sent off to distant camps with loads of trade goods, to gather from them the robes which they had prepared, or to buy horses and mules.

Of these traders there were seven or eight, of whom the following are remembered: Murray, an Irishman known to the Indians as Pau-ē-sīh´, Flat Nose; Fisher, an American, Nō-mā-nī´, Fish; Hatcher, a Kentuckian, Hē-hīm´nī-hō-nāh´, Freckled Hand; Thomas Boggs, a Missourian, Wŏhk´po-hŭm´, White Horse; John Smith, a Missourian, Pŏ-ō-om´ mats, Gray Blanket; Kit Carson, a Kentuckian, Vī-hiu-nĭs´, Little Chief, and Charles Davis, a Missourian, Ho-nīh´, Wolf.

L. Maxwell, Wō-wĭhph´ pai-ī-sīh´, Big Nostrils, was

the superintendent or foreman at the fort, but had nothing to do with the trading. He looked after the herds and laborers and fort matters in general.

Murray, who was a good hunter and trapper, and a brave man, was one of the two more important men among the traders. He usually remained at the fort, and was almost always left in charge when the train went to the States. Hatcher, however, was probably the best trader, and the most valued of the seven.

Each of these traders had especial friendly relations with some particular tribe of Indians, and each was naturally sent off to the tribe that he knew best. Besides this, often when villages of Indians came and camped somewhere near the post, the chiefs would request that a particular man be sent to their village to trade. Sometimes to a very large village two or three traders would be sent, the work being more than one man could handle in a short period of time.

When it was determined that a trader should go out, he and the chief clerk talked over the trip. The trader enumerated the goods required, and these were laid out, charged to him, and then packed for transportation to the camp. If the journey were over level prairie, this transportation was by wagon, but if over rough country pack-mules were used. If on arrival at the camp the trader found that the trade was going to be large, and that he required more goods, he sent back his wagon, or some of his animals, to the post for additional supplies. When he returned from his trip and turned in his robes, he was credited with the goods that he had received. The trade for robes ended in the spring, and during the summer the traders often went to different villages to barter for horses and mules.

A certain proportion of the trade with the Indians was for spirits, but this proportion was small. The Indians demanded liquor, and though Colonel Bent was strongly opposed to giving it to them, he knew very well that unless he did something toward satisfying their demands, whiskey traders from Santa Fé or Taos might come into the territory and gratify the Indians' longing for drink, and at the same time take away the trade from the fort. Two or three times a year, therefore, after many visits from the chiefs, asking for liquor, promising to take charge of it and see to its distribution, and to be responsible that payment should be made for it, a lot of liquor would be sent out to a camp, packed in kegs of varying sizes. A trader coming into the villages would deposit his load in the lodge of the chief. The Indians wishing to trade would come to the lodge and offer what they had to trade, and each would be assigned a keg of a certain size, sufficient to pay for the robes, horses, or mules that he sold. Each Indian then tied a piece of cloth or a string to his keg, so as to mark it as his, and it remained in the chief's lodge, unopened for the present. When the trade had been completed, the trader left the village, and not until he had gone some distance did the chief permit the Indians to take their kegs of liquor. Sometimes while the traders were in a camp trading ordinary goods, a party of men from Taos or Santa Fé would come into the camp with whiskey, and then at once there would be an end of all legitimate business until the Indians had become intoxicated, drunk all the spirits, and become sober again. No trader ever wished to have whiskey in the camp where he was working.

We commonly think of the trade at one of these old forts as being wholly for furs, but at Bent's Fort this was not the case. In later times furs—that is to say, buffalo robes—were indeed a chief article of trade, and were carried back to the States to be sold there; but a great trade also went on in horses and mules, of which the Indians possessed great numbers, and of which they were always getting more. These horses and mules were taken back to the settlements and sold there, but they were also sold to any one who would buy them. The cavalyard was a part of every train which returned to the States, the animals being herded by Mexicans and being in charge of a trader, who disposed of them when they reached the settlements.

The Indians frequently paid for their goods in horses and mules, but this was not the only source from which horses came. About 1845 William Bent sent his brother, George Bent, with Tom Boggs and Hatcher, down into Mexico to trade for horses and mules. They brought back great herds, and with them a celebrated rider known at the fort, and in later years to

all the Cheyennes, as One-eyed Juan, whose sole occupation was breaking horses, a vocation which he followed until he was too old to get into the saddle. It
was said of him that when he wished to show off he
would put a saddle on a wild horse, and placing a
Mexican dollar in each one of the huge wooden stirrups, would mount the horse, and no matter what the
horse might do, these dollars were always found under
the soles of the rider's feet when the animal stopped
bucking.

While the chief market at which the horses and mules
were sold was St. Louis, yet on at least one occasion
Hatcher took a herd of horses which had been bought
wild from the Comanches and broken by the Mexicans
at the fort over to Taos and Santa Fé, and sold them
there. Occasionally they sold good broken horses to
the Indians for robes.

It must be remembered that a large proportion of
these horses purchased from the Indians, and especially
from the Comanches, were wild horses taken by the
Comanches from the great herds which ran loose on
the ranches in Mexico. Practically all these horses
bore Mexican brands.

After the emigration to California began, herds of
horses and mules were sent up to the emigrant trail on
the North Platte River, to be sold to emigrants on their
way to California. On one occasion Hatcher, with a
force of Mexican herders, was sent up there in charge
of a great herd of horses and mules, and remained along-

side the trail until he had disposed of all his animals. He carried back with him the gold and silver money received for them in leather panniers, packed on the backs of animals.

Before starting on another similar trip, Hatcher said to Colonel Bent: "It is useless to load down our animals with sugar, coffee and flour, to carry up there. We will take only enough to last us to the trail, and there we can buy all we need from the emigrants. Moreover, they have great numbers of broken-down horses, and it would be a good idea to buy these for little or nothing, and then drive them back here and let them get rested and fat, and then we can take them up there and sell them again." The wisdom of this was at once apparent, and the suggestion was followed out.

Important members of the fort household were Chipita; Andrew Green, the bourgeois's cook; the old French tailor, whose name is forgotten, and the carpenter and the blacksmith.

Chipita was the housekeeper and laundress, the principal woman at the post, and the one who, on the occasion of dances or other festivities, managed these affairs. She was a large, very good-natured, and kindly woman, and is said to have been half French and half Mexican. She spoke French readily. She was married to one of the employees of the fort.

Andrew Green, the black cook, has already been spoken of as having ultimately been set free.

The old French tailor had come up from New Orleans.

He had a shop in one of the rooms of the fort, where he used to make and repair clothing for the men.   Much of this clothing was of buckskin, which he himself dressed, for he was a good tanner.

In winter the teamsters and laborers usually spent their evenings in playing cards and checkers in the quarters by the light of tallow candles, the only lights they had to burn.   These candles were made at the fort, Chipita doing the work.   They were moulded of buffalo tallow, in old-fashioned tin moulds, perhaps a dozen in a set.   The work of fixing the wicks in the moulds occupied considerable time.   The tallow was then melted, the refuse skimmed from it, the fluid grease poured into the moulds, and the wicks, which hung from the top, were cut off with a pair of scissors.   Then the moulds were dipped in a barrel of water standing by, to cool the candles, and presently they were quite hard, and could be removed from the moulds, ready for use.

In the winter Chipita would sometimes vary the monotony of the life by getting up a candy-pulling frolic, in which the laborers and teamsters all took part, and which was more or less a jollification.   During the afternoon and evening the black New Orleans molasses, which was used in the Indian trade, was boiled, and after supper the people gathered in one of the rooms and pulled the candy.   Candy such as this was a great luxury, and was eagerly eaten by those who could get it.

The work of the carpenter and blacksmith, whose shops stood at the back of the fort, was chiefly on the wagons, which they kept in good order. For them winter was the busy season, for it was their duty to have everything in good order and ready for the train to start out in April.

In the store of the fort—presumably for sale to travellers or for the use of the proprietors—were to be found such unusual luxuries as butter-crackers, Bent's water-crackers, candies of various sorts, and, most remarkable of all, great jars of preserved ginger of the kind which fifty or sixty years ago used to be brought from China. Elderly people of the present day can remember, when they were children, seeing these blue china jars, which were carried by lines of vegetable rope passed around the necks of the jars, and can remember also how delicious this ginger was when they were treated to a taste of it.

At the post were some creatures which greatly astonished the Indians. On one of his trips to St. Louis St. Vrain purchased a pair of goats, intending to have them draw a cart for some of the children. On the way across the plains, however, one of them was killed, but the one that survived lived at the fort for some years and used to clamber all over the walls and buildings. The creature was a great curiosity to the plains people, who had never before seen such an animal, and they never wearied of watching its climbing and its promenading along the walls of the fort. As it grew older it became cross, and seemed to take pleasure in scattering little groups of Indian children and chasing them about. The Southern Cheyennes went but little into the mountains at this time, and but few of them had ever seen the mountain sheep.   If they had, they would not have regarded the domestic goat with so much wonder.

The post was abundantly supplied with poultry, for pigeons, chickens, and turkeys had been brought out there, and bred and did well.   At one time George Bent brought out several peacocks, whose gay plumage and harsh voices astonished and more or less alarmed the Indians, who called them thunder birds, Nŭn-ūm'ā-ē-vĭ'kĭs.

There was no surgeon at the fort, Colonel Bent doing his own doctoring.   He possessed an ample medicine-chest, which he replenished on his trips to St. Louis. He had also a number of medical books, and no doubt these and such practical experience as came to him with the years made him reasonably skilful in the rough medicine and surgery that he practised.   With the train he carried a small medicine-chest, which occasionally came into play.

For many years Bent's Fort was the great and only gathering-place for the Indians in the Southwestern plains, and at different times there were large companies of them present there.

At one time no less than three hundred and fifty lodges of Kiowa Apaches were camping near the fort on the south side of the river, and at another, according to Thomas Boggs, six or seven thousand Cheyennes were camped there at one time. When the Kiowas, Comanches, and Apaches were camped about the fort the number of Indians was very large. It must be remembered that prior to 1849 the Indians of the Southwest had not been appreciably affected by any of the new diseases brought into the country by the whites. This was largely due to the forethought of William Bent, who, by his action in 1829, when smallpox was raging at his stockade, protected the Cheyennes and Arapahoes at least, and very likely other Indians, from the attacks of this dread disease.

Shortly after the great peace between the Cheyennes, Arapahoes, Kiowas, Comanches, and Apaches, which was made in 1840, the two great camps moved up to Bent's Fort, the Cheyennes and Arapahoes camping on the north side of the river, the Kiowas, Comanches, and Apaches on the south. It was a great gathering of Indians, and the feasting, singing, dancing, and drumming were continuous. Though peace had just been made, there was danger that some of the old ill feeling that had so long existed between the tribes yet remained. Colonel Bent, with his usual wisdom, warned his employees that to these camps no spirits whatever should be traded. He recognized that if the Indians got drunk they would very likely begin to quarrel again, and a collision between members of tribes formerly hostile might lead to the breaking of the newly made peace. This was perhaps the greatest gathering of the Indians that ever collected at Fort William. How many were there will never be known.

Such, briefly, is the story of Bent's Fort, the oldest, largest, and most important of the furt rading posts on the great plains of the United States. Unless some manuscript, the existence of which is now unknown, should hereafter be discovered, it is likely to be all that we shall ever know of the place that once held an important position in the history of our country.

Bent's Fort long ago fell to ruins, but it has not been wholly forgotten. Up to the year 1868 the buildings were occupied as a stage station, and a stopping-place for travellers, with a bar and eating-house; but soon after that, when the railroad came up the Arkansas River, and stage travel ceased, the old post was abandoned. From that time on, it rapidly disintegrated under the weather.

In the autumn of 1912 I stood on this historic spot, still bare of grass, and marked on two sides by remains of the walls, in some places a mere low mound, and in others a wall four feet high, in which the adobe bricks were still recognizable. Here and there were seen old bits of iron, the fragment of a rusted horseshoe, of a rake, and a bit of cast-iron which had been part of a stove and bore letters and figures which could be made out as portions of the words "St. Louis, 1859."

The land on which the fort stood was owned by a public-spirited citizen, Mr. A. E. Reynolds, of Denver, Col., and here within the walls of the old fort he has placed a granite stone to mark its site and to commemorate its history. He has given the land over to the care of the Daughters of the American Revolution to be used as a public park for the counties of Otero and Bent, Colo.

William Bent, whose life was devoted to the upbuilding of the Southwest, will always be remembered as the one who placed on that fertile and productive empire the stamp "settled."

GEORGE FREDERICK RUXTON, HUNTER

GEORGE FREDERICK RUXTON, HUNTER

SOME time about 1840 George Frederick Ruxton, a young Englishman, was serving in Canada as an officer in a British regiment. In 1837, when only seventeen years of age, he had left Sandhurst to enlist as a volunteer in the service of Spain, where he served with gallantry and distinction in the civil wars and received from Queen Isabella II the cross of the first class of the Order of San Fernando. The monotony of garrison duty in Canada soon palled on one who had taken part in more stirring scenes, and before long he resigned his commission in his regiment and sought new fields of adventure.

He was a man fond of action and eager to see new things. His earliest project was to cross Africa, and this he attempted, but without success.

He next turned toward Mexico as a field for adventure, and he has painted a fascinating picture, both of life there at the time of the Mexican War and of life in the mountains to the north. The two small volumes of his writings are now out of print, but they are well worth reading by those who desire to learn of the early history of a country that is now well known, and which within fifty years has changed from a region without population to one which is a teeming hive of industry.

In Ruxton's *Adventures in Mexico and the Rocky Mountains* is a singularly vivid account of the author's journeyings from England, by way of the Madeira Islands, Barbadoes and others of the Antilles, to Cuba, and so to Vera Cruz, more fully called the Rich City of the True Cross; or as often, and quite aptly—from the plague of yellow fever which so constantly ravaged it— the City of the Dead. From Vera Cruz he travelled north, passing through Mexico, whose coast was then blockaded by the gringoes of North America, then through the country ravaged by marauding Indians, and at last, leaving Chihuahua and crossing by way of El Paso into New Mexico, he reached what is now the Southwestern United States. Through this country he passed—in winter—north through the mountains, meeting the trappers and mountaineers of those days and the Indians as well, crossed the plains, and finally reached St. Louis, and from there passed east to New York.

Although untrained in literature, Ruxton was a keen observer, and presented his narrative in most attractive form. He saw the salient characteristics of the places and the people among whom he was thrown, and commented on them most interestingly. He gives us a peculiarly vivid picture of Mexico as it was during its early days of stress and strain, or from the time of its independence, for within the last twenty-five years there had been not far from two hundred and fifty revolutions. This state of things, as is well known, continued for a dozen years after the Mexican War, or

until the great Indian Juarez became ruler of the
country and put down lawlessness and revolution with
a strong hand. From his day until the expulsion of
his great successor Porfirio Diaz Mexico was fortunate
in her rulers.

Just after Ruxton reached Vera Cruz General Santa
Anna, ex-President of Mexico, reached the city, having
been summoned to return after his expulsion of a year
before. Santa Anna was received with some form and
ceremony, but with no applause; and before he had
been long ashore was cross-examined by a representative of the people in very positive fashion, and sub-
mitted meekly to the inquisition.

It is hardly to be supposed that Ruxton, who had
been a British soldier, would be blind to the extraordinary appearance and absolute lack of discipline of the
Mexican troops, and his description of the soldiers,
their equipment, and the preparations for the reception
of Santa Anna is interesting. "The crack regiment of
the Mexican army—*el onze*, the 11th—which happened
to be in garrison at the time, cut most prodigious capers
in the great plaza several times a day, *disciplinando*—
drilling for the occasion. Nothing can, by any possi-
bility, be conceived more unlike a soldier than a Mexican *militar*.   The regular army is composed entirely of
Indians—miserable-looking pigmies, whose grenadiers
are five feet high. Vera Cruz, being a show place, and
jealous of its glory, generally contrives to put decent
clothing, by subscription, on the regiment detailed to

garrison the town; otherwise clothing is not considered indispensable to the Mexican soldier. The muskets of the infantry are (that is, if they have any) condemned Tower muskets, turned out of the British service years before. I have seen them carrying firelocks without locks, and others with locks without hammers, the lighted end of a cigar being used as a match to ignite the powder in the pan. Discipline they have none. Courage a Mexican does not possess; but still they have that brutish indifference to death, which could be turned to account if they were well led, and officered by men of courage and spirit."

Toward the end of the rainy season Ruxton, with a *mozo*, started for the north. He travelled on horseback, and his way was made difficult by the condition of the roads, which were heavy from rain, and by the presence in the country of troops on their way to the war, which made the accommodations, bad at best, still worse.

Concerning the city of Mexico and its inhabitants of the better class he speaks with some enthusiasm, but the hotels were villainous, the city unsafe for strangers after night, and at that time a blond man—a *guero*— was constantly taken for a Texan or a Yankee, and was subject to attack by any of the people.

In the city of Mexico Ruxton purchased horses from a Yankee horse-dealer named Smith, and set out with a pack-train for the farther north. His accounts of his travels, the difficulties of the way, the inns at which he stopped, and the cities that he passed through are extremely interesting. Of the manufacture of the national drink, *pulque*, the favorite beverage of the Mexicans, he says: "The maguey, American aloe—*Agave americana*—is cultivated over an extent of country embracing 50,000 square miles. In the City of Mexico alone the consumption of pulque amounts to the enormous quantity of 11,000,000 of gallons per annum, and a considerable revenue from its sale is derived by Government. The plant attains maturity in a period varying from eight to fourteen years, when it flowers; and it is during the stage of inflorescence only that the saccharine juice is extracted. The central stem which incloses the incipient flower is then cut off near the bottom, and a cavity or basin is discovered, over which the surrounding leaves are drawn close and tied. Into this reservoir the juice distils, which otherwise would have risen to nourish and support the flower. It is removed three or four times during the twenty-four hours, yielding a quantity of liquor varying from a quart to a gallon and a half.

"The juice is extracted by means of a syphon made of a species of gourd called *acojote*, one end of which is placed in the liquor, the other in the mouth of a person, who by suction draws up the fluid into the pipe and deposits it in the bowls he has with him for the purpose. It is then placed in earthen jars and a little old pulque —madre de pulque—is added, when it soon ferments, and is immediately ready for use. The fermentation occupies two or three days, and when it ceases the pulque is in fine order.

"Old pulque has a slightly unpleasant odour, which heathens have likened to the smell of putrid meat, but, when fresh, is brisk and sparkling, and the most cooling, refreshing, and delicious drink that ever was invented for thirsty mortal; and when gliding down the dust-dried throat of a way-worn traveller, who feels the grateful liquor distilling through his veins, is indeed the 'licor divino,' which Mexicans assert, is preferred by the angels in heaven to ruby wine."

Wherever Ruxton passed, his fair hair and complexion and his excellent arms were subjects of wonder; the first to the women and children, the second to the men. His double-barrelled rifles seem especially to have impressed the men.

As he passed farther and farther north, he heard more and more concerning the raids of the Indians, and at the ranch of La Punta, where he stopped to witness the sport of tailing the bull, he heard from one of the inhabitants an account of the raid of the previous year, in which a number of peons were killed and some women and children carried away to the north. He says: "The ranchero's wife described to me the whole scene, and bitterly accused the men of cowardice in not defending the place. This woman, with two grown daughters and several smaller children, fled from the rancho before the Indians approached, and concealed themselves under a wooden bridge which crossed a stream near at hand. Here they remained for some hours, half dead with terror: presently some Indians approached their place of concealment: a young chief stood on the bridge and spoke some words to the others. All this time he had his piercing eyes bent upon their hiding-place, and had no doubt discovered them, but concealed his satisfaction under an appearance of indifference. He played with his victims. In broken Spanish they heard him express his hope 'that he would be able to discover where the women were concealed— that he wanted a Mexican wife and some scalps.' Suddenly he jumped from the bridge and thrust his lance under it with a savage whoop; the blade pierced the woman's arm and she shrieked with pain. One by one they were drawn from their retreat.

" '*Dios de mi alma!*'—what a moment was this!— said the poor creature. Her children were surrounded by the savages, brandishing their tomahawks, and she thought their last hour was come. But they all escaped with life, and returned to find their houses plundered and the corpses of friends and relations strewing the ground.

" '*Ay de mi!*'—what a day was this! '*Y los hombres,*' she continued, '*qui no son hombres?*'—And the men— who are *not* men—where were they? '*Escondidos como los ratones*'—hidden in holes like the rats. '*Mire!*' she said suddenly, and with great excitement: 'look at these two hundred men, well mounted and armed, who are now so brave and fierce, running after the poor bulls; if twenty Indians were to make their appearance where would they be? *Vaya! vaya!*' she exclaimed, '*son cobardes*'—they are cowards all of them.

"The daughter, who sat at her mother's feet during the recital, as the scenes of that day were recalled to her memory, buried her face in her mother's lap, and wept with excitement.

"To return to the toros. In a large corral, at one end of which was a little building, erected for the accommodation of the lady spectators, were inclosed upwards of a hundred bulls. Round the corral were the horsemen, all dressed in the picturesque Mexican costume, examining the animals as they were driven to and fro in the inclosure, in order to make them wild for the sport—*alzar el corage*. The ranchero himself, and his sons, were riding amongst them, armed with long lances, separating from the herd, and driving into another inclosure, the most active bulls. When all was ready, the bars were withdrawn from the entrance of the corral, and a bull driven out, who, seeing the wide level plain before him, dashed off at the top of his speed. With a shout, the horsemen pursued the flying animal, who, hearing the uproar behind him, redoubled his speed. Each urges his horse to the utmost, and strives to take the lead and be first to reach the bull. In such a crowd, of course, first-rate horsemanship is required to avoid accidents and secure a safe lead. For some minutes the troop ran on in a compact mass—a sheet could have covered the lot. Enveloped in a cloud of

dust, nothing could be seen but the bull, some hundred
yards ahead, and the rolling cloud. Presently, with a
shout, a horseman emerged from the front rank; the
women cried '*Viva!*' as, passing close to the stage, he
was recognized to be the son of the ranchera, a boy of
twelve years of age, sitting his horse like a bird, and
swaying from side to side as the bull doubled, and the
cloud of dust concealed the animal from his view.
'*Viva Pepito! viva!*' shouted his mother, as she waved
her reboso to encourage the boy; and the little fellow
struck his spurs into his horse and doubled down to his
work manfully. But now two others are running neck
and neck with him, and the race for the lead and the
first throw is most exciting. The men shout, the
women wave their rebosos and cry out their names:
'*Alza—Bernardo—por mi amor, Juan Maria—Viva Pe-
pitito!*' they scream in intense excitement. The boy at
length loses the lead to a tall, fine-looking Mexican,
mounted on a fleet and powerful roan stallion, who
gradually but surely forges ahead. At this moment
the sharp eyes of little Pepe observed the bull to turn
at an angle from his former course, which movement
was hidden by the dust from the leading horseman. In
an instant the boy took advantage of it, and, wheeling
his horse at a right angle from his original course, cut
off the bull. Shouts and vivas rent the air at sight of
this skillful maneuver, and the boy, urging his horse
with whip and spur, ranged up to the left quarter of
the bull, bending down to seize the tail, and secure it

under his right leg, for the purpose of throwing the animal to the ground. But here Pepe's strength failed him in a feat which requires great power of muscle, and in endeavouring to perform it he was jerked out of his saddle and fell violently to the ground, stunned and senseless. At least a dozen horsemen were now striving hard for the post of honour, but the roan distanced them all, and its rider, stronger than Pepe, dashed up to the bull, threw his right leg over the tail, which he had seized in his right hand, and, wheeling his horse suddenly outwards, upset the bull in the midst of his career, and the huge animal rolled over and over in the dust, bellowing with pain and fright."

Pushing northward through Mexico, Ruxton passed into a country with fewer and fewer inhabitants. It was the borderland of the Republic, where the Indians, constantly raiding, were killing people, burning villages, and driving off stock. The author's adventures were frequent. He was shot at by his *mozo*, or servant, who desired to possess his property. He met wagon-trains coming from Santa Fé, owned and manned by Americans. He lost his animals, was often close to Indians, yet escaped without fighting them, assisted in the rescue of a number of American teamsters who had endeavored to strike across the country to reach the United States, and many of whom had perished from hunger and thirst; and finally, while on this good errand, was robbed of all his property by thieves in the little village where he had left it. His journal of travel is pleasantly interspersed with traditions of the country and accounts of local adventures of the time.

Reaching Chihuahua, he found the shops stocked with goods brought from the United States by way of Santa Fé, it being profitable to drive the wagon-trains south as far as Chihuahua, rather than to sell their loads in Santa Fé. This Santa Fé trade, always subject to great risks from attacks by Indians and other dangers of the road, was made still more difficult from the extraordinary customs duties laid by the Mexican officials, who, without reference to the nature of the goods carried, assessed a duty of $500 on each wagon, no matter what its size or its contents.

Of Chihuahua as it was in those days Ruxton writes with enthusiasm: "In the sierras and mountains," he says, "are found two species of bears—the common black, or American bear, and the grizly bear of the Rocky Mountains. The last are the most numerous, and are abundant in the sierras, in the neighbourhood of Chihuahua. The carnero cimarron—the big-horn or Rocky Mountain sheep—is also common on the Cordillera. Elk, black-tailed deer, cola-prieta (a large species of the fallow deer), the common red deer of America, and antelope, abound on all the plains and sierras. Of smaller game, peccaries (javali), also called cojamete, hares, and rabbits are everywhere numerous; and beavers are still found in the Gila, the Pecos, the Del Norte, and their tributary streams. Of birds—the faisan, commonly called paisano, a species of pheasant:

the quail, or rather a bird between a quail and a partridge, is abundant; while every variety of snipe and plover is found on the plains, not forgetting the *gruya*, of the crane kind, whose meat is excellent. There are also two varieties of wolf—the white, or mountain wolf; and the coyote, or small wolf of the plains, whose long-continued and melancholy howl is an invariable adjunct to a Mexican night encampment."

At the time that the author passed through Chihuahua that province was in a state of more or less excitement, expecting the advance of the "Americanos" from New Mexico, which province had been occupied by the United States forces (Santa Fé having been entered Aug. 18, 1846, by Gen. S. W. Kearny), and following the troops was a caravan of 200 traders' wagons bound for Chihuahua. Ruxton was travelling northward, directly toward the American troops, and bore despatches for the American commander; he was therefore treated with extreme courtesy in Chihuahua and went on his way. He has something to say about the Mexican troops stationed here at Chihuahua, whom Colonel Doniphan, two or three months later, with 900 volunteers, defeated with a loss of 300 killed and as many wounded, capturing the city of Chihuahua, and without "losing *one man* in the campaign." As a matter of fact, one man was killed on the United States side, while the Mexican losses were given as 320 killed, 560 wounded, and 72 prisoners.

It was in November that the author bade adieu to

Chihuahua and set out for Santa Fé. Though the country through which he journeyed was infested with Indians, yet now and then a Mexican village was passed, occupied by people who were poor both in pocket and in spirit, and satisfied merely to live. When the Rio Grande, which in old times was commonly called the Del Norte, was passed, Ruxton was in what is now the United States. It was then Mexican territory, however, and at El Paso there were Mexican troops, and also a few American prisoners. From here, for some distance northward, Indian "sign" was constantly seen, chiefly of Apaches, who made it their business and their pleasure to ravage the region.

On the Rio Grande, a few days' journey beyond El Paso, a surveying party under the command of Lieutenant Abert, of the United States Engineers, was met with, and near him was camped a great part of the traders' caravan which was on its way to Chihuahua. The scene here must have been one of interest. The wagons were corralled, making a fort, from which Indians or Mexicans could be defied, and the large and wild-looking Missourians formed a striking contrast to the tiny Mexicans, with whom the author had so long been mingling. The American troops in this and neighboring camps were volunteers, each one of whom thought himself quite as good as his commanding officers, and anything like discipline was unknown. Ruxton was greatly impressed by this, and commented freely on it, declaring that—"the American can never be made a soldier; his constitution will not bear the restraint of discipline; neither will his very mistaken notions about liberty allow him to subject himself to its necessary control."

No doubt the troops which conquered Mexico were a good deal of a mob, and won their victories in a great measure by the force of individual courage, and through the timidity and still greater lack of organization of the troops opposed to them. On the other hand, Ruxton seems to have felt much admiration for the officers in command of the regular army. He speaks of West Point, and declares that the military education received there is one "by which they acquire a practical as well as theoretical knowledge of the science of war"; and that, "as a class, they are probably more distinguished for military knowledge than the officers of any European army; uniting with this a high chivalrous feeling and a most conspicuous gallantry, they have all the essentials of the officer and soldier."

Ruxton spent some time hunting about this camp. One day he had a shot at a large panther which he did not kill, and later he found a turkey-roost. After a short delay here he started northward again. One of his servants had deserted him some time before, and now he sent the other back to Mexico because he was already suffering from the severity of the climate. The author's animals had now been travelling so long together that they required little or no attention in driving. Of course the operation of packing for a single man was slow and difficult. Continuing northward, he reached Santa Fé, where, however, he did not stop long.

It was now winter, and the weather cold and snowy, but the intrepid traveller had no notion of waiting for more genial days. He has much to say about the Indians in the neighborhood, and especially of the Pueblos, whose stone villages and peculiar methods of life greatly interested him. He found the Mexicans of New Mexico no more attractive than those with whom he had had to do farther to the southward, but seems to have felt a certain respect, if not admiration, for the Canadian and American trappers who had married among these people. Some of these men advised him strongly against making the effort to reach Fort Leavenworth at this season of the year, but he kept on. The journey was difficult, however. His animals, natives of the low country and of the tropics, were unused to mountain travel; each frozen stream that they came to was a cause of delay. The work of getting them on was very laborious, and every two or three days Ruxton froze his hands. He was now approaching the country of the Utes, who at that time were constantly raiding the settlements of northern New Mexico, killing the Mexicans and taking their horses. His purpose was to strike the Arkansas River near its head waters, and to reach the Bayou Salado, an old rendezvous for trappers and a great game country. The cold of the mountain country grew more and more bitter, and the constant winds made it almost impossible for the men to keep from freezing. Indeed, sometimes the cold was so severe that Ruxton found it necessary to put blankets on his animals to keep them from perishing. For days at a time snow, wind, and cold were so severe that it was impossible to shoot game, as he could not bend his stiffened fingers without a long preliminary effort.

During a part of his journey from Red River north he had been constantly followed by a large gray wolf, which evidently kept with him for the remains of the animals killed, and for bits of food left around camp.

At length the Huerfano River was passed and a little later the Greenhorn, where there was a camp of one white trapper and two or three French Canadians. A few days later the Arkansas was reached, and then the trading-post known as the Pueblo. Here Ruxton became a guest of John Hawkins, a well-known mountaineer of the time, and here he spent the remainder of the winter hunting on the Fontaine-qui-bouille and in the Bayou Salado.

Ruxton had many hunting adventures, and some narrow escapes from Indian fighting. Much of what he writes of this period has to do with the animals of the region, for at that time the country swarmed with game. The rapidity with which wolves will devour an animal is well known to those familiar with the olden time, but not to the people of to-day.

"The sagacity of wolves is almost incredible. They will remain around a hunting camp and follow the hunters the whole day, in bands of three and four, at less than a hundred yards distance, stopping when they stop, and sitting down quietly when game is killed, rushing to devour the offal when the hunter retires, and then following until another feed is offered them. If a deer or antelope is wounded, they immediately pursue it, and not unfrequently pull the animal down in time for the hunter to come up and secure it from their ravenous clutches. However, they appear to know at once the nature of the wound, for if but slightly touched, they never exert themselves to follow a deer, chasing those only which have received a mortal blow.

"I one day killed an old buck which was so poor that I left the carcase on the ground untouched. Six coyotes, or small prairie wolves, were my attendants that day, and of course, before I had left the deer twenty paces, had commenced their work of destruction. Certainly not ten minutes after, I looked back and saw the same six loping after me, one of them not twenty yards behind me, with his nose and face all besmeared with blood and his belly swelled almost to bursting. Thinking it scarcely possible that they could have devoured the whole deer in so short a space, I had the curiosity to return, and, to my astonishment, found actually nothing left but a pile of bones and hair, the flesh being stripped from them as clean as if scraped with a knife. Half an hour after I killed a large blacktail deer, and as it was also in miserable condition, I took merely the fleeces (as the meat on the back and

ribs is called), leaving four-fifths of the animal untouched. I then retired a short distance, and, sitting
down on a rock, lighted my pipe, and watched the operations of the wolves. They sat perfectly still until I
had withdrawn some three-score yards, when they scampered, with a flourish of their tails, straight to the
deer. Then commenced such a tugging and snarling
and biting, all squeaking and swallowing at the same
moment. A skirmish of tails and flying hair was seen
for five minutes, when the last of them, with slouching
tail and evidently ashamed of himself, withdrew, and
nothing remained on the ground but a well-picked
skeleton. By sunset, when I returned to camp, they
had swallowed as much as three entire deer."

Although Ruxton was no longer travelling, he was
not yet free from danger from storms, and an extraordinary night passed in a snow-storm followed the loss of
his animals on a hunting trip. Horses and mules had
disappeared one morning, and he and his companion
had set out to find them. This they did, and when they
overtook the animals, shortly after noon, he says: "I
found them quietly feeding . . . and they suffered me to
catch them without difficulty. As we were now within
twenty miles of the fort, Morgan (his companion), who
had had enough of it, determined to return, and I
agreed to go back with the animals to the *cache*, and
bring in the meat and packs. I accordingly tied the
blanket on a mule's back, and, leading the horse, trotted
back at once to the grove of cottonwoods where we

had before encamped. The sky had been gradually overcast with leaden-coloured clouds, until, when near sunset, it was one huge inky mass of rolling darkness: the wind had suddenly lulled, and an unnatural calm, which so surely heralds a storm in these tempestuous regions, succeeded. The ravens were winging their way toward the shelter of the timber, and the coyote was seen trotting quickly to cover, conscious of the coming storm.

"The black threatening clouds seemed gradually to descend until they kissed the earth, and already the distant mountains were hidden to their very bases. A hollow murmuring swept through the bottom, but as yet not a branch was stirred by wind; and the huge cottonwoods, with their leafless limbs, loomed like a line of ghosts through the heavy gloom. Knowing but too well what was coming, I turned my animals toward the timber, which was about two miles distant. With pointed ears, and actually trembling with fright, they were as eager as myself to reach the shelter; but, before we had proceeded a third of the distance, with a deafening roar, the tempest broke upon us. The clouds opened and drove right in our faces a storm of freezing sleet, which froze upon us as it fell. The first squall of wind carried away my cap, and the enormous hailstones beating on my unprotected head and face, almost stunned me. In an instant my hunting shirt was soaked, and as instantly frozen hard; and my horse was a mass of icicles. Jumping off my mule—for to ride was impossible—I tore off the saddle blanket and covered my head. The animals, blinded with the sleet, and their eyes actually coated with ice, turned their sterns to the storm, and, blown before it, made for the open prairie. All my exertions to drive them to the shelter of the timber were useless. It was impossible to face the hurricane, which now brought with it clouds of driving snow; and perfect darkness soon set in. Still, the animals kept on, and I determined not to leave them, following, or, rather, being blown, after them. My blanket, frozen stiff like a board, required all the strength of my numbed fingers to prevent its being blown away, and although it was no protection against the intense cold, I knew it would in some degree shelter me at night from the snow. In half an hour the ground was covered on the bare prairie to the depth of two feet, and through this I floundered for a long time before the animals stopped. The prairie was as bare as a lake; but one little tuft of greasewood bushes presented itself, and here, turning from the storm, they suddenly stopped and remained perfectly still. In vain I again attempted to turn them toward the direction of the timber; huddled together, they would not move an inch; and, exhausted myself, and seeing nothing before me but, as I thought, certain death, I sank down immediately behind them, and, covering my head with the blanket, crouched like a ball in the snow. I would have started myself for the timber, but it was pitchy dark, the wind drove clouds of frozen snow into my

face, and the animals had so turned about in the
prairie that it was impossible to know the direction to
take; and although I had a compass with me, my hands
were so frozen that I was perfectly unable, after
repeated attempts, to unscrew the box and consult it.
Even had I reached the timber, my situation would
have been scarcely improved, for the trees were scattered wide about over a narrow space, and, consequently,
afforded but little shelter; and if even I had succeeded
in getting firewood—by no means an easy matter at
any time, and still more difficult now that the ground
was covered with three feet of snow—I was utterly
unable to use my flint and steel to procure a light, since
my fingers were like pieces of stone, and entirely without feeling.

"The way the wind roared over the prairie that night
—how the snow drove before it, covering me and
the poor animals partly—and how I lay there, feeling
the very blood freezing in my veins, and my bones pet-
rifying with the icy blasts which seemed to penetrate
them—how for hours I remained with my head on my
knees and the snow pressing it down like a weight of
lead, expecting every instant to drop into a sleep from
which I knew it was impossible I should ever awake—
how every now and then the mules would groan aloud
and fall down upon the snow, and then again struggle
on their legs—how all night long the piercing howl of
wolves was borne upon the wind, which never for
an instant abated its violence during the night,—I would

not attempt to describe. I have passed many nights alone in the wilderness and in a solitary camp—have listened to the roarings of the wind and the howling of wolves, and felt the rain or snow beating upon me with perfect unconcern: but this night threw all my former experiences into the shade, and is marked with the blackest of stones in the memoranda of my journeyings.

"Once, late in the night, by keeping my hands buried in the breast of my hunting shirt, I succeeded in restoring sufficient feeling into them to enable me to strike a light. Luckily my pipe, which was made out of a huge piece of cottonwood bark, and capable of containing at least twelve ordinary pipefuls, was filled with tobacco to the brim; and this I do believe kept me alive during the night, for I smoked and smoked until the pipe itself caught fire and burned completely to the stem.

"I was just sinking into a dreamy stupor, when the mules began to shake themselves and sneeze and snort; which hailing as a good sign, and that they were still alive, I attempted to lift my head and take a view of the weather. When with great difficulty I raised my head, all appeared dark as pitch, and it did not at first occur to me that I was buried deep in snow; but when I thrust my arm above me, a hole was thus made, through which I saw the stars shining in the sky and the clouds fast clearing away. Making a sudden attempt to straighten my almost petrified back and limbs, I rose, but, unable to stand, fell forward in the snow, frightening the animals, which immediately started away. When I gained my legs I found that day was just breaking, a long gray line of light appearing over the belt of timber on the creek, and the clouds gradually rising from the east, and allowing the stars to peep from patches of blue sky. Following the animals as soon as I gained the use of my limbs, and taking a last look at the perfect cave from which I had just risen, I found them in the timber, and, singularly enough, under the very tree where we had *cached* our meat. However, I was unable to ascend the tree in my present state, and my frost-bitten fingers refused to perform their offices; so that I jumped upon my horse, and, followed by the mules, galloped back to the Arkansa, which I reached in the evening, half dead with hunger and cold.

"The hunters had given me up for lost, as such a night even the 'oldest inhabitant' had never witnessed. My late companion had reached the Arkansa, and was safely housed before it broke, blessing his lucky stars that he had not gone back with me."

It was at this time that the news of the Pueblo Indian rising in the valley of Taos was received and that Governor Charles Bent and other white men had been killed.

At this time the fur of the beaver had been supplanted by other and cheaper materials, so that beaver fur, which formerly brought eight dollars a pound, now brought but one dollar. For this reason many, if not

most, of the trappers had for the time being ceased
their work, and had settled down on farms in the mountains, where, though professing to farm, they raised
little from the ground except corn, but subsisted almost
entirely on the game, which was enormously abundant. The author has much to say about the trappers
and their ways of life, and this is one of the spirited
pictures of the craft that he paints:

"On starting for a hunt, the trapper fits himself out
with the necessary equipment, either from the Indian
trading-forts, or from some of the petty traders—
coureurs des bois—who frequent the western country.
This equipment consists usually of two or three horses
or mules—one for saddle, the others for packs—and
six traps, which are carried in a bag of leather called
a *trap-sack*. Ammunition, a few pounds of tobacco,
dressed deer-skins for moccasins, &c., are carried in a
wallet of dressed buffalo-skin, called a possible-sack.
His 'possibles' and 'trap-sack' are generally carried on
the saddle-mule when hunting, the others being packed
with the furs. The costume of the trapper is a hunting-
shirt of dressed buckskin, ornamented with long fringes;
pantaloons of the same material, and decorated with
porcupine-quills and long fringes down the outside of
the leg. A flexible felt hat and moccasins clothe his
extremities. Over his left shoulder and under his right
arm hang his powder-horn and bullet-pouch, in which
he carries his balls, flint and steel, and odds and ends of
all kinds. Round the waist is a belt, in which is stuck

a large butcher-knife in a sheath of buffalo-hide, made fast to the belt by a chain or guard of steel; which also supports a little buckskin case containing a whetstone. A tomahawk is also often added; and, of course, a long heavy rifle is part and parcel of his equipment. I had nearly forgotten the pipe-holder, which hangs round his neck, and is generally a gage d'amour, and a triumph of squaw workmanship, in shape of a heart, garnished with beads and porcupine-quills.

"Thus provided, and having determined the locality of his trapping-ground, he starts to the mountains, sometimes alone, sometimes with three or four in company, as soon as the breaking up of the ice allows him to commence operations. Arrived on his hunting-grounds, he follows the creeks and streams, keeping a sharp look-out for 'sign.'

"During the hunt, regardless of Indian vicinity, the fearless trapper wanders far and near in search of 'sign.' His nerves must ever be in a state of tension, and his mind ever present at his call. His eagle eye sweeps round the country, and in an instant detects any foreign appearance. A turned leaf, a blade of grass pressed down, the uneasiness of the wild animals, the flight of birds, are all paragraphs to him written in nature's legible hand and plainest language. All the wits of the subtle savage are called into play to gain an advantage over the wily woodsman; but with the natural instinct of primitive man, the white hunter has the advantages of a civilized mind, and, thus provided, seldom fails to outwit, under equal advantages, the cunning savage.

"Sometimes, following on his trail, the Indian watches him set his traps on a shrub-belted stream, and, passing up the bed, like Bruce of old, so that he may leave no tracks, he lies in wait in the bushes until the hunter comes to examine his carefully-set traps. Then, waiting until he approaches his ambushment within a few feet, whiz flies the home-drawn arrow, never failing at such close quarters to bring the victim to the ground. For one white scalp, however, that dangles in the smoke of an Indian's lodge, a dozen black ones, at the end of the hunt, ornament the camp-fires of the rendezvous.

"At a certain time, when the hunt is over, or they have loaded their pack-animals, the trappers proceed to the 'rendezvous,' the locality of which has been previously agreed upon; and here the traders and agents of the fur companies await them, with such assortment of goods as their hardy customers may require, including generally a fair supply of alcohol. The trappers drop in singly and in small bands, bringing their packs of beaver to this mountain market, not unfrequently to the value of a thousand dollars each, the produce of one hunt. The dissipation of the 'rendezvous,' however, soon turns the trapper's pocket inside out. The goods brought by the traders, although of the most inferior quality, are sold at enormous prices:—Coffee, twenty and thirty shillings a pint-cup, which is the usual measure; tobacco fetches ten and fifteen shillings a plug; alcohol, from twenty to fifty shillings a pint; gunpowder, sixteen shillings a pint-cup; and all other articles at proportionately exorbitant prices.

"A trapper often squanders the produce of his hunt, amounting to hundreds of dollars, in a couple of hours; and, supplied on credit with another equipment, leaves the rendezvous for another expedition, which has the same result time after time; although one tolerably successful hunt would enable him to return to the settlements and civilized life, with an ample sum to purchase and stock a farm, and enjoy himself in ease and comfort the remainder of his days.

"An old trapper, a French Canadian, assured me that he had received fifteen thousand dollars for beaver during a sojourn of twenty years in the mountains. Every year he resolved in his mind to return to Canada and, with this object, always converted his fur into cash; but a fortnight at the 'rendezvous' always cleaned him out, and, at the end of twenty years, he had not even credit sufficient to buy a pound of powder.

"These annual gatherings are often the scene of bloody duels, for over their cups and cards no men are more quarrelsome than your mountaineers. Rifles, at twenty paces, settle all differences, and, as may be imagined, the fall of one or other of the combatants is certain, or, as sometimes happens, both fall to the word 'fire.' "

Ruxton made many solitary hunting trips away from the fort—Pueblo—and of one of these, to the head of the Fontaine-qui-bouille, he paints a pleasing picture:

"Never was there such a paradise for hunters as this lone and solitary spot. The shelving prairie, at the bottom of which the springs are situated, is entirely surrounded by rugged mountains, and, containing perhaps two or three acres of excellent grass, affords a safe pasture to their animals, which would hardly care to wander from such feeding, and the salitrose rocks they love so well to lick. Immediately overhead, Pike's Peak, at an elevation of 12,000 feet above the level of the sea, towers high into the clouds; whilst from the fountain, like a granitic amphitheatre, ridge after ridge, clothed with pine and cedar, rises and meets the stupendous mass of mountains, well called 'Rocky,' which stretches far away north and southward, their gigantic peaks being visible above the strata of clouds which hide their rugged bases.

"This first day the sun shone out bright and warm, and not a breath of wind ruffled the evergreen foliage of the cedar groves. Gay-plumaged birds were twittering in the shrubs, and ravens and magpies were chattering overhead, attracted by the meat I had hung upon a tree; the mules, having quickly filled themselves, were lying round the spring, basking lazily in the sun; and myself, seated on a pack, and pipe in mouth, with rifle ready at my side, indolently enjoyed the rays, which reverberated (*sic*) from the white rock on which

I was lying, were deliciously warm -and soothing. A piece of rock, detached from the mountainside and tumbling noisily down, caused me to look up in the direction whence it came. Half a dozen big-horns, or Rocky Mountain sheep, perched on the pinnacle of a rock, were gazing wonderingly upon the prairie, where the mules were rolling enveloped in clouds of dust. The enormous horns of the mountain sheep appeared so disproportionably heavy, that I every moment expected to see them lose their balance and topple over the giddy height. My motions frightened them, and, jumping from rock to rock, they quickly disappeared up the steepest part of the mountain. At the same moment a herd of blacktail deer crossed the corner of the glade within rifle shot of me, but, fearing the vicinity of Indians, I refrained from firing before I had reconnoitred the vicinity for signs of their recent presence.

"Immediately over me, on the left bank of the stream, and high above the springs, was a small plateau, one of many which are seen on the mountainsides. Three buffalo bulls were here quietly feeding, and remained the whole afternoon undisturbed. I saw from the sign that they had very recently drunk at the springs, and that the little prairie where my animals were feeding was a frequent resort of solitary bulls."

A mountain hunter rather than one of the plains, Ruxton nevertheless devotes some space to buffalo hunting. He points out what has so often been written of since his time, that the buffalo was hard to kill, not because it had so much vitality, but because the inexperienced hunter so seldom shot it in the right place. Thus he says:

"No animal requires so much killing as a buffalo. Unless shot through the lungs or spine, they invariably escape; and, even when thus mortally wounded, or even struck through the very heart, they will frequently run a considerable distance before falling to the ground, particularly if they see the hunter after the wound is given. If, however, he keeps himself concealed after firing, the animal will remain still, if it does not immediately fall. It is a most painful sight to witness the dying struggles of the huge beast. The buffalo invariably evinces the greatest repugnance to lie down when mortally wounded, apparently conscious that, when once touching mother earth, there is no hope left him. A bull, shot through the heart or lungs, with blood streaming from his mouth, and protruding tongue, his eyes rolling, bloodshot, and glazed with death, braces himself on his legs, swaying from side to side, stamps impatiently at his growing weakness, or lifts his rugged and matted head and helplessly bellows out his conscious impotence. To the last, however, he endeavours to stand upright, and plants his limbs farther apart, but to no purpose. As the body rolls like a ship at sea, his head slowly turns from side to side, looking about, as it were, for the unseen and treacherous enemy who has brought him, the lord of the plains, to such a pass. Gouts of purple blood spurt

INDIAN SIGNALLING "BUFFALO DISCOVERED"

from his mouth and nostrils, and gradually the failing limbs refuse longer to support the ponderous carcase; more heavily rolls the body from side to side, until suddenly, for a brief instant, it becomes rigid and still; a convulsive tremor seizes it, and, with a low, sobbing gasp, the huge animal falls over on his side, the limbs extended stark and stiff, and the mountain of flesh without life or motion.

"The first attempts of a 'greenhorn' to kill a buffalo are invariably unsuccessful. He sees before him a mass of flesh, nearly five feet in depth from the top of the hump to the brisket, and consequently imagines that, by planting his ball midway between these points, it must surely reach the vitals. Nothing, however, is more erroneous than the impression; for to 'throw a buffalo in his tracks,' which is the phrase of making a clean shot, he must be struck but a few inches above the brisket, behind the shoulder, where alone, unless the spine be divided, a death-shot will reach the vitals. I once shot a bull, the ball passing directly through the very centre of the heart and tearing a hole sufficiently large to insert the finger, which ran upwards of half a mile before it fell, and yet the ball had passed completely through the animal, cutting its heart almost in two. I also saw eighteen shots, the half of them muskets, deliberately fired into an old bull, at six paces, and some of them passing through the body, the poor animal standing the whole time, and making feeble attempts to charge. The nineteenth shot, with the muzzle touching his body, brought him to the ground. The head of the buffalo-bull is so thickly covered with coarse matted hair, that a ball fired at half a dozen paces will not penetrate the skull through the shaggy frontlock. I have frequently attempted this with a rifle carrying twenty-five balls to the pound, but never once succeeded.

"Notwithstanding the great and wanton destruction of the buffalo, many years must elapse before this lordly animal becomes extinct. In spite of their numerous enemies, they still exist in countless numbers, and, could any steps be taken to protect them, as is done in respect of other game, they would ever remain the life and ornament of the boundless prairies, and afford ample and never-failing provision to the travelers over these otherwise desert plains. Some idea of the prodigious slaughter of these animals may be formed, by mentioning the fact that upwards of one hundred thousand buffalo robes find their way annually into the United States and Canada; and these are the skins of *cows* alone, the bull's hide being so thick that it is never dressed. Besides this, the Indians kill a certain number for their own use, exclusive of those whose meat they require; and the reckless slaughter of buffalo by parties of white men, emigrants to the Columbia, California, and elsewhere, leaving, as they proceed on their journey, thousands of untouched carcases on the trail, swells the aggregate of this wholesale destruction to an enormous amount."

The keen scent of the buffalo and its apparent poor
sight were noticed by Ruxton, as they have been by
so many others.   What is perhaps not generally known,
because it has been forgotten, is that when running,
the buffalo commonly swings its head from one side
to the other, apparently in the effort to see what is
going on on either side and perhaps, to some extent,
behind it.   Other characteristics—its harmlessness,
and its occasional unconcern in the presence of danger
—are also shown here.

"There are two methods of hunting buffalo—one on
horseback, by chasing them at full speed, and shooting
when alongside; the other by 'still hunting,' that is,
'approaching,' or stalking, by taking advantage of the
wind and any cover the ground affords, and crawling
to within distance of the feeding herd.   The latter
method exhibits in a higher degree the qualities of the
hunter, the former those of the horseman.   The buffalo's head is so thickly thatched with long, shaggy hair
that the animal is almost precluded from seeing an
object directly in its front; and if the wind be against
the hunter he can approach, with a little caution, a
buffalo feeding on a prairie as level and bare as a billiard-table.   Their sense of smelling, however, is so
acute, that it is impossible to get within shot when to
windward, as, at the distance of nearly half a mile, the
animal will be seen to snuff the tainted air, and quickly
satisfy himself of the vicinity of danger.   At any other
than the season of gallantry, when the males are, like

all other animals, disposed to be pugnacious, the buffalo is a quiet, harmless animal, and will never attack unless goaded to madness by wounds, or, if a cow, in sometimes defending its calf when pursued by a horseman; but even then it is seldom that they make any strong effort to protect their young.

"When gorged with water, after a long fast, they become so lethargic that they sometimes are too careless to run and avoid danger. One evening, just before camping, I was, as usual, in advance of the train, when I saw three bulls come out of the river and walk leisurely across the trail, stopping occasionally, and one, more indolent than the rest, lying down whenever the others halted. Being on my hunting-mule, I rode slowly after them, the lazy one stopping behind the others, and allowing me to ride within a dozen paces, when he would slowly follow the rest. Wishing to see how near I could get, I dismounted, and, rifle in hand, approached the bull, who at last stopped short, and never even looked round, so that I walked up to the animal and placed my hand on his quarter. Taking no notice of me, the huge beast lay down, and while on the ground I shot him dead. On butchering the carcase I found the stomach so greatly distended, that another pint would have burst it. In other respects the animal was perfectly healthy and in good condition."

Ruxton was not only an earnest hunter and a hardy traveller, but he was also a keen observer, and living as he did for long periods in the open air and among the wild animals, he saw many curious things.

"The first mountain-sheep I killed, I got within shot of in rather a curious manner. I had undertaken several unsuccessful hunts for the purpose of procuring a pair of horns of this animal, as well as some skins, which are of excellent quality when dressed, but had almost given up any hope of approaching them, when one day, having killed and butchered a black-tail deer in the mountains, I sat down with my back to a small rock and fell asleep. On awaking, feeling inclined for a smoke, I drew from my pouch a pipe, and flint and steel, and began leisurely to cut a charge of tobacco. Whilst thus engaged I became sensible of a peculiar odour which was wafted right into my face by the breeze, and which, on snuffing it once or twice, I immediately recognized as that which emanates from sheep and goats. Still I never thought that one of the former animals could be in the neighbourhood, for my mule was picketed on the little plateau where I sat, and was leisurely cropping the buffalo-grass which thickly covered it.

"Looking up carelessly from my work, as a whiff stronger than before reached my nose, what was my astonishment at seeing five mountain-sheep within ten paces, and regarding me with a curious and astonished gaze! Without drawing a breath, I put out my hand and grasped the rifle, which was lying within reach; but the motion, slight as it was, sufficed to alarm them, and with a loud bleat the old ram bounded up the mountain, followed by the band, and at so rapid a pace that all my attempts to 'draw a bead' upon them were ineffectual. When, however, they reached a little plateau about one hundred and fifty yards from where I stood, they suddenly stopped, and, approaching the edge, looked down at me, shaking their heads, and bleating their displeasure at the intrusion. No sooner did I see them stop than my rifle was at my shoulder, and covering the broadside of the one nearest to me. An instant after and I pulled the trigger, and at the report the sheep jumped convulsively from the rock, and made one attempt to follow its flying companions; but its strength failed, and, circling round once or twice at the edge of the plateau, it fell over on its side, and, rolling down the steep rock, tumbled dead very near me. My prize proved a very fine young male, but had not a large pair of horns. It was, however, 'seal' fat, and afforded me a choice supply of meat, which was certainly the best I had eaten in the mountains, being fat and juicy, and in flavour somewhat partaking both of the domestic sheep and buffalo."

Among other notes about this species Ruxton speaks of several attempts that had been made to secure the young of mountain sheep and transport them to the States. None of these, however, had been successful. Old Bill Williams even took with him into the mountains a troop of milch goats, by which to bring up the young sheep, but, though capturing a number of lambs, he did not succeed in reaching the frontier with a single one.

He reports also the superstition of the Canadian trappers concerning the carcajou, which we know as the wolverene, and tells of a reported battle which an old Canadian trapper said that he had had with one of these animals, and which lasted upward of two hours, during which he fired a pouchful of balls into the animal's body, which spat them out as fast as they were shot in. Two days later, in company with the same man, the author, in looking over a ridge, saw a wolverene, and shot at it, as it was running off, without effect. For this he was derided by the Canadian, who declared that if he had shot fifty balls at the carcajou it would not have cared at all.

One night, when camped on the Platte, the author woke up, and looking out of his blanket, saw sitting before the fire a huge gray wolf, his eyes closed and his head nodding in sheer drowsiness.

The last day of April, Ruxton set out to cross the plains for Fort Leavenworth, intending to return to England. Soon afterward they reached Bent's Fort, and a little later were joined by a number of Frémont's men, and by Kit Carson, who were returning from California. They passed a Cheyenne camp, and before very long were well out on the plains and in the buffalo country. Concerning the abundance of these animals Ruxton tells the same extraordinary stories that all old-timers relate. He hunted buffalo both by "approaching" and by running; and tried many experiments with these great beasts. One night the camp was almost run down by a vast herd of buffalo, but all hands being aroused, they managed, by firing their guns and making all the noise they could, to split the herd, so that the two branches passed around them.

At length the party approached Council Grove, and the more humid country, where the eastern timber was found, which, to Ruxton and to the Missourians of the party, looked like old friends.

Ruxton was a true outdoor man, loving the wilderness for itself alone, accepting whatever of toil, exposure, or hardship might come to him, feeling amply repaid for these annoyances by the joy of independence, of the beauties that surrounded him, and of the absolute physical well-being which was a part of this life.

The days when an existence such as is pictured in his accounts of the Rocky Mountains could be enjoyed are long past, yet there are still living some men who can absolutely sympathize with the feeling expressed in the following paragraphs:

"Apart from the feeling of loneliness which any one in my situation must naturally have experienced, surrounded by stupendous works of nature, which in all their solitary grandeur frowned upon me, and sinking into utter insignificance the miserable mortal who crept beneath their shadow; still there was something inexpressibly exhilarating in the sensation of positive freedom from all worldly care, and a consequent expansion of the sinews, as it were, of mind and body, which made me feel elastic as a ball of Indian rubber, and in a state of such perfect *insouciance* that no more dread of scalping Indians entered my mind than if I had been sitting in Broadway, in one of the windows of Astor House. A citizen of the world, I never found any difficulty in investing my resting-place, wherever it might be, with all the attributes of a home; and hailed, with delight equal to that which the artificial comforts of a civilized home would have caused, the, to me, domestic appearance of my hobbled animals, as they grazed around the camp, when I returned after a hard day's hunt. By the way, I may here remark, that my *sporting* feeling underwent a great change when I was necessitated to follow and kill game for the support of life, and as a means of subsistence; and the slaughter of deer and buffalo no longer became *sport* when the object was to fill the larder, and the excitement of the hunt was occasioned by the alternative of a plentiful feast or a banyan; and, although ranking under the head of the most red-hot of sportsmen, I can safely acquit myself of ever wantonly destroying a deer or buffalo unless I was in need of meat; and such consideration for the feræ naturæ is common to all the mountaineers who look to game alone for their support. Although liable to an accusation of barbarism, I must confess that the very happiest moments of my life have been spent in the wilderness of the far West; and I never recall but with pleasure the remembrance of my solitary camp in the Bayou Salado, with no friend near me more faithful than my rifle, and no companions more sociable than my good horse and mules, or the attendant coyote which nightly serenaded us. With a plentiful supply of dry pine-logs on the fire, and its cheerful blaze streaming far up into the sky, illuminating the valley far and near, and exhibiting the animals, with well-filled bellies, standing contentedly at rest over their picket-pins, I would sit cross-legged enjoying the genial warmth, and, pipe in mouth, watch the blue smoke as it curled upwards, building castles in its vapoury wreaths, and, in the fantastic shapes it assumed, peopling the solitude with figures of those far away. Scarcely, however, did I ever wish to change such hours of freedom for all the luxuries of civilized life, and, unnatural and extraordinary as it may appear, yet such is the fascination of the life of the mountain hunter, that I believe not one instance could be adduced of even the most polished and civilized of men, who had once tasted the sweets of its attendant liberty and freedom from every worldly care, not regretting the moment when he exchanged it for the monotonous life of the settlements, nor sighing, and sighing again, once more to partake of its pleasures and allurements.

"Nothing can be more social and cheering than the welcome blaze of the camp fire on a cold winter's night, and nothing more amusing or entertaining, if not instructive, than the rough conversation of the single-

SKINNING A BUFFALO

minded mountaineers, whose simple daily talk is all of exciting adventure, since their whole existence is spent in scenes of peril and privation; and consequently the narration of their every-day life is a tale of thrilling accidents and hairbreadth 'scapes, which, though simple matter-of-fact to them, appear a startling romance to those who are not acquainted with the nature of the lives led by these men, who, with the sky for a roof and their rifles to supply them with food and clothing, call no man lord or master, and are free as the game they follow."

Some little time was spent at Fort Leavenworth, where Ruxton found the change from the free life of prairie and mountain very unpleasant. He suffered still more when he reached St. Louis, and was obliged to assume the confining garb of civilization, and above all, to put his feet into shoes.

Ruxton's journey from St. Louis to New York was uneventful, and in July he left for England, which he reached in the middle of August, 1847.

It was after this that he wrote a series of sketches, entitled "Life in the Far West," which were afterward published in *Blackwood's Magazine,* and finally in book form in England and America. These sketches purport to give the adventures of a trapper, La Bonté, during fifteen years' wandering in the mountains, and set forth trapper and mountain life of the day. They show throughout the greatest familiarity with the old-time life. The author's effort to imitate the dialect spoken by the trappers makes the conversation not always easy to read; but they are most interesting as faithful pictures of life in the mountains between 1830 and 1840—at the end of the days of the beaver.

A BOY IN INDIAN CAMPS

A BOY IN INDIAN CAMPS

I

AMONG THE CHEYENNES

ONE of the most charming books written about
the early plains is Lewis H. Garrard's *Wah-
To-Yah and the Taos Trail*. It is the narrative of a boy, only seventeen years old, who, in 1846,
travelled westward from St. Louis with a train led by
Mr. St. Vrain, of the firm of Bent, St. Vrain & Co., and
after some time spent on the plains and in Cheyenne
camps, proceeded westward to New Mexico and there
saw and heard of many of the events just antecedent to
the Mexican War.

It is an interesting fact that the book, which, in its
interest and its fidelity to nature and to early times,
equals the far more celebrated *California and Oregon Trail* of Parkman, tells of the events of the same
year as Parkman's volume, but deals with a country
to the south of that traversed by him who was to become one of the greatest historians of America. The
charm of each volume lies in its freshness. Neither

could have been written except by one who saw things with the enthusiastic eyes of youth, who entered upon each adventure with youth's enthusiasm, and who told his story with the frankness and simplicity of one who was very young. After all, the greatest charm of any literature lies in the simplicity with which the story is told, and in both these delightful volumes is found this attractive quality.

Garrard reached St. Louis on his way to the Rocky Mountains in July, 1846, and there became acquainted with the firm of Pierre Chouteau, Jr., & Co., so well known in the fur trade of the West. Here, too, he met Kenneth McKenzie, one of the first traders with the Blackfeet Indians, and Mr. St. Vrain.

To the modern reader it seems odd to see it stated in the first two lines of the book that a part of the necessary preparations for the trip before him was the "laying in a good store of caps, fine glazed powder, etc.," but in those days the percussion cap was still a new thing, and of the guns used west of the Missouri River the great majority still used the flint to strike fire to the charge.

Besides Garrard, there were others in St. Vrain's company, who were new to the plains. Of these one was Drinker, a Cincinnati editor; another, a Mr. Chadwick. Besides these there were General Lee of St. Louis, a friend or two of St. Vrain's, and various employees of the traders.

Bent's train was encamped not far from Westport,

and here Garrard got his first taste of wild life, sleeping on the ground in the open.   Here, too, he saw his first Indians, the Wyandottes, who, in 1843, had been moved westward from their homes in Ohio.   Here, of course, he met those who for months were to be his travelling companions, and he paints us a fresh picture of them in these pleasing words:

"There were eighteen or twenty Canadian Frenchmen (principally from St. Louis) composing part of our company, as drivers of the teams.   As I have ever been a lover of sweet, simple music, their beautiful and piquant songs in the original language fell most harmoniously on the ear, as we lay wrapped in our blankets.

"On the first of September, Mr. St. Vrain's arrival infused some life into our proceedings, but nothing more worthy of note occurred, except riding and looking at horses, of which Drinker and I were in need; one of which, Frank De Lisle, '*le maitre de wagon*,' sold me for fifty dollars, whom, from his fanciful color, brown and white spots, and white eyes, was designated by the descriptive though not euphonious name of, '*Paint*.'   He was a noted buffalo chaser, and I anticipated much excitement through his services.

"The way the mules were broken to wagon harness would have astonished the 'full-blooded' animals of Kentucky and other horse-raising States exceedingly. It was a treatment none but hardy Mexican or scrub mules could survive.   They first had to be lassoed by our expert Mexican, Blas, their heads drawn up to a wagon wheel, with scarce two inches of spare rope to relax the tight noose on their necks, and starved for twenty-four hours to subdue their fiery tempers; then harnessed to a heavy wagon, lashed unmercifully when they did not pull, whipped still harder when they ran into still faster speed, until, after an hour's bewilderment, and plunging and kicking, they became tractable and broken down—a labor-saving operation, with the unflinching motto of 'kill or cure.' "

The pulling out of the train from near Westport was an interesting and exciting event. Teamsters were shouting to their newly yoked bulls; the herders were driving along the caballada; mounted men were hurrying back and forth; the leader of the company and his wagon-master were constantly passing to and fro from one end of the train to the other, seeing how things went, and looking for weak spots among the teams and the wagons. A few days later came the first rain-storm —a dismal occasion to the young traveller on the plains. There are few old plainsmen but can still recall something of the discomfort of a long day's travel in the storm; of the camping at night with clothing thoroughly wet and bodies thoroughly chilled, and the sitting or lying, or perhaps even sleeping in the wet clothing. "The wagons being full of goods, and we without tents, a cheerless, chilling, soaking, wet night was the consequence. As the water penetrated, successively, my blanket, coat, and shirt, and made its way down my back, a cold shudder came over me; in the gray, foggy morning a more pitiable set of hungry, shaking wretches were never seen. Oh! but it was hard on the poor greenhorns!"

At Council Grove, which they reached the last of September, the train remained for two days, and as this was the last place travelling westward where hardwood could be procured, the men felled hickories and oaks for spare axle-trees, and swung the pieces under their wagons. Young Garrard was an eager hunter, and set out from camp in search of wild turkeys, whose cries he could hear, but he got none.

Here is another picture of that early life which may call up in the minds of some readers pleasant memories of early days when they, too, were a part of such things: "So soon as a faint streak of light appears in the east, the cry *turn out* is given by De Lisle; all rise, and, in half an hour, the oxen are yoked, hitched and started. For the purpose of bringing everything within a small compass, the wagons are corralled; that is, arranged in the form of a pen, when camp is made; and as no animals in that country are caught without a lasso, they are much easier noosed if driven in the corral. There, no dependence must be placed in any but one's self; and the sooner he rises, when the cry is given, the easier can he get his horse.

"Like all persons on the first trip, I was green in the use of the lasso, and Paint was given to all sorts of malicious dodging; perhaps I have not worked myself into a profuse perspiration with vexation a hundred and one times, in vain attempts to trap him.

"Not being able to catch my horse this morning, I hung my saddle on a wagon and walked, talking to the loquacious Canadians, whose songs and stories were most acceptable. They are a queer mixture, anyhow, these Canadians; rain or shine, hungry or satisfied, they are the same garrulous, careless fellows; generally caroling in honor of some brunette Vide Poche, or St. Louis Creole beauty, or lauding, in the words of their ancestry, the soft skies and grateful wine of La Belle France, occasionally uttering a *sacré*, or *enfant de garce*, but suffering no cloud of ill humor to overshadow them but for a moment. While walking with a languid step, cheering up their slow oxen, a song would burst out from one end of the train to the other, producing a most charming effect."

The train was now approaching the buffalo range, and before long several buffalo were seen. Now, too, they had reached a country where *"bois de vaches"*— buffalo chips—were used for fuel, and the collecting of this was a part of the daily work after camp was made. More and more buffalo were seen, and before long we hear of the plain literally covered with them, and now, as buffalo were killed more often, Garrard is introduced to a prairie dish which no one will ever eat again. He says: "The men ate the liver raw, with a slight dash of gall by way of zest, which, served *à la Indian*, was not very tempting to cloyed appetites; but to hungry men, not at all squeamish, raw, warm liver, with raw marrow, was quite palatable.

"It would not do," he continues, "for small hunting parties to build fires to cook with; for, in this hostile Indian country, a smoke would bring inquiring friends. Speaking of hostile Indians, reminds me of a question related by one of our men: at a party, in a Missouri frontier settlement, a lady asked a mountaineer, fresh from the Platte, 'if hostile Indians are as savage as those who serve on foot!'

"Returning to camp the prairie was black with the herds; and, a good chance presenting itself, I struck spurs into Paint, directing him toward fourteen or fifteen of the nearest, distant eight or nine hundred yards. We (Paint and I) soon neared them, giving me a flying view of their unwieldy proportions, and, when within fifteen feet of the nearest I raised my rifle half way to the face and fired. Reloading, still in hot pursuit (tough work to load on a full run), I followed, though without catching up. One feels a delightfully wild sensation when in pursuit of a band of buffalo, on a fleet horse, with a good rifle, and without a hat, the winds playing around the flushed brow, when with hair streaming, the rider nears the frightened herd, and, with a shout of exultation, discharges his rifle. I returned to the party highly gratified with my first, though unsuccessful, chase, but Mr. St. Vrain put a slight damper to my ardor, by simply remarking—

"'The next time you "run meat" don't let the horse

go in a trot and yourself in a gallop' (I had, in my eagerness, leaned forward in the saddle, and a stumble of
the horse would have pitched me over his head); by
which well-timed and laconic advice, I afterward prof-
ited."

From this time on there was much chasing of buffalo,
but little killing of them, except by the old hands.   The
young ones, of course, neither knew how to shoot nor
where to shoot, and our author naïvely remarks, after
one of his chases: "To look at a buffalo, one would
think that they could not run with such rapidity; but,
let him try to follow with an ordinary horse, and he is
soon undeceived."

During the efforts of the greenhorns to kill buffalo
this incident occurred: "Mr. Chadwick (of St. Louis,
on his first trip, like several of us, for pleasure),
seeing a partially blind bull, concluded to 'make meat'
of him; crawling up close, the buffalo scented him
and pitched about every way, too blind to travel
straight or fast. Chad fired; the mad animal, directed by the rifle report, charged. How they did
'lick it' over the ground! He pursued, yelling, half in
excitement, half in fear, till they were close to the
wagons, where the pursuer changed tack, only to be
shot by one of the teamsters with a nor'-west fusil."

It is natural enough that the boy author, while
travelling for the first time through the buffalo range,
should think and write chiefly about buffalo, yet he
finds time to tell of the prairie-dog towns through

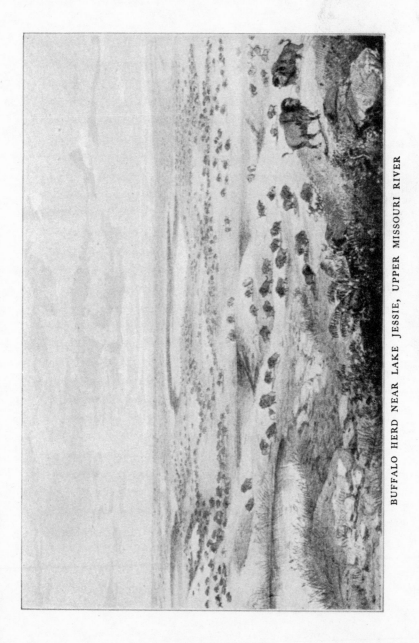

BUFFALO HERD NEAR LAKE JESSIE, UPPER MISSOURI RIVER

which they passed, and of the odd ways of the dogs and
the curious apparent companionship or at least co-
habitation of the snakes and the prairie owls with
them.   As they passed through this region north of
the Arkansas in the hot, dry weather of the early fall,
they suffered sometimes from thirst.   The first grave
passed by the train aroused melancholy and sympathetic feelings in the boy's heart.

One day Garrard went out hunting with Mr. St.
Vrain and another, and a band of buffalo were discovered on their way to water.   Here Garrard first
found himself near a wounded bull, and the picture
that he paints of the monster is a true and a striking
one.   "Mr. St. Vrain, dismounting, took his rifle, and
soon was on the 'approach,' leaving us cached behind
a rise of the ground to await the gun report.   We laid
down with our blankets, which we always carried
strapped to the saddle, and, with backs to the wind,
talked in a low tone, until hearing Mr. St. Vrain's gun,
when we remounted.   Again and again the rifle was
heard, in hasty succession, and hastening to him, we
found a fat cow stretched, and a wounded male limp-
ing slowly off.   The animals were tied to the horns
of our cow; and, with butcher knives, we divested the
body of its fine coat; but, finding myself a 'green hand,'
at least not an adept, in the mysteries of prairie butchering, I mounted Paint for the wounded fellow, who
had settled himself, with his fore legs doubled under
him, three hundred yards from us.   Mine was a high

pommeled, Mexican saddle, with wooden stirrups; and, when once seated, it was no easy matter to be dislodged. Paint went up within twenty yards of the growling, wounded, gore-covered bull, and there stood trembling, and imparting some of his fear to myself.

"With long, shaggy, dirt-matted, and tangled locks falling over his glaring, diabolical eyes, blood streaming from nose and mouth, he made the most ferocious looking object it is possible to conceive; and, if nurses could portray to obstinate children in true colors the description of a mad buffalo bull, the oft-repeated 'bugaboo' would soon be an obsolete idea.

"While looking with considerable trepidation on the vanquished monarch of the Pawnee plains, he started to his feet; and, with a jump, materially lessened the distance between us, which so scared Paint that he reared backward, nearly sliding myself and gun over his tail; and before the bridle rein could be tightened, ran some rods; but, turning his head, and setting the rowels of my spurs in his flanks, I dashed up within thirty feet of the bull; and at the crack of the gun, the 'poor buffler' dropped his head, his skin convulsively shook, his dark eyes, no longer fired with malignancy, rolled back in the sockets, and his spirit departed for the region of perpetual verdure and running waters, beyond the reach of white man's rifle or the keen lance of the prairie warrior."

And then the picture with which he closes the chapter covering the march through the buffalo range!

How boyish, and yet how charming and how true
it is!

"Good humor reigned triumphant throughout
camp. Canadian songs of mirth filled the air; and at
every mess fire, pieces of meat were cooking *en appolas;*
that is, on a stick sharpened, with alternate fat and
lean meat, making a delicious roast. Among others,
boudins were roasting without any previous culinary
operation, but the tying of both ends, to prevent the
fat, as it was liquified, from wasting; and when pronounced 'good' by the hungry, impatient judges, it
was taken off the hot coals, puffed up with the heat
and fat, the steam escaping from little punctures, and
coiled on the ground, or a not particularly clean saddle blanket, looking for all the world like a dead snake.

"The fortunate owner shouts, 'Hyar's the doin's,
and hyar's the 'coon as *savys* "poor bull" from "fat
cow"; freeze into it, boys!' And all fall to, with ready
knives, cutting off savory pieces of this exquisitely ap-
petizing prairie production.

"At our mess fire there was a whole side of ribs
roasted. When browned thoroughly we handled the
long bones, and as the generous fat dripped on our
clothes, we heeded it not, our minds wrapped up with
the one absorbing thought of satisfying our relentless
appetites; progressing in the work of demolition, our
eyes closed with ineffable bliss. Talk of an em-
peror's table—why, they could imagine nothing half
so good! The meal ended, the pipe lent its aid to

complete our happiness, and, at night we retired to the comfortable blankets, wanting nothing, caring for nothing."

Late in October the train met with the advance guard of a party of Cheyenne warriors, then on the war-path for scalps and horses against the Pawnee nation. These were the first really wild Indians that Garrard had seen, and their picturesqueness and unusual appearance greatly interested him. In those days the Cheyennes had never been at war with the white people, and they were on terms of especial friendliness with Bent and St. Vrain, from whose trading posts they obtained their supplies. A little later, on the way to Bent's Fort, they passed a Cheyenne medicine lodge, with its sweat-house, and later still Indian graves on scaffolds which rested on the horizontal limbs of the cottonwood trees. A day or two after this they reached Fort William, or Bent's Fort, where they met William Bent, in his day one of the best-known men of the southern plains. A few days were spent there, and then came the most interesting adventure that the boy had had.

Early in November he started for the Cheyenne village with John Smith, who, with his wife, his little boy Jack, and a Canadian, were setting out for the village to trade for robes.

John Smith is believed to have been the first white man ever to learn the Cheyenne language, so as to be able to interpret it into English. When he made his appearance on the plains we do not know, but he was there in the '30's, and for many years was employed by Bent and St. Vrain to follow the Indians about and trade with them for robes. Early in his life on the plains he had married a Cheyenne woman and established intimate relations with the tribe, among whom he remained for many years. He was present in the camp of the Cheyennes during the Chivington massacre at Sand Creek, in 1864, at which time his son, Jack, the child mentioned by Garrard in this volume, was killed by the soldiers, being shot in the back by a soldier who saw his shadow on the lodge skins and fired at it. It is said that John Smith himself came very near being killed, and had a hard time in talking the Colorado soldiers out of killing him. He has a son now living at Pine Ridge.

The small party journeyed on toward the village, and while Pierre, the Canadian, drove the wagon, and the woman and her child rode in silence, Smith and Garrard kept up a lively conversation. Smith was anxious to learn all about the "States" and life there, while Garrard replied to him with inquiries about Indians and their ways. And so, day after day, they journeyed over the plain until the cone-shaped lodges of the village came in sight, to be reached a few hours later. Riding into the camp, they halted at the lodge of one of the principal men, and unsaddling and unpacking their animals there, entered it with their goods, and according to custom established themselves in the back part, which was at once given up to them by the host.   And now began an entirely new life for Garrard —a life into which he threw himself with the whole-hearted enthusiasm of a healthy lad, and which he thoroughly enjoyed.   The days and evenings in the camp; the moving from place to place over the prairie; the misfortunes which happened to the men unaccus-tomed to such life, are all described.   Vivid glimpses of the marching Indian column are given in the follow-ing paragraphs:

"The young squaws take much care of their dress and horse equipments; they dashed furiously past on wild steeds, astride of the high-pommeled saddles. A fancifully colored cover, worked with beads or porcupine quills, making a flashy, striking appearance, extended from withers to rump of the horse, while the riders evinced an admirable daring, worthy of Amazons.   Their dresses were made of buckskin, high at the neck, short sleeves, or rather none at all, fitting loosely, and reaching obliquely to the knee, giving a relieved, Diana look to the costume; the edges scalloped, worked with beads, and fringed.   From the knee, down-ward, the limb was encased in a tightly fitting leggin, terminating in a neat moccasin—both handsomely worked with beads.   On the arms were bracelets of brass, which glittered and reflected in the radiant, morning sun, adding much to their attractions.   In their pierced ears, shells from the Pacific shore, were pendant; and, to complete the picture of savage taste and profusion, their fine complexions were eclipsed by a coat of flaming vermillion.

"Many of the largest dogs were packed with a small quantity of meat, or something not easily injured. They looked queerly, trotting industriously under their burdens; and, judging from a small stock of canine physiological information, not a little of the wolf was in their composition. These dogs are extremely muscular and are compactly built.

"We crossed the river on our way to the new camp. The alarm manifested by the *ki-kun* (children) in the lodge-pole drays, as they dipped in the water, was amusing; the little fellows, holding their breaths, not daring to cry, looked imploringly at their inexorable mothers, and were encouraged by words of approbation from their stern fathers. Regaining the grassy bottom, we once more went in a fast walk.

"The different colored horses, the young Indian beaux, the bold, bewildering belles, and the newness of the scene were gratifying in the extreme to my unaccustomed senses. After a ride of two hours we stopped, and the chiefs, fastening their horses, collected in circles, to smoke the pipe and talk, letting their squaws unpack the animals, pitch the lodges, build fires, arrange the robes, and, when all was ready, these 'lords of creation' dispersed to their several homes to wait until their patient and enduring spouses prepared some food. I was provoked, nay, angry, to see the lazy, overgrown men, do nothing to help their wives; and, when the young women pulled off their bracelets and finery, to chop wood, the cup of my wrath was full to overflowing, and, in a fit of honest indignation, I pronounced them ungallant and savage in the true sense of the word. A wife, here, is, indeed, a helpmeet."

Bravery, endurance, and hardihood were in those days a part of the education of each Indian boy, and here is a glimpse of the training received by a baby, which should fit him for the hardships that each warrior must endure. This was the grandson of the Vippo-nah, a boy six or seven months old:

"Every morning, his mother washed him in cold water, and sent him out to the air to make him hardy; he would come in, perfectly nude, from his airing, about half frozen. How he would laugh and brighten up, as he felt the warmth of the fire! Being a boy, the parents have great hopes of him as a brave and chief (the acme of Indian greatness); his father dotes upon him, holding him in his arms, singing in a low tone, and in various ways, showing his extreme affection."

One of the subjects discussed by Garrard and John Smith before they reached the Cheyenne village was prairie foods. Smith spoke of the excellence of dog meat, while Garrard declared that it must be horrible, saying that buffalo meat was unquestionably the most delicate food in this or any other country. Smith agreed that buffalo was the best, but that dog meat was the next, and offered to bet that he would make

Garrard eat dog meat in the village and make him declare that it was good. How John Smith carried out his threat is told in the following paragraphs:

"One evening we were in our places—I was lying on a pile of outspread robes, watching the blaze, as it illumined the lodge, which gave the yellow hue of the skins of which it was made, a still brighter tinge; and, following with my eye, the thin blue smoke, coursing, in fantastic shapes, through the opening at the top of the cone; my thoughts carrying me momentarily everywhere; now home; now enjoying some choice edible, or, seated by a pleasant friend, conversing; in short, my mind, like the harp in Alexander's feast, the chords of which, touched by the magic hand of memory, or flight of fancy, alternately depressed, or elevated me in feeling. Greenwood and Smith, sitting up, held in 'durance vile' the ever present pipe. Their unusual laughter attracted my attention, but, not divining the cause I joined in the conversation. It was now quite late, and feeling hungry, I asked what was on the fire.

"'Terrapins!' promptly replied Smith.

"'Terrapins?' echoed I, in surprise, at the name. 'Terrapins! How do you cook them?'

"'You know them hard-shell land terrapin?'

"'Yes.'

"'Well! the squaws go out to the sand buttes and bring the critters in and cook 'em in the shell alive —those stewin' thar ar cleaned first. Howsomever, they're darned good!'

"'Yes, hos, an' that's a fact, wagh!' chimed in Greenwood.

"I listened, of course, with much interest to their account of the savage dish, and waited, with impatience for a taste of that, the recital of whose merits sharpened my already keen appetite. When the squaw transferred the contents of the kettle to a wooden bowl, and passed it on to us, our butcher knives were in immediate requisition. Taking a piece, with hungry avidity, which Smith handed me, without thought, as to what part of the terrapin it was, I ate it with much gusto, calling 'for more.' It was extremely good, and I spoke of the delicacy of the meat, and answered all their questions as to its excellency in the affirmative, even to the extent of a panegyric on the whole turtle species. After fully committing myself, Smith looked at me a while in silence, the corners of his mouth gradually making preparations for a laugh, and asked:

" 'Well, hos! how do you like dogmeat?' and then such hearty guffaws were never heard. The stupefaction into which I was thrown by the revolting announcement, only increased their merriment, which soon was resolved into yells of delight at my discomfiture.

"A revulsion of opinion, and dogmeat too, ensued, for I could feel the 'pup' crawling up my throat; but saying to myself—'that it was good under the name of terrapin,' 'that a rose under any other name would smell as sweet,' and that it would be prejudice to stop, I broke the shackles of deep-rooted antipathy to the canine breed, and, putting a choice morceau on top of that already swallowed, ever after remained a stanch defender and admirer of dogmeat. The conversation held with Smith, the second day of our acquaintance, was brought to mind, and I acknowledged that 'dog' was next in order to buffalo."

Life in the Cheyenne camp went on interestingly. Garrard began to make a vocabulary of the Cheyenne language, and soon to speak it in a broken fashion which caused his auditors to shriek with laughter. He watched them at the sign language, amused them with games and the few books which he possessed, went to feasts, noted the odd implements and ways of his camp mates, and set down all that happened, together with his boyish reflections on the incidents.

The discipline practised by John Smith on his son Jack will bear repeating. It seems that the child had taken to crying one night, much to the annoyance of four or five chiefs who had come to the lodge to talk and smoke. "In vain did the mother shake and scold him with the severest Cheyenne words, until Smith, provoked beyond endurance, took the squalling youngster in hands; he 'shu-ed' and shouted, and swore, but Jack had gone too far to be easily pacified. He then sent for a bucket of water from the river, and poured cupfull after cupfull on Jack, who stamped and screamed, and bit, in his puny rage. Notwithstanding, the icy stream slowly descended until the bucket was emptied, another was sent for, and again and again the cup was replenished and emptied on the blubbering youth. At last, exhausted with exertion, and completely cooled down, he received the remaining water in silence, and, with a few words of admonition, was delivered over to his mother, in whose arms he stifled his sobs, until his heart-breaking grief and cares were drowned in sleep. What a devilish mixture Indian and American blood is!"

Garrard was a healthy, natural boy, and with all a boy's love of fun. He mingled readily and naturally in the sports and amusements of the young people of the Cheyenne camp and heartily enjoyed it. In those days the white trader in the Indian camp was regarded as a great man, and was treated with respect, to retain which he carried himself with much dignity. But Garrard cared nothing for this respect, and made no effort to preserve this dignity. He danced and sang with the boys and girls, and the women were astonished to find a white person so careless of appearances, though they liked him all the better for it.

On one occasion in the winter there was much excitement in the Cheyenne camp. A war-party was returning, and all the men, women, and children blackened their faces and went out to meet them. The returning warriors advanced in triumph, for they had three scalps, borne on slender willow wands, and hanging from each scalp was a single tuft of hair which told that they were Pawnees. Now there was great rejoicing in the camp, and many dances to celebrate the victory and to rejoice over the triumph that the tribe had made over its enemies. "The drum, at night, sent forth its monotony of hollow sound, and our Mexican, Pedro, and I, directed by the booming, entered a lodge, vacated for the purpose, full of young men and squaws, following one another in a continuous circle, keeping the left knee stiff, and bending the right with a half-forward, half-negative step, as if they wanted to go on and could not, accompanying it, every time the right foot was raised, with an energetic, broken song, which, dying away, was again and again sounded—hay-a-hay, hay-a-hay, they went—laying the emphasis on the first syllable. A drum, similar to, though larger than, a tamborine, covered with parfleche, was beat upon with a stick, producing with the voices a sound not altogether disagreeable. . . .

"During the day, the young men, except the dancers, piled up dry logs in a level, open space near, for a grand demonstration. At night, when it was fired, I folded my blanket over my shoulders, *comme les sauvages*, and went out. The faces of many girls were brilliant with vermillion; others were blacked, their robes, leggins and skin dresses, glittering with beads and porcupine quill work. Rings and bracelets of shining brass encircled their taper arms and fingers, and shells dangled from their ears. Indeed, all the finery collectable was piled on in barbarous profusion, though a few, in good taste or through poverty, wore a single band, and but few rings; and with jetty hair, parted in the middle, from the forehead to the neck, terminating in two handsome braids. . . .

"The girls, numbering two hundred, fell into line together, and the men, of whom there were two hundred and fifty, joining, a circle was formed, which 'traveled' around with the same shuffling step already described. The drummers, and other musicians (twenty or twenty-five of them) marched in a contrary direction, to, and from, and around the fire, inside the large ring; for, at the distance kept by the outsiders, the area was one hundred and fifty feet in diameter. There Appolonian emulators chanted the great deeds performed by the Cheyenne warriors; as they ended, the dying strain was caught up by the hundreds of the outside circle, who, in fast-swelling, loud tones, poured out the burden of their song. At this juncture, the march was quickened, the scalps of the slain were borne aloft and shaken in wild delight, and shrill warnotes, rising above the furious din, accelerated the pulsation, and strung high the nerves. Time-worn shields, careering in mad holders' hands, clashed, and keen lances, once reeking in Pawnee blood, clanged. Braves seized one another with an iron grip, in the heat of excitement, or chimed more tenderly in the chant, enveloped in the same robe with some gentle maiden as they approvingly stepped through one of their own original polkas.

"Thirty of the chiefs, and principal men were ranged by the pile of blazing logs. By their invitation, I sat

A CHEYENNE INDIAN CAMP

down near 'Old Bark,' and smoked death and its concomitant train of evils to those audacious tribes, who doubt the courage or supremacy of the brave, the great, and powerful Cheyenne nation.

"The pipe was lavishly decorated with beaver strips, beads, and porcupine; the mixture of tobacco and bark, was prepared with unusual care for this, their grand gala night."

It would be interesting to follow Garrard through his life in the Cheyenne camp, but space forbids this. He was called away from this interesting life by the news which came from the West of the death at the hands of the Pueblos of Governor Charles Bent, in New Mexico. Fugitives who had escaped the attack had come to Fort William and told what had happened, and soon after, William Bent, with twenty-three men, started for the Mexican settlements. They passed far to the southward of Pike's Peak, met a few United States soldiers and volunteers, and toward the middle of February were joined by Sublette, with two companions, who reported forty thousand men enlisted for Mexico. Toiling through the mountains in true winter weather, the party marched on until they came to one of Bent's ranches and at last reached Taos. From this on, the author's route was much among the Mexicans of the various towns until, at last, turning his face eastward, he came back across the mountains, and once more found himself in the Cheyenne village, whence soon afterward he set out for the East.

II

AN ATTACK BY COMANCHES

ALTHOUGH Garrard had seen plenty of Indians, and had been present at more than one skirmish, he had not yet taken part in a real Indian fight, though he had long wished to do so. On the way back this desire was gratified, and the boy, with his eighteenth birthday only just behind him, paints in one of the last chapters of his book a spirited picture of the alarms, surprises, narrow escapes, and swift changes of an Indian raid on the moving wagon-trains near the Pawnee Fork of the Arkansas. His trip on the plains ended in an exciting fighting climax, and we can fancy that it gave the boy material for talk and for delightful recollections during the rest of his life.

"We were started early. The wagons traveled in double file, so that in case of an attack from the leagued Camanches and Arapahoes, whose propinquity was as well-known as dreaded, they would not be strung along too great a space. The caballada was driven and kept between these two lines of the train.

"Late in the afternoon, when the sun was fast sinking to its golden-hued, silver-flecked bed, and the drooping ears of the flagging mules betokened weariness, objects were seen directly before us in the trace. Keen-eyed Barton, in calling our attention to them, uttered his opinion in the single significant word, '*Injuns!*'

" 'Indians, say you, Barton?' inquired the colonel, looking in the direction pointed, 'Indians? Upon my word I believe so. Come on, we'll reconnoiter, and say nothing to the train until the fact is ascertained—indeed, I hope not'—and, striking spurs into his large brown California mule, he loped forward, followed by some eight or ten of us. We soon ascertained, beyond a doubt, enough danger to lessen our party to five—the colonel, Barton, Brown, McCarty, and myself, who kept on until within less than a quarter of a mile of the large party of mounted warriors. That portion of our men who had put back with all possible speed, set the train in a ferment by their prodigious narrations.

"In front, on the opposite rise of ground, was a sight to make the stoutest heart among us quail; for the Indian force, displayed within long rifleshot, numbered, according to our unanimous estimate, four hundred strong, glittering with gay pennons, bright lance-heads, and savage ornaments. Young braves rode their plunging barbs restlessly to and fro. The shrill and startling notes of preparation reached us but too plainly; and we hurried back to await for the expected charge. The train was in almost inextricable confusion, but the colonel soon restored order. The wagons, mules, and men advanced to the brow of the hill and made a corâl: that is, the two front wagons came together, and the inside forewheels of those following, were made to touch the outside hindwheel of the one immediately in front. In this manner, a secure but irregular oval pen was formed, into which were driven the oxen, the caballada, and the riding animals, thus leaving the men free to devote their whole attention to the enemy. There was little noise, but much alacrity, and considerable trepidation among the poor teamsters, thirty of whom were without firearms. We had scarcely finished our preparations for defense, when the Indians, with poised lances, furiously charged upon us. For some time they circled around our corâl with guns unslung, and white shields continually shifted to protect their bodies. At last they drew rein; and, on each side of our party, commenced a lively demonstration, sending their balls singing through the air; some overhead, some perforating the wagons and wagon-sheets, and some knocking the fur from our hide-bound oxen.

"We were drawn up in line outside, fronting the main body, two hundred and fifty yards distant. We gave them several rounds, one-half of us reserving fire until the discharged arms were reloaded. The Indians scattered after our rather ineffectual volleys, and their position became more menacing, their war-whoops more dissonant and savage than before. We posted ourselves about the wagons, each man to his liking. Lieutenant Brown, with five men, took a position on a knoll fifty yards from us, and kept up an incessant firing, which was warmly reciprocated by the foe. It became exciting; the warriors galloping furiously, bent down, now on this side, now on that, until nothing of their person could be seen but the heel and part of the leg thrown across the cantle of the saddle. From under the horse's neck would issue a smoke-cloud, as we heard the sighing of the ball as it cut its way overhead, or knocked the dust from the dry plain. Sharply-sighted rifles gave ready answer; cheers rang out from our exhilarated party, and unfortunate oxen, stung by furrowing bullets from lumbering escopetas, plunged and horned each other from side to side of the crowded corâl.

"A California Indian, belonging to Colonel Russell, ran, with gun in hand, far out toward the foiled enemy, making the Indian sign of insult and derision; and, in Spanish, abusing them most scandalously. He came back before long, in no small hurry, with three of the outraged foe at his heels, who were in return repelled at fullest speed by us. A ball overhead, causes even the coolest man to dodge involuntarily, however surely he may know that the whistling bullet has already missed him. This is especially the case in a desultory scattered fire. Many a hearty laugh was had at the ludicrous positions into which we found ourselves thrown by these badly-aimed missiles.

"The Indians detained us an hour, and then, re-linquishing their *coup* attempts, moved off toward the west, to our extreme gratification. Had the charge been made before the corâl was formed, they would have scalped the whole party, for our force was small, and composed for the most part of green teamsters. Yoking up, we reached camp, by the river's side, hot, thirsty, and irritated at our meager 'satisfaction.'

"June 19th. The train proceeded with much caution. Indian spies watched us in the distance, hanging like wolves on our rear; the gleam of their lances was often seen among the sandbuttes beyond the river. They were evidently intending to make another descent, on the first fair opportunity. Our flankguards were on the alert, and the day ended without a conflict. The country was sparsely wooded with cottonwood and boxelder, and *bois de vaches* supersedes substantial fuel for several days travel through the region of the 'Coon Creeks.'

"Our animals were saddled, hitched, and the train in motion, after an early cup of coffee. The air brisk and cool, and the sky clear, gave promise of a fair day's travel; and even uneasy fears of Camanche attack were not sufficient to check our joyous feelings. It was the duty of the horsemen to push forward at mealtime, select a camp, and wait for the arrival of the train. Near noon, we entered a large 'bottom,' horseshoe-shaped, around which the river made a circuit of three miles or more. The wagons kept the trace across the neck, and a party, composed of Colonel Russell, Mr. Coolidge, and myself, on mules, and three others, on horses, followed the course of the stream to gather fuel. This I laid across the pommel of the colonel's saddle, as I collected it, and he was already loaded with sufficient to boil our cup of coffee and fry the slice of pork for which we were well prepared by several hours' fasting, when, all at once, the three horsemen strung out in a straight shoot for the wagons, without a word to us. 'Hallo!' shouted we, 'what's your hurry?' The fast receding men said nothing, but pointed to the southwest, in which direction there approached, at full speed, a war-party of about forty, endeavoring to cut us off from the wagons which were then corâlling in great confusion. Dusky figures, and light puffs of smoke, showed faintly in the distance, the attack on the straggling train. No time was to be lost in rejoining our company, and back we spurred, to the tune of Camanche take the hindmost. The lines of the Indian attack and our return were convergent, and it was a mere question of speed whether we lost our topknots or gained the corâl. The pursuers already had the advantage. The colonel threw down his wood, and I replaced the old cap on my rifle with a fresh one, determined that one should 'go under' before my 'hair was lifted.' I led the retreat, mounted on a small irongray mule—a native of the California savannas—who bounded most gallantly—for a mule—over the prairie. Colonel Russell followed in my wake, but Coolidge was still behind. Our pace seemed snail-like, and we jammed our rifle butts into the flanks of the poor beasts most unmercifully.

" 'Come on, Coolidge,' shouted the Colonel to the frightened trader, 'come on, we'll soon be safe.'

"'Yes, yes! but this fool animal isn't worth a cuss for running,' and with that, he gave the poor mule another '*chug*' with his sharp riflestock. No exertion was spared, no incentive was neglected, to urge our dull beasts along; and though there was but small chance for escaping a lance thrust, we answered loudly their yells. When within three hundred yards of the wagon, I looked back, and saw Coolidge far behind, with several Indians close upon him, the foremost brandishing his lance. I shouted to the colonel that Coolidge was gone, and immediately we jerked our animals around. The colonel aimed hastily, fired, and galloped back to the corâl. I spurred on to cover Coolidge's retreat, who came lumbering with the *owgh-owgh-he-a* of his pursuers close to his ear. When I drew rein, and placed it between my teeth, my mule, contrary to all precedent and custom, stood stock still, while I took steady aim, at the nearest savage, who, flying along with eager look and harsh yell, was striving to make a sure blow. His band followed on his track, at distances various as their horses' speed. Coolidge, with eyes staring with fright, bent close down to his mule's neck. When I first drew bead on the Camanche's painted hide, he was approaching in a quartering direction to my right; as the gentleman was rather fleshy about the umbilical region, and tender withal, to make a sure shot, I kept the silver bead at my rifle point, at that particular spot, until he had passed to the left. With the report the yellow devil's legs twitched in pain (I was so close to him that I could see even his features with disagreeable distinctness), and throwing up his horse's head, he galloped off to the river. Those who watched, say that he did not come back.

"Reloading at full speed, Coolidge and I hurried into the corâl, which was just being closed. We dismounted, merely giving each other a look of congratulation; for the rattling of the guns, and the warwhoops and yells of the men, drowned our voices, and left us nothing to do but fight. For that work, with a good will, and quite systematically, we prepared ourselves. The Colonel's party were firing with much earnestness. A short distance of the place where we were gathering wood, a large force was descending the sand buttes, glittering with bright gun-barrels, swords, and lances—a well-armed band. They crossed the river in a trot, which was quickened into a charge as they reached the bank, and, at one hundred and fifty yards distance, they opened their fire. For a few minutes, rifles, warwhoops, escopetas, hurrahs, contended in discordant strife—a tumult of wild sounds. But they could not stand our well-directed fire, and fell back. They left no dead on the field. This is never done, and the only token of the effect of our balls was, by the wounded precipitately leaving the immediate scene of action. To give straightout evidence of injury, by show of pain, or otherwise, is a breach of their code of honor—an infringement severely rebuked by the taunts of the tribe

—a weakness not soon forgotten or forgiven by the old chiefs, whose duty and care it is, to sustain, by precept and example, the national bravery and hardihood. They consider not the death, merely, of an enemy, a victory—a *coup* must be counted. On a horse-stealing expedition, this is a horse; in battle, a scalp; and the trophies must be shown at home, before the warrior is allowed to decorate his robe with the black hand. When an Indian falls too far gone to rescue himself, his friends rush up and bear him off between their fleet steeds.

"They rallied and again circled around us, with their white shields protecting their bodies, tossing their spears, and showing off their beautiful horses, and their own graceful persons, to the best advantage. Their intention was to make a charge on the first vulnerable point, but we, being too well guarded, they, after many feints, fell back. I sat flat on the ground, my rifle resting on the spoke of a wagon-wheel—firing as often as an Indian came within range—and, when the painted, warwhooping target *vamosed* for safer quarters, at the crack of the gun, certainly no other than a smile of satisfaction lit up my face. If none fell outright, it was not that any qualms of conscience prevented my taking cool and sure aim, at those who, after chasing a mile, and nearly scaring the life out of us, were then keeping us penned in the hot sun without water.

"One Indian, who, from his distinguished, though scanty, dress, was a 'brave' of the first order, came close into our lines, throwing himself behind the body of his horse, so as to show nothing but a hand and foot; but, as he raised himself, one of the colonel's men cut, with his rifleball, a neatly-dressed skin, that hung at his neck, which we picked up after the fight, as our only trophy. They now tossed their balls into us from a long distance, by elevating their pieces, being convinced that our corâl could not be broken without great loss of life. Two teamsters, about this time getting scared at the whistling missiles, crept, for security, into an empty wagon. They had scarcely made themselves comfortable, when a ball, crashing through both sides of their defense, buried itself in the side of a poor steer. The terrified Neds tumbled out, greeted by the roars of the men around.

" 'That's what you get for your cussed cowardice,' drawled out one of the fellows.

"'Well, I'll be darned, if that wasn't a grazer,' ejaculated Charley McCarty. 'Feel if you haven't got a hole in your dogskin—I'd hate to be as bad scared as you, by thunder!'

"We were detained upward of two hours. Our fatigued and heated oxen were nearly dropping with thirst. The savages filed slowly up the sand buttes on the other side of the river, and we proceeded to camp, each man talking of his own shots.

"June 22. We expected to reach the Pawnee Fork during the morning's march, and as there were bluffs near the camp, and several streams intervening, thickset with timber, favorable for ambuscade, the advance guard preceded the train a quarter of a mile. We were on the alert, our eyes searching every object, our guns ready to fire, as with bridle-rein firmly grasped, we galloped along in the bright summer morning. Our exposed position, and the continual expectation of the Camanche yell, kept us excited wildly enough, although no foe delayed our march. By noontide, the saddles were off—the wagons corâlled, and the tent pitched once more. Among the remains of the old camps, I found the skull and skeleton of an Indian. The sinews, well gnawed by the wolves, were not yet dry, and the skin and hair still graced the head, which, passed from hand to hand by the curious, was, at last, tossed into the turbulent waters of the flooded Pawnee Fork. The Camanche, whose head this was, had been killed a few days previous, in an encounter with traders. One or two others 'went under' at the same time, but their bodies had been rescued.

"On the opposite side of the creek, a train from the States was stopped like ourselves by the risen waters. I accompanied some of our men over to it. We swam across, holding our shirts and buckskins in one hand. At the camp we found a government train, some traders' wagons, any quantity of gaping men, and a *whitewoman*—a real whitewoman! and we gazed upon her with great satisfaction and curiosity. After gleaning the 'news,' we returned in a full run to the creek, and, crossing as before, retailed our scanty information.

"The next day was beautiful, and we waited impatiently for the slow-receding stream to become fordable. The men scattered on both banks, the grazing cattle and caballadas, with the white wagon-tops of the three camps, made a serene and lovely scene. About ten o'clock, an immense drove of buffalo was seen running in the prairie to the southwest. Some of our party set off in pursuit on their horses, while twenty or thirty of us ran down to intercept them as they crossed the creek. A faint cry of Indians! Indians! Indians! from the camp reached those nearest the muleguard, and by them it was repeated and wafted on to us, who, hardly knowing whether to *câche* in the undergrowth, or to run for camp, stood for a moment undecided, and then 'streaked it' for the wagons. Turning our eyes to the furthest train on the hill, we perceived it in great commotion. Fifty Indians were charging among them with their lances, recoiling from the light volumes of smoke at times, and again swallowing up the little force with their numbers and shutting them in from our sight. Others were stampeding the oxen. After a conflict of several minutes, they retreated, bearing with them a dead warrior, behind the bluff hill which jutted boldly from the opposite shore.

"Our teamsters, during the fight, looked on with mouth and eyes open, in wonderment, regardless of their own cattle, still feeding in a deeply-fringed savanna. Tall cottonwood timber, overgrown with the luxuriant vine and thick-set underbrush, impervious to the eye, confined our stock to this secluded spot. The creek, half encircling it with a grand sweep, added its protection. A lightguard of three men watched the grazing herd. We were still congratulating ourselves on our escape, when from the guard, we heard the cry that the Indians were swimming the creek and driving off the oxen. More than half the camp started in full run to protect them. As we rounded the angle of the stream, yells were heard, then the dusky forms of a few Indians were seen; and, by the time we were within long gunshot, some sixty were among the luckless herd, goading them into a lumbering gallop. The colonel's party led the van, and would have saved the cattle, had the teamsters supported them. But, they hanging back, we told them that their oxen might go to ———. Hurrying back to camp, Colonel Russell mounted his force and went in pursuit; but, in vain, we tried to repair the loss that negligence and cowardice had effected. Our ride rescued only thirty oxen, and gave us a view of the retreating savages, thrusting their lances into the remainder. In that unfortunate half hour, the train lost one hundred and sixty steers; which, at the purchase price—one half less than they were worth on the prairie—was a damage of four thousand dollars, together with a total loss of from five to seven thousand more, in the necessary abandonment of the wagons— the natural result of sending on the plains a set of green men, commanded by as raw a director, poorly and scantily armed with government blunderbusses, and

meagerly furnished with from eight to fifteen rounds
of cartridges each, which were often wasted on game or
targets long before reaching the Indian country.   And
this was not the only instance of miserable economy,
as the official reports show.

"Our train was in a sad condition; half a yoke to
each wagon.   Mr. Coolidge was really to be pitied—
nearly four hundred miles from the States, with but
two oxen to haul four large wagons, heavily loaded with
robes and peltries.   The colonel carried a few packs
(as many as he was able); he bargained with one of
the outward-bound trains to take some back to Mann's
Fort, and the rest he câched.   The government people crowded their 'kits' and provision in three wagons; and, toward evening of the next day, we crossed
the creek which had now subsided, leaving twenty-six
wagons and any amount of extras, to the Indians and
the wolves.   Toward sundown, as we were hitching
up to travel in the night, a party of dragoons, filing
down the hill, made camp near.   Lieutenant J. Love,
commanding, was informed of the outrage, and promised satisfaction.   We stopped a moment at the train,
with which the first fight had occurred.   One poor fellow, named Smith, from Van Buren County, Missouri,
had been lanced seven times through the neck and
breast.   He killed the Indian that fell, while on his
back and already wounded."

Garrard's trip on the plains ended in true story-
book fashion, and, we can fancy, gave the boy material

for reminiscence and story-telling for many a long year.

This book, and many another of the period, mention constantly, and in most familiar fashion, names that to old-timers in the West are familiar as household words—men whom, in their old age, we ourselves perhaps knew; men with whose sons and daughters we have lived as contemporaries. But the generation that knew these old-timers, Carson, Bridger, Jack Robinson, Jim and John Baker, Bent, St. Vrain, Sublette, Hugh Monroe, Ike Edwards, Bill Gary, Symonds, Beaubien, La Jeunesse, Rowland, and a hundred others whose names could be given, has for the most part passed away.

These names belong to the history of the early West. Soon they will be historic only, for those who have known them will also have crossed the Great Divide, and there will be none who can recall their personality.

THE SOLITARY HUNTER

THE SOLITARY HUNTER

I

PRAIRIE TRAVEL

IN the year 1847 John Palliser, an Irishman, sailed from Liverpool by the good ship "Cambria" for an extended trip in America to make acquaintance with "our Trans-Atlantic brethren, and to extend my visit to the regions still inhabited by America's aboriginal people—now, indeed, driven far westward of their rightful territories and pressed backward into that ocean of prairies extending to the foot of the great Rocky Mountains."

Palliser was a young man of good family, the son of Colonel Wray Palliser, of Comragh, County Waterford. Like so many of his race, he was energetic, quick-witted, forceful, and possessed a great fund of humor. He seems to have been first of all a hunter, and like all successful hunters to have been a keen and close observer. Some time after his return to England he wrote a book giving his experiences of adventure in the Far West. It is one of the best books of hunting adventure ever written—terse, always to the point, modest, giving facts and conclusions, and very little

about his own views of life. The book has long been
out of print and is now not easily obtained, but it is
really a model in the picture that it paints of old-time
conditions and in the self-effacement of the author.

Palliser has long been forgotten. Almost equally
forgotten are two of his shipmates, whose names at
one time were familiar enough throughout the civilized
world. These were "General Tom Thumb" and P. T.
Barnum, who was bringing Tom Thumb back to the
United States after a season of exhibition in Europe.

The "Cambria" touched for coal at Halifax and then
came on to Boston and New York, where the traveller
stopped at the Astor House, which, he says, is "far
larger than any hotel I ever beheld in the old world."
From New York he went down to Philadelphia, Balti-
more, Cumberland, and Wheeling, and from there down
the Ohio River to the Mississippi and to St. Louis and
New Orleans. His whole journey, though described
briefly, is full of effective touches, and his comments
and criticisms are keen but kindly. To a description
of New Orleans he gives some space, and speaks with
cordial warmth of the friendliness and hospitality of
the Creole inhabitants.

From New Orleans he went up the Mississippi and
Arkansas (spelled phonetically Arkansor) Rivers, and
spent some time hunting small game, deer, bear, and,
by good fortune, killed a fine panther. A more or less
amusing tale, which Palliser quotes from an experience
of his brother a year before, is worth repeating.

"One day, when comfortably seated with Jackson and his family, in the neighbourhood of Lake Jefferson, a little nigger come running in, shouting, 'Oh, massa! terrible big alligator; him run at me.' When we got him to speak a little more coherently, it appeared that he had been bathing in the lake, and that an alligator had suddenly rushed at him, and when the boy, who luckily was not in deep water, had escaped by running to land, the brute had actually pursued him for some distance along the shore. We instantly loaded our rifles and started off in quest of the monster, accompanied by the boy, who came as guide. After carefully exploring the bank and reeds, though unsuccessfully, we concealed ourselves, in hopes of seeing him rise to the top of the water when he thought the coast was clear; but as we waited a long time without any result, we proposed what certainly was a most nefarious project; namely, to make the boy strip off his clothes and start him into the water again as a bait for the alligator. It was some time before we could get the boy to come round to our view of the matter: his objections to our plan were very strong, and his master's threats failed completely, as indeed they generally did; for he was the kindest-hearted man in the world to his negroes. At last I coaxed him with a bright new dollar. This inducement prevailed over his fears, and the poor boy began to undress, his eyes all the while reverting alternately from the water to the dollar, and from the dollar to the water. We told him we did not want him to go in so deep as to be obliged to swim. 'By golly, then, me go for dollare'; and in he walked, but had hardly reached water higher than his knees, when crash went the reeds, and the little fellow cut in towards our place of concealment at an astonishing pace, pursued by the alligator. The savage beast, as before, came right out on the bank, where we nailed him with two capital shots through the head, that effectually checked his career. He struggled violently, but uselessly, to regain his congenial element, and, after two or three furious lashes of his ponderous tail, sullenly expired. The triumph of the boy was complete."

Palliser next went to Louisville, Ky., and after a pause in that State to inspect the Mammoth Cave, returned to Louisville, where he took the boat for St. Louis to make preparations for his Rocky Mountain trip. He locates in St. Louis that excellent story which has been so often told in the last sixty years about the two great talkers who were matched on a bet to see which should outtalk the other.

"Old Mr. Cohen was universally considered a great talker, so much so, that he even admitted it himself; but this evening a formidable rival appeared against him in the person of a strange character from Kentucky, who fairly met him on his own ground, and after supper evinced such unceasing powers of conversation, that old Mr. Cohen was unable to get in a word, and was fain to claim a hearing. 'Let me speak, let me speak,' he gasped several times but with no avail; till, at last, the fool's argument was resorted to, and a bet made which should talk the longest. An umpire was chosen to determine which of the two loquacious combatants should be the winner; but, as might naturally be supposed, none of us had the patience to sit out the contest, so we went off to bed, leaving a plentiful supply of brandy, sugar, and iced water. Next morning, at a quarter past five, victory was declared for Missouri, the umpire returning at that hour and finding the Kentucky man fast asleep in his arm chair, and old Mr. Cohen sitting up close beside him and whispering in his ear."

Palliser soon started for Independence, Mo., the great outfitting point for the fur trade in those days, when the plains and mountains were free. At Independence he met Mr. Kipp—James Kipp—one of the best-known traders of early days and the builder of some of the first trading posts far up the river. For twenty years before this, it had been James Kipp's practice to go down the river in the summer with the fur company's flotilla of mackinaw boats, and in the autumn to ride north again to the mouth of Yellowstone River, a distance of something like fifteen hundred miles. James Kipp is the bourgeois mentioned by Catlin as his host among the Mandans when, in 1834, he was painting on the upper river.

The party that set out from Independence on the 2d of September numbered seventeen or eighteen, of whom the greater number were French Creoles and

Canadians to whom Palliser pays the wholly deserved
compliment that they were "docile, patient, enduring
fellows with constitutions like iron, well practiced in
journeys of this kind and character." Their beds and
supplies were carried on pack-animals, and they travelled for some days through a country very thinly
settled and occupied in part by the Mormons. "The
last spot where we saw white faces was the Council
Bluffs, the trading post and the residence of a Government Agent, where we remained a day supplying ourselves with coffee, sugar, and biscuit, salt pork, and
beans, as we did not expect for some time yet to reach
a good hunting country."

The camps made after they had passed out of the
settled region, where they lived at farm-houses, showed
a method of life wholly new to Palliser, and one which
to many Americans is as unknown to-day as it was to
him. "A little before sunset, we unsaddled and un-
packed our horses, placing the packs and saddle of each
rider in a separate pile, at equal distances, so as to
form a circular enclosure about ten paces in diameter;
and after watering and 'hobling' the horses, i.e. at-
taching the fore and hind legs on one side together by
means of an iron chain, with a leathern strap around
the fetlock, to prevent their straying, we turned them
loose to graze; not till then considering ourselves at
liberty to attend to our own comforts. Our first business was, then, to cut and gather wood, and to light a
fire in the centre of the circle, fetching some water in

the kettles, and putting the meat on to cook, and making our beds of saddle-cloths, blankets, and buffalo robes: this done, we roasted our coffee berries, and having wrapped them in a piece of deer or buffalo skin, and pounded them in the stump of a tree with the back of a hatchet, put them in our coffee pot and boiled them; and the meat being cooked by the time this process was over, and the coffee made, we fell to with great appetite. After supper, we lighted our pipes, and then each turned in when he felt inclined, and, with his feet to the fire, slept as only travellers in the prairie can sleep. Before day we were up again, unhobled and watered our horses, loaded the packs, and were all in the saddle by sunrise." The morning halt for breakfast was made about eleven o'clock, the horses were allowed to graze, and at one the train started again, to travel until dark.

The country through which they were passing had been thoroughly hunted by Indians, and the camp was out of meat, and had no food except beans. However, the fall migration of the wild fowl was on; at least the lakes and streams were occupied by plenty of ducks. Palliser set out with two of the hunters to try to kill some of these, but found that neither of the men could shoot on the wing. "It was amusing to see how astounded they were at my knocking over a fine mallard, that came wheeling over our heads; they insisted on its being a chance shot, and would not be persuaded to the contrary, until I brought down several successively; and at last, with a most satisfactory right and left, silenced their scepticism completely. They were greatly delighted; '*Mais comment diable, monsieur, faites-vous cela?*' said one hardy old veteran to me. I offered to instruct him, but could not get him to fire rapidly enough, as he was afraid of wasting his ammunition, which was very expensive."

On this journey they saw the approach of a prairie fire—a splendid and terrible sight—but succeeded in cutting it off by back-firing. The old French voyageurs declare that the Indians were travelling about. This experience suggested to Palliser a description given him by a brother sportsman of a fire which he had witnessed. "We had seen, during the latter part of our day's journey, a remarkable appearance in the eastern horizon; and during supper observed a smell of burning, and a few light cinders fell about the camp, and presently we remarked that the luminous appearance in the east had very much augmented. There being a little hill in front of us, we could not see distinctly what caused it; but having consulted together, we agreed that it proceeded from a prairie on fire, which, however, was a long way off. About eight o'clock the smell of burning and the glare having materially increased, we walked up to the top of the hill, when a spectacle presented itself to us the most grand that can well be conceived. The whole horizon, from north to south, was one wall of fire, blazing up in some places to a great height, at others merely smouldering in the grass. It was, however, at least, eight miles off; but the wind seemed to set in our direction, so we instantly returned, and took measures to preserve the camp. We were in a corner, as it were, on the bank of the stream, with a good deal of brushwood running up on our left, and the ground sloping up gradually from the creek to the top of the hill. Our guides, on looking at the fire, said that it would not harm us—'*Ce n'est rien —le vent change.*' In short, they would do nothing. In about twenty minutes, however, it approached so near that there was no time to be lost, and all hands were immediately employed in burning a road across the face of the hill, so as to stop the fire at that part. A more picturesque scene could hardly be imagined. The night was very dark, but as far as the eye could reach, all across the horizon, about four miles in front of us, was a broad, bright, lurid glare of fire, with a thick canopy of smoke hanging over it, whose fantastic wreaths, as they curled in the breeze, were tinged with the red reflection of the flames. Even at that distance we could hear the crackling and rushing of the fire, which, as it advanced, caused a strong wind, and every now and then a brighter flame would shoot high up into the black cloud of smoke over the top of the hill, illuminating for an instant our tents and waggons in the dark hollow, and giving a momentary glimpse of the horses which were picketed on the side of the rise, on the crest of which the figures of the men engaged in lighting the opposition fire (which, as it became too extended, they beat down with blankets, only suffering it to burn a space about twelve feet broad, right across the line of the advancing conflagration), stood out in strong relief against the glowing wall of light beyond them; and as they ran about, tossing their arms, and waving the blankets and little torches of lighted grass, they looked in the distance like demons rather than men. We had no time to look at the picturesque, however, for every moment (owing to their previous obstinacy in neglecting to take precaution in time) became more pregnant with danger, and by the time they had burned as much as would only about half cover the camp, the fire was raging in the bottom at the other side of the hill. I ran up for an instant to the top, and shall never forget the scene. Although still half a mile off, the fire seemed close to me, and the heat and smoke were almost intolerable, while the dazzling brightness of the flames made it painful to look at them; they were in three lines nearly parallel, the first of which was just below me, burning with a rushing noise, and crackling as it caught the dry grass, that gave an idea of total destruction which it is impossible to convey, and stretching away over hill and dale for twelve or fourteen miles on each side of me, lighting up the sides of the hills and the little groves of wood far away. The two lines in the rear were not so much connected, and seemed rather licking up any little spots of grass which had escaped at first. Every now and then a prairie hen would flirr past, flying in a

wild uncertain manner, as if fear had almost deprived
it of the use of its wings; while all the songsters of the
grove were wheeling about among the trees, uttering
the most expressive cries of alarm, and the melancholy hooting of several owls, and wailing yells of the
wolves, together with the shouts and cries of the men,
almost drowned occasionally by the roaring of the
flames, added to the savage grandeur of the scene, and
one could have fancied the end of all things was at
hand. On returning to the camp, I found all hands
cutting the lassoes and halters of the mules, some of
which galloped off instantly into the river, where they
remained standing till the hurricane of flame had
passed over; the others, seemingly trusting themselves
instinctively more to man than to their own energies
in such an emergency, followed us up the space which
we had burned, and remained quietly there, trembling
indeed, but without an effort to escape. By the time
the animals were collected in this spot, the fire was
blazing on the top of the hill, and we all rushed away
with blankets to arrest its progress, if possible, at the
part which we had left unguarded; all our efforts would
have been in vain, however, and our tents and everything else must have been consumed, but that, just at
that weak point, the grass suddenly became thin and
scanty, with much stony ground, and we had the satisfaction of seeing the flames stopped there and turned
off to the northward along the edge of the brushwood.
It was really terrific to be, as we were, trying to break

it down in the very middle of the blaze (which, after all, was so narrow that where the flames were not high, you could jump across it); we were, indeed, nearly suffocated by the smoke and heat. As soon as we perceived the fire turned off, we returned to the camp and horses, and all danger was over; but the sight of the three lines of fire stretching up the rising grounds behind the camp, just like the advance of a vast army, was magnificent; and it was still more extraordinary to watch the manner in which the fire passed itself on, as it were, over the tops of the highest trees, to the height of at least forty or fifty feet. The whole scene lasted altogether about two hours, and nothing could be conceived more awfully grand. The extraordinary rushing and crackling sound of the flames was one of the most terrific parts of it, and when one considers that the grass is nowhere more than five or six feet high, it is difficult to imagine how the flame blazes up to such a vast height as it did. The contrast presented, two hours afterwards, was most striking. Instead of the brilliant glare of the fire, and lurid appearance of the sky, there reigned an impenetrable darkness, earth and sky being alike shrouded in a black gloom, which could almost be felt; not a star was to be seen, and the air retained a suffocating, sulphureous smell, as if Satan himself had passed over the earth. We could not distinguish objects at ten paces' distance, and were right glad when a fresh breeze came gently breathing over the prairie, dissipating the murky vapors still hanging in the atmosphere; and a fine starlit sky, with a sharpish frost, at length relieved us from the close, choking feeling we had experienced for hours before.   This prairie fire had travelled at the rate of five miles an hour, bringing with it a strong gale of wind; for, otherwise, the night was quite calm, both before and after it had passed over."

At Fort Vermilion the Kipp party found a camp of Sioux who were dancing in triumph over the scalp of a woman.   With these Indians they at once established friendly relations.   The Sioux had a woman captive, whom Palliser and Kipp purchased and set free.   Here some of their best horses were stolen, not perhaps by the Indians of this camp, but by others.

Game was scarce and the white men were requested by the Indians who were about to start out on their autumn buffalo-hunt to travel with them, and not to move on in advance lest they should frighten the game, if any were about.   The old-time moving of an Indian camp, with its men marching at the head and on the flanks and the women with their travois in the column, is well described.   Scouts had been sent on in advance by the Indians to look for buffalo, and orders were given that no one should pass far beyond the camp.

Palliser went out on foot to try to kill some ducks along a little stream, and while looking for the birds was startled by the sound of a gun just behind and the whistle of a bullet passing near his head.   The shot

was fired by an Indian not far from him. Palliser ran
to him and threatened to shoot him if he tried to reload his gun. Another Indian who came up acted as
mediator, and explained what had happened. Palliser
had not fully understood the order issued by the chiefs,
and the man who shot at him was no doubt a "soldier,"
trying to make the white man go into camp.

The next day the Indians turned off toward the
buffalo and the white men went on, and not very long
after reached Fort Pierre, the site of the present city
of Pierre, S. D. Not long after leaving Fort Pierre,
early in October, they came upon buffalo, which Palliser is careful to note should be called bison, and on
the 27th of October reached Fort Union, then the chief
depot of the American Fur Company's trade through
the upper Missouri.

II

BUFFALO-RUNNING

Buffalo were plenty and here Palliser had his first
run. His views on buffalo-hunting—that extinct sport
—are quite worth quoting:

"Buffalo-hunting is a noble sport, the animal being
swift enough to give a good horse enough to do to close
with him; wheeling round with such quickness as to
baffle both horse and rider for several turns before there
is any certainty of bringing him down. Added to
which, there is the danger of being charged by one old

bull while in pursuit of another; this, however, they will not often do, unless when blown by the awkwardness of a bad hunter, in chasing them too far, when they turn and get desperate.

"The first object in approaching a herd of buffalo should be, to get as near as possible before charging them; then, rush in with your horse at full speed, single out one animal, and detach him from the herd, which you will soon do, and after a turn or two be able to get a broadside shot, when you should endeavour to strike him behind the fore-shoulder. While reloading, slacken your horse's speed to a hand gallop. The general method of loading is to empty the charge from the horn slung round your neck into the palm of your hand, whence you can more easily pour it down the barrel; you then take a bullet wet out of your mouth, and throw it down upon the powder; by which means you avoid the necessity of using the ramrod, a most inconvenient process when riding fast on horseback. I found it from experience better to dispense with both powderhorn, ramrod, and copper caps altogether, and use a light self-priming flint gun, carrying the powder loose in the skirt pockets of my shooting-coat, and thereby having no further delay than to thrust my hand in for it and empty it down the barrel of my gun; accuracy in quantity at such close quarters being of small importance. Taking the bullet from the mouth is both the quickest and safest method of loading; quicker than fumbling for it in your pocket, and safer, because its being wet causes it to stick for a moment without rolling forward on depressing the muzzle to take aim; and my brother sportsmen are doubtless aware of the danger of leaving an empty space in the barrel between the powder and the ball. I would not, however, recommend any one to depend too much upon the detention of the wet bullet, but to fire immediately on lowering the muzzle. I ought here to mention, that in running buffalo, you never bring the gun to your shoulder in firing, but present it across the pummel of the saddle, calculating the angle with your eye and steadying yourself momentarily by standing in the stirrups as you take aim. This is difficult to do at first, and requires considerable practice; but the facility once acquired, the ease and unerring steadiness with which you can shoot is most satisfactory, and any one accustomed to this method condemns ever afterward the lifting of a gun to the shoulder whilst riding at speed, as the most awkward and unscientific bungling.

"We drew up our horses, and proceeded to skin and cut up the animals, and were soon joined by the drays despatched from the fort for the purpose of taking home the meat. What we had killed that day was very good and tolerably fat. I have before adverted to the excellence of bison beef, and the superiority of its fat over that of the domestic ox; but before leaving the subject, I will state two instances in which I myself saw this superiority fully established.

"Old Mr. Kipp, at Christmas, thinking to give all the employés and voyageurs of the Fur Company at Fort Union a great treat, had for some time previously been fattening up a very nice small-boned heifer cow, which was killed in due time, in prime condition. All who had been reckoning on the treat this would afford them, sat down in high expectation of the ensuing feast; but after eating a little while in silence, gradually dropped off one by one to the bison meat, which was also on the table, and were finally unanimous in condemning the beef, which they said was good enough, but nothing remarkable, and the fat sickening. A plate-full of it was also given, as ordinary buffalo beef, to an Indian woman in another room at the fort, on the same occasion: she pronounced it good food, but, said she, 'it is both coarse and insipid'; and the fat, if she were to eat much of it, would make her sick.

"I mention these circumstances, having been one of the very few who have seen the comparative merits of the two meats tested by Europeans, Americans, and Indians at the same time, and heard the unanimous verdict in favour of the wild bison."

It is worth noting that Indians who are old enough to have known buffalo all declare that the flesh of domestic cattle tastes badly and has an evil smell. This, to be sure, may mean no more than that the flesh and fat have an unusual taste and smell, which is disagreeable, because unusual. Probably, however, no one who has habitually eaten buffalo meat but will acknowledge that it is far more tender and delicate than the flesh of domestic cattle.

During the winter hunting was continuous. Indians constantly came to the post to trade or to beg. An interesting visitor was old Bill Williams, a famous trapper of that day, who had long been believed dead. He was one of a party attacked by Blackfeet, when all except Williams had been killed.

This winter Palliser witnessed a fight between the Sioux and the Assiniboines which seems to have resulted in a draw, though one Sioux was killed. These Sioux, by the way, were very troublesome and had shot many of the milch cows, and, more serious than all, a fine thoroughbred bull which belonged at the post.

"The loss of this handsome, noble animal was universally regretted in the fort, for besides his great value as their only means of continuing the breed of domestic cattle in that remote region, he proved most useful in drawing home many a heavy load of meat, and much of the wood for the fuel in the fort; as a tribute to his memory, I must here record a single combat of his with a bison, which, according to the description of his keeper, 'Black Joseph,' must have been truly Homeric.

"About three months previous to my arrival at Fort Union, and in the height of the buffalo breeding season, when their bulls are sometimes very fierce, Joe was taking the Fort Union bull, with a cart, into a

"BISON AND BULL, NOW IN MORTAL COMBAT, MET MIDWAY WITH A SHOCK THAT MADE THE EARTH TREMBLE"

point on the river above the fort, in order to draw
home a load of wood, which had been previously cut
and piled ready for transportation the day before,
when a very large old bison bull stood right in the cart
track, pawing up the earth, and roaring, ready to dispute the passage with him.   On a nearer approach, instead of flying at the sight of the man that accompanied
the cart, the bison made a headlong charge.   Joe had
barely time to remove his bull's head-stall and escape
up a tree, being utterly unable to assist his four-footed
friend, whom he left to his own resources.   Bison and
bull, now in mortal combat, met midway with a shock
that made the earth tremble.   Our previously docile
gentle animal suddenly became transformed into a
furious beast, springing from side to side, whirling
round as the buffalo attempted to take him in flank,
alternately upsetting and righting the cart again,
which he banged from side to side, and whirled about
as if it had been a band-box.   Joe, safe out of harm's
way, looked down from the tree at his champion's
proceedings, at first deploring the apparent disadvantage he laboured under, from being harnessed to a cart;
but when the fight had lasted long and furious, and it
was evident that both combatants had determined
that one or other of them must fall, his eyes were
opened to the value of the protection afforded by the
harness, and especially by the thick strong shafts of
the cart against the short horns of the bison, who,
although he bore him over and over again down on his

haunches, could not wound him severely. On the other hand, the long sharp horns of the brave Fort Union bull began to tell on the furrowed sides of his antagonist, until the final charge brought the bison, with a furious bound, dead under our hero's feet, whose long fine-drawn horn was deep driven into his adversary's heart. With a cheer that made the woods ring again, down clambered Joe, and while triumphantly caressing, also carefully examined his chivalrous companion, who, although bruised, blown, and covered with foam, had escaped uninjured.

"It required all Joe's nigger eloquence to persuade the bull to leave the slain antagonist, over whom he long stood watching, evidently expecting him to get up again to renew the combat, Joe all the time coaxing him forward with, 'Him dear good bull, him go home now, and do no more work to-day,' which prospect, black Joe, in common with all his sable brethren, considered as the acme of sublunary felicity."

During this winter the people at Fort Union were attacked by an epidemic which laid up many of them. Those who were not incapacitated by illness were, therefore, obliged to hunt the harder to supply the post with food, for in that country and at that time food meant meat almost exclusively. Buffalo-running in winter is often hard work, and when to the winter weather are added the difficulties of deep snow, the work becomes not only hard but dangerous. Some incidents of a winter run are given in Palliser's account of his killing some meat four or five miles from the post. He "had a splendid run, flooring a cow and wounding a bull, which I left for the present, and then stretching away at full speed, I pursued after another uncommonly fine fat cow. She gave me an awful chase, turning and doubling incessantly. My little horse was sorely at a disadvantage in the snow and began to show symptoms of distress; but I could not manage to get a broadside shot. At last making one more push, I got pretty close behind her and raising myself in my stirrups fired down upon her. . . . She dropped at the report, the bullet breaking her spine. My little horse, unable to stop himself, rolled right over her, making a complete somersault, and sending me, gun and all, flying clean over both of them into a snowdrift. I leaped up, ran back to my horse, which I caught without much difficulty, and was glad to find no more hurt than myself. My gun was filled with snow, of course, but otherwise uninjured."

The friendly relations between the domestic cattle and the buffalo caused Palliser much surprise, for he was unaware that cattle and buffalo associate intimately and sometimes interbreed.

Cases have been recorded where buffalo in their stampede have carried off considerable numbers of cattle, which became as wild as the buffalo with which they associated. Another point new to Palliser, and perhaps not well understood by naturalists at present, is the fact that buffalo do not, as a rule, use their hoofs to remove the snow from the ground, but push the snow aside with the nose. Palliser says: "I was still more astonished, on attentively observing this friendly intercourse, to see our little calves apparently preferring the companionship of the bison, particularly that of the most colossal bulls, to that of their own species. I took an opportunity one morning of investigating the reason of this more closely, and availing myself of some broken ground, beyond which I saw three of our poor little half-starved calves in company with two gigantic bulls, I crept up very carefully, and lay under the brow of a hill, not fifty yards from the nearest in order to observe them, and was not long in discovering that the bison has the power of removing the snow with his admirably-shaped shovel-nose so as to obtain the grass underneath it. His little companions, unable to remove the frozen obstacle for themselves, were thankfully and fearlessly feeding in his wake; the little heads of two of them visible every now and then, contesting an exposed morsel under his very beard. It was an interesting sight, and I crept softly away again, so as not to disturb them.

"Although the bison scrapes the snow with his nose, I do not think he does so with his hoofs. I have frequently seen the snow, where buffalo have been feeding, stained with slight signs of blood, and after having shot them, found the noses of both cow and bull sore from the constant shovelling."

Buffalo-hunting was not without its excitement. On

a certain day, for example, with an Indian, he killed three bulls, one of which was shot four times, and though seeming very weak did not fall, so that Palliser determined to finish him.

"Walking up therefore to within thirty paces of him, till I could actually see his eyes rolling, I fired for the fourth time directly at the region of the heart, as I thought, but to my utter amazement up went his tail and down went his head, and with a speed that I thought him little capable of, he was upon me in a twinkling. I ran hard for it but he rapidly overhauled me, and my situation was becoming anything but pleasant. Thinking he might, like our own bulls, shut the eyes in making a charge, I swerved suddenly to one side to escape the shock, but, to my horror, I failed in dodging him, for he bolted round quicker than I did, and affording me barely time to protect my stomach with the stock of my rifle, and to turn myself sideways as I sustained the charge, in the hopes of getting between his horns, he came plump upon me with a shock like an earthquake. My rifle-stock was shivered to pieces by one horn, my clothes torn by the other; I flew into mid-air, scattering my prairie-hens and rabbits, which had hitherto hung dangling by leathern thongs from my belt, in all directions, till landing at last, I fell unhurt in the snow, and almost over me—fortunately not quite—rolled my infuriated antagonist, and subsided in a snowdrift. I was luckily not the least injured, the force of the blow having been perfectly deadened by the enormous mass of fur, wool, and hair, that clothed his shaggy head-piece."

It was here that Palliser saw his first elk, which he describes with great detail, and whose whistle in the breeding season he declares to be the most beautiful sound in all the animal creation; it is like the sound of an enormous soft flute, uttered in a most coaxing tone.

In his hunting in the buffalo range, where, of course, wolves were most abundant, Palliser, as might be supposed, saw many wolves. He speaks with enthusiasm of the splendid white skins which he secured and brought into the post. In several cases he observes that wolves will eagerly devour the carcasses of their own kind. He notes also that they sometimes sleep so soundly that a man may walk up quite close to them. This is something that happened occasionally to all hunters. A hunting companion on one occasion walked to within a few feet of a sleeping deer, and commented in low tones to his companion on the soundness of its slumbers.

During this winter at Fort Union Palliser purchased a mongrel hauling, or travois, dog, sired by a white wolf. The animal was particularly shy of white men, and the old woman who sold it was obliged to catch the dog twice and deliver it a second time. Palliser wanted the dog to haul his travois on a journey he was about to make with two voyageurs. His companions had a pair of mules harnessed to a sleigh. He notes that the mules, of course, must be fed on cottonwood bark, since the grass was now deeply covered with snow. Palliser's dog—Ishmah by name—like his master, had to depend for food on the rifle. Shortly after starting, Palliser and his two companions separated, he and the dog to go up the river to Fort Mackenzie alone. He travelled chiefly on the ice, using due care to avoid the air-holes which are so frequent and so dangerous, and never leaving the river for any great distance. In the valley, shelter from the terrible storms of the high prairie may always be found. Here the two companions, who by this time had come thoroughly to understand each other, found the journey comfortable and very pleasant.

Ishmah's friendly relation with the wolves was sometimes very annoying, for often he ran off and played with the young wolves, chasing and being chased by them in turn. One afternoon, however, Ishmah followed a wolf off on the prairie, dragging behind him the travois loaded with everything that Palliser then possessed. He followed, shouting, but the dog had disappeared, and darkness soon obliged the owner to turn back toward the river. He was a long way from timber and all about him was a vast barren waste of snow. The situation was anything but agreeable. "I was about one hundred miles from any known habitation, and nearly one hundred and fifty from my destination, destitute of robe and blankets, with but very little powder in my horn, and only two bullets in my pouch. In short, I was in a pretty considerable

sort of a 'fix,' and had nothing for it but to make
tracks again with all speed for the timber. Fortunately, I found my way back to the river without much
difficulty. It was a beautiful moonlight night, which
enabled me to collect some fallen wood, and having
lighted a fire, I seated myself beside it, and began to
consider the probabilities of my ever reaching a trading-
post alive, in the event of Ishmah not returning, and
how I should economise my ammunition and increase
my rate of travelling so as to effect this object. My
prospects were dismal enough, nor did I feel cheered
as the cold north breeze froze the perspiration which
had run down my forehead and face, and formed
icicles in my beard and whiskers, that jingled like
bells as I shook my head in dismissing from my mind
one project after another. At last resigning myself
to my fate I took out my pipe, determined to console
myself with a smoke, when, alas! on feeling for tobacco I found that was gone too. This was the climax of my misfortune! I looked to the north star
and calculated by the position of the Plough that it
must have been about ten o'clock, the time at which
in England we have our knees under the mahogany,
surrounded by friends, discussing a bottle of the best,
and awaiting the summons to tea in the drawing-room.
I tried to see a faint similarity to the steam of the tea-
urn in the smoke from the snow-covered wood on my
dreary fire, and endeavoured to trace the forms of
sweet familiar faces in the embers, till I almost heard

ISHMAH, THE TRAVOIS DOG

the rustling of fresh white crepe dresses round me,
when, hark! I did hear a rustle—it approaches nearer,
nearer, and I recognize the scraping of Ishmah's travail on the snow; another moment and the panting
rascal was by my side! I never felt so relieved, and
laughed out loud from sheer joy, as I noticed the con-
sciousness he showed by his various cringing movements of having behaved very badly.   I was too well
pleased, however, at his reappearance to beat him,
particularly when I found nothing of his harness and
load either missing or injured in the slightest degree.
Even the portion of meat which I had secured from the
last deer I shot was untouched; so that I had nothing
to do but unpack the travail, make my bed, and cook
our supper."

Palliser was greatly interested in the Indians that
he saw, and tried to understand something of their
ways of thought. He quotes a woman whom he called
to look through a telescope as saying: "The white man
know of this—here she moved her hand as if writing
—what happens very far off, and with this—touching
the telescope—they see what is a long way off; now
have they invented anything by which they can hear
what is saying a long way off?" This seems a more
or less reasonable inquiry for the telephone of modern
times.

It was at White River Post that Palliser met an
Indian who later became one of his best friends and of
whom he had much to say. They hunted together and

on their first hunt killed a fine wolf which made them several meals. Palliser was unwilling to eat this food until he saw the relish with which his companion was consuming it; but having made the first step and learning how toothsome it was, he hesitated no longer.

Hunting was constantly kept up during the winter, for life depended on it. The weather was, as usual, uncertain. Palliser, whose stock of copper caps had run low, now went from the White River Post to Larpenteur's Post on Knife River with a party which McKenzie was sending to Fort Union. He wished also to visit Mr. Chardon, who was in command at the Minitaree Fort. The party set out on a fine sunny morning, and the heat was so great that one of them—Frederick—who was stout, walked in his shirt-sleeves puffing and blowing like a grampus.

At the Grand Detour—the Big Bend—they attempted to make the cut-off, which is only fourteen miles across, instead of following the river-bank for about forty miles. Palliser tried to persuade his companions to go the long way, showing them what a bad position they would be in if caught in a snow-storm on the prairie. However, the Indians believed that spring had come, and they started and finally camped on a little stream in the bed of which the snow was deeply drifted.

"Night was then coming on, and it began to rain slightly; but we brightened up the fire again, little knowing what was in store for us. Shortly after dark

the wind veered round to the north-east, accompanied
by snow, and at last it blew so hard as to oblige us to
put out the fire, especially on account of the gunpowder. Owing to our exposed situation, the wind merci-
lessly drove sparks, and even lighted brands, whirling
amongst us, turn which way we would, as the eddies
of wind drove furiously down the gullies against our
little encampment from all points of the compass.
Old Peekay and his wife collected every blanket and
skin they could muster. I seized my buffalo-robe and
blankets, called Ishmah to me, round whom I put my
arms, and hugging him close to my breast, shivered
through the night.

"Never shall I forget the horrible hours of suspense
I passed, expecting every instant the feeling of sleep to
overpower me, knowing the fatal consequences and
fearing an inability to resist it. I found my faithful
dog an invaluable friend, and really believe he was
the means of saving my life; for I seemed to feel the
caloric, as it issued from him, preserve my body from
turning into stone. Day at last dawned, and the wind
abated. We contrived to move to a less-exposed situation, where we lighted a roaring fire, and warmed
ourselves, then renewed our journey, reaching the opposite extremity of the Grand Detour by nightfall.

"Our supper that night was a very scanty one of
dried buffalo-meat, the last of the provision with which
Martin had supplied us. As for the unfortunate dogs
that accompanied the Indian Peekay and his squaw,

they, poor wretches had not eaten a morsel for weeks; and so awful an array of starved spectres never were seen."

Fortunately, the next day a bull was killed, and, wonderfully enough, by an old Indian who that morning had made a special prayer for food. The Indian was old and infirm and had not fired a gun or killed game for many years, but certainly in this case his prayer was answered.

Palliser found Mr. Chardon very ill with a violent attack of rheumatism, but extremely glad to receive his guest. To this post a little later came Boucharville, one of the most celebrated hunters and trappers of the region. He was a French Canadian of the best type, but had recently suffered great misfortunes, having lost his horses through the severity of the winter, had his traps stolen by Indians, barely escaped capture by a war-party, and finally broken the sight of his rifle.

This man Palliser engaged to make a trip back to Fort Union and thence on horseback up the Yellowstone River, intending at the close of the trip to make bull-hide boats and transport their skins and other effects back to Fort Union by water. For this trip two additional men were hired, a stout Canadian named Pérey and a half-breed named Paquenode. Palliser and Boucharville were to do the hunting; the other two were to keep the camp, mind the horses, and cook. In the meantime it was early in April and the wild-fowl were beginning to arrive from the South.

Palliser was keen to shoot some but had no shot. He tried to manufacture it and finally did so by beating out lead quite flat, cutting it into little bars, and again cutting these into little cubes an eighth of an inch each way. These were put in a small metal boiler in the kitchen of the Fort with some smooth stones and ashes and the boiler was revolved until the sharp corners were worn off the cubes and they approached the spherical. With this imperfect ammunition, good execution was done, for of course the birds were extremely abundant.

III

UP THE YELLOWSTONE RIVER

THE ice broke up in the Missouri on the 17th of April, and as the rising water forced up the ice, the explosion was like distant thunder. For over thirty hours the river rushed by in a furious torrent, carrying enormous blocks of ice and roaring with a splendid sound as the masses passed along, forcing everything before them.

Soon after this the party started for Fort Union. They had very little food; some dried meat, a little bag of biscuits, some coffee, and a quart bottle of molasses to sweeten the coffee. During the march they had opportunities to secure eggs from the nests of the water-fowl, which were already laying, but even with this help, on the fifth day they were reduced to one biscuit each.

"Early next morning we were passing along the side of the river, very hungry, and making a short march with the intention of hunting in the afternoon. Pérey carried a double-barrelled gun loaded with buck-shot, and was walking near the pack-horse, Ishmah and his travail following me, when we were astonished by the sudden appearance of four antelopes climbing up the bank close at hand. Owing to the steepness of the bank, they did not come in sight of us until they had reached the summit; the moment they did so they wheeled round, but not before Pérey fired and shot one, which rolled down the bank into the water, and was carried down the stream. Boucharville and I tugged at our gun-covers; his he could not remove quickly enough; I tore away the thong of mine—which had run into a knot—with my teeth, and cocked my rifle. By this time the other three antelopes were swimming away in the broad stream; a little eddy in the rapid current turned one of them broadside to me; I fired, hitting the animal between wind and water, behind the shoulder,—its head drooped, as, floating dead on the surface of the water, it was carried down the stream after its companion. Pérey then performed a splendid feat; he ran down the side of the river far enough to enable him to undress,—which he partly did in running,—jumped into the half-frozen water, along which the blocks of ice were still at intervals coursing, striking out boldly, laid his hand on the first carcass, then with great exertion reached the second as it floated by, and brought both into the bank: this was the more fortunate, for half a minute more would have swept them past the bend into the rapids beyond where the scene occurred, and involved not only the loss of our game, but a considerable risk to this brave fellow.

"The two antelopes afforded us quite a sufficiency of food to last until our arrival at Fort Union, which we reached early on the ninth day after our departure from the Minitarées."

At Fort Union food was scarce. The Indians camped there were afraid to venture away from the post to hunt, and immediately about the post white hunters and Indians had been hunting until all the game had been killed or driven away.

It did not take long to get together such supplies as might be had for Palliser's party—saddles, bridles, ammunition, a couple of traps, some coffee, sugar, and salt. It was necessary to cross the Missouri River from north to south below the mouth of the Yellowstone. This done, a few miles would take them into a land of plenty, a region where game was abundant; but the crossing would be difficult. The river was high and the water still cold. While going down the river they were fortunate enough to see deer and a little later some elk, of which they secured two. Their abundance now made them think of the starvation back at Fort Union and, packing up their surplus meat, they took it back to the fort to exchange for certain much needed things. Among these things were fishhooks, awls, needles, and, most important of all, an excellent four-oared skiff.

With the boat they succeeded in taking their horses and party across the Missouri, and this done they cached their precious skiff, burying it under the willows on the south bank of the Yellowstone, close to its junction with the Missouri.

Almost at once they found themselves in a country of abundant game, and of this game the antelope chiefly impressed the author. Of them he said: "These march in line, sometimes for several miles together, and, by imitating the movements of their leader, exhibit the most striking effects, resembling military evolutions: they simultaneously whirl round their white breasts and red flanks, like the 'Right face!—Left face!' of a regiment on parade. Obedient to the motions of their leader, when he stops, all stop: he stamps and advances a step, the slight similar impulse waves all down along the line; he then gives a right wheel, and round go all their heads for one last look; finally, he gives the right face about, and away 'their ranks break up like clouds before a Biscay gale.' Stately wapiti wandered on the plain, feeding not far from the willows, to whose friendly shelter in they crashed the moment we presented ourselves to their view. And as we approached steep frowning cliffs, overhanging the river, I saw, for the first time, the wild sheep or grosse corne of the Rocky Mountains, balancing themselves, chamois-like, on the tops of most inaccessible crags, whither they had rushed on first catching sight of us." He repeats the ancient fable that the sheep horns are so large and solid as to enable the animal to safely fling himself on his head from considerable heights.

He made a hunt for this new game and succeeded in killing a great ram, while Boucharville got two lambs, at this season much better food than the ram, for the sheep in early spring, feeding largely on the wild leeks, often tastes of this so strongly as to be almost uneatable.

In this land of plenty the party had a pleasant, easy time and lived like fighting-cocks. Palliser's clothing by this time was falling to pieces, and he was obliged to replace it by a coat made of an elk-skin, and trousers of the hides of blacktail deer. While in camp here Indians appeared on the other side of the river, but did not discover the hunters. However, the half-breed Paquenode, who appears to have been a natural coward, was frightened nearly to death and even tried to seize the best horse in the party in order to run away.

It was now late in May, and Palliser determined to build some boats and return to Fort Union, and then, taking up the skiff buried at the mouth of the Yellowstone, to row down to the Minitarée Fort about two hundred and eighty miles. The skeletons of the boats were made of willows, and these frames covered with bull-hides. After the canoes were loaded, Palliser and Boucharville occupied the first boat and towed the

second.   He sent the other men back to Fort Union
with the horses.

Late one evening, as they were floating down the
river, they heard voices, and presently passed an Indian camp unobserved, and landing a little below it
quietly returned to the vicinity and found the party
to consist of two old men, an old woman, and ten
young people.   After a little observation, the two white
men walked into the Crow camp, where the terrified
children ran away screaming.   The fears of the Indians were soon allayed, for Boucharville could talk
Crow, and the relations between the two parties became
very cordial.

While at Fort Union Palliser sent his horses by an
Indian friend down to Fort Berthold, while he, with
two of his three men, raised the buried skiff and started
down the river.   On their way an attack was threatened by a war-party of Indians, while the men were
out looking for mountain sheep.   Boucharville and
Palliser retreated to the camp and there took up a
position in the timber, and the Indians, after some
threatening demonstrations, made up their minds that
the position was too strong to be attacked and moved
off.   Later, the travellers came upon two white trappers whose arms had become useless and who were
then engaged in making bows and arrows with which
to kill game.   These two, Gardépée and Dauphin,
were competent young men and made a valuable ad-
dition to the party.   It was only the next day when

Palliser, while skinning a deer that he had killed, was called by Dauphin, and as he ran toward him and passed over a hill he saw a bear standing on his hind legs looking about him, while Dauphin, hidden behind a rock, was industriously snapping his useless pistol at the bear. When he saw Palliser the bear ran, but was brought back by Dauphin, who imitated the call of a buffalo-calf, so that Palliser shot at him, but only hit him in the flank.

"The bear clawed at the spot where the ball struck him, and charged up to within twenty paces of us, while I was reloading; whereupon Dauphin snapped his pistol again at him without effect. Fortunately for us, Bruin was only a two-year-old, and afraid to rush in, though large enough to have smashed both of us, defenceless as we were at the moment, and, before I could get on my percussion cap, bolted over the brow of the hill. I was still so thoroughly blown from my run over the rocky ground, that I gave up my heavy rifle to Dauphin, who threw down the useless pistol, and started in chase, I following him. He soon got a shot at the bear, who turned round, clawed at the wound, gave a savage growl, and ran into one of those little clumps which always mark a watercourse in the hilly country. I took the rifle again, loaded, and pursued the enemy right into the clump, in spite of the remonstrances of Dauphin, and, getting a sight of him first, gave him a finishing shot between eye and ear. Although he was but a young bear, only in his third year, it was with great difficulty that we could drag him out; he measured five feet four inches from rump to the muzzle, and his claws were three inches and three-quarters long. Had he been fully grown, and possessed of that amount of courage and ferocity with which the old grisly bears, both male and female, are endowed, it would certainly have fared badly with us that day. However, we skinned our prize with great satisfaction; and I was exceedingly pleased with the pluck and daring of my companion, who had been twice charged by the bear, and whose pistol had twice snapped."

A day or two later Palliser and Dauphin had a fine buffalo-chase which led them a long way. They started in pursuit of a new-born buffalo-calf, and this is what happened:

"The cow, of course, went off, and at a tolerable pace, followed by the calf, at an astonishing rate for so young a beast. Dauphin wanted to shoot the mother, in order not only to shorten the race, but to increase our chance of rearing the calf, by cutting off the cow's udder when dead; but that, of course, I would not allow, and ended the discussion by knocking up the muzzle of the rifle which he was using with the barrel of my gun. Then bidding him follow my example, I threw down my gun to lighten myself, calling on Boucharville to take care of the two; and drawing our belts a hole tighter, we dashed off again up hill and down dale, till at last we stretched away right out along the prairie for five or six miles.   By-and-by the little calf began to shows symptoms of failing, and the cow, allowing her instinct of self-preservation to overcome her maternal attachment, made the best of her way off, and crossing some inequalities in the ground, was lost to the sight of her offspring.   The little fellow then stopped; whereupon Dauphin, who possessed a wonderful facility for imitating the calls of animals, immediately began to grunt like a buffalo-cow, and to our great amusement the little beast turned about, cocked up his tail, and came galloping back to us.   We then turned about, and to our great delight it frisked round us all the way into the camp.   I was most anxious to get it to the fort as early as possible, for I knew that if I could do so in time, I might by chance be able to rear it on pounded Indian corn and lukewarm water."

The next day another calf was captured out of a herd which was crossing the river, and now Palliser had a pair which he hoped he might succeed in getting to Europe—as later he did.   For the first day or two of their captivity these little calves were fed on strong broth, but there were domestic cows at the fort and these reared the calves.

Shortly after Palliser's arrival at the fort, Mr. Chardon died, having first requested Palliser to write his will.   Boucharville, when sounded on the question of making another hunt, declared that he would go wherever Palliser wished to; and the next day they took the horses across the river with the skiff, intending

to hunt up the Little Missouri River and to look for
grizzly bears in the Turtle Mountains.   On the fourth
day of their journey from Fort Berthold they reached
the Turtle Mountains.   Here they found a war lodge,
built by a party of Minitarées the year before, and
took possession of it.   Boucharville, an experienced
man, did not like to remain in this debatable land,
which was on the border of the Sioux and Minitarée
territory, and began at once to figure on when they
could get away.

Here bear, antelope, elk, and sheep were extremely
abundant and food was always plentiful.   One day
while Palliser was beginning to skin an elk, just killed,
Boucharville, who was about to clean his gun, was
charged by a grizzly, and escaped her by dashing into
a clump of rose-bushes.   The bear, which had cubs with
her, charged after Palliser, who was running toward
his horse, which he feared would be lost if it smelt the
bear.   When he reached the horse he stopped and
faced the bear, which also stopped and stood up, and
then turned and ran.   Palliser shot at the bear, but
hit her too far back.   She stopped to bite at her wound
and gave him time to load again.   Just as he was putting a copper cap on the nipple the bear rose on her
hind legs, and he sent a bullet through her heart.
Palliser was very lucky in that his horse did not pull
back or shy, and that there was nothing to disturb his
aim.   When the horse was brought to the bear and the
skin put upon him, he paid no attention and showed

"JUST AS HE WAS PUTTING A COPPER CAP ON THE NIPPLE THE BEAR ROSE ON HER HIND LEGS"

no signs of fear, a very unusual thing, for horses are commonly very much afraid even of bear-skins.

After they reached camp Dauphin started out to capture one of the young bears, but as Palliser thought the chances of finding them were very slight he did not go with him, but afterward regretted this. Dauphin killed one of the little bears and tried to take the other alive, but it fought fiercely, tearing his clothes and cutting him with its claws. Dauphin had armed himself with a stout club, but, even so, had done no more than make a draw of the battle. They now started back toward the Little Missouri and on the way saw a bear, which, to Palliser's very great disgust, was lost by the eagerness of Dauphin.

At the Little Missouri Palliser went duck-shooting with his smooth-bore gun, but coming on the old carcass of a bull found all about it large bear tracks, some of which looked very fresh. He drew his charges of shot and rammed down a couple of balls, and followed the tracks from the prairie until at last he discovered a large bear walking slowly along. "I approached as near as I could without his perceiving me, and, lying down, tried Dauphin's plan of imitating the lowing of a buffalo-calf. On hearing the sounds, he rose up, displaying such gigantic proportions as almost made my heart fail me; I croaked again, when, perceiving me, he came cantering slowly up. I felt that I was in for it, and that escape was impossible, even had I declined the combat; so cocking both barrels of my Trulock, I remained kneeling until he approached very near, when I suddenly stood up, upon which the bear, with an indolent roaring grunt, raised himself once more upon his hind-legs, and just at the moment when he was balancing himself previously to springing on me, I fired, aiming close under his chin: the ball passing through his throat, broke the vertebræ of the neck, and down he tumbled, floundering like a great fish out of water, till at length he reluctantly expired. I drew a long breath as I uncocked my left barrel, feeling right glad at the successful issue of the combat. I walked round and round my huge prize, surveying his proportions with great delight; but as it came on to rain, I was obliged to lose no time in skinning him. I got soaked through before I succeeded in removing his tremendous hide, and then found it too heavy for me to take away; so I was obliged to return to camp without the trophy of my conquest. It was dark when I arrived. Boucharville and Dauphin had built a most comfortable little hut of logs and bark, and having laid down the skins and spread our beds inside, with the saddles at our heads for pillows, and a good roaring fire outside at our feet, we fell heartily to our supper of elk meat and coffee.

"At daybreak next morning I repaired on horseback to the scene of my conflict with the bear, and found, to my great delight, on my arrival at the spot, that neither the skin nor the carcass of the bear had been touched by the wolves. This fact confirmed to me the testi-

mony of the hunters and trappers of these parts, as
to the great awe in which the grisly bear is held by the
wolves and lesser animals of prey. If a bear kills an
animal, or finds a dead carcass on the prairie, he appro-
priates it; and though many a hungry prowler passing
by may look wistfully at the choice morsel, it is like
the eastern monarch's share, 'taboo'; and even when the
mountain monarch is absent, the print of his paw is a
seal sufficient for its security. It cost me considerable
exertion to place the reeking hide on my saddle; but
I succeeded at last, and climbing on the top of it, lighted
my pipe and rode back into camp. Riding along, towards noon we descried another bear, a lean, hungry-
looking monster, prowling about searching for *pommes
blanches*, and, to judge from his appearance, likely to
afford us a pretty severe fight. In approaching him,
we did not take any precaution to avoid giving him our
wind, concluding, from my former experience, that he
would not decline the combat; but in this instance I
was mistaken, for rushing away down a ravine, he was
soon lost to our view. This result, although it disappointed me at the time, yet gave me a further insight
into the disposition and habits of the animal, and agreed
with the accounts I had heard from many hunters and
trappers with whom I had previously conversed on the
subject; namely, that a grisly bear will, in most instances, run away from a man on getting his wind,
unless previously wounded, or under such circumstances as to make him think that he cannot escape.

Old Mr. Kipp, of Fort Union, told me that once, when on one of his numerous journeys from the States, he was in the Indian country, and had gone out of camp with his double-barrelled gun to look for ducks; he was seen from a distance by a grisly bear, who came cantering towards him. The day was fine, and the old gentleman did not know which way the wind blew, but had sufficient presence of mind to pluck off some of the woolly material of which his blue blanket capote was composed, and throw it into the air; and marking the direction of the current ran a little distance round, till he got full in the line of it, and then stood bolt upright facing Bruin, who rose on his hind-legs for a moment, surveying the tough old man, and then shuffled off, shaking his head as if he considered him meat rather too savoury for his palate."

There were other adventures with grizzly bears and Palliser recounts a story told by Boucharville about a bear which sprang upon the leading bull of a herd of buffalo and killed it. Other accounts have been given of such battles where the bull killed the bear.

The time for Palliser's return was now at hand, and loading his skins into boats made of buffalo-hide he floated down the river to the Minitarée post, where James Dawson the old fur trader was now in charge. A little later, boarding the Fur Company's steamer "Martha," he took his way with all his trophies down the river and at last reached St. Louis, and his prairie hunt was over.

The publication of his book, *The Solitary Hunter*, had unexpected results. Some time after its appearance, the British Colonial Office chose Palliser to command an expedition to explore British North America and to topographically determine the boundary line between the British possessions and the United States, from Lake Superior west to the Cascade Range. This expedition was in the field for three years or more. Papers reporting its progress were published by Parliament in 1859, and finally, about 1863, the British Government published Palliser's detailed journal, containing reports on the geography, agricultural resources, and commercial possibilities of far western America. Later Palliser was a magistrate for County Waterford and, for a time, served as high sheriff of that county.

THE COUNCIL AT FORT BENTON

THE COUNCIL AT FORT BENTON

WILLIAM T. HAMILTON, who died in 1908, was perhaps the very last survivor of that old-time race of trappers whose courage, skill, and endurance led to the discovery, exploration, and settlement of that vast territory which we now call the Empire of the West. He left St. Louis in 1842 with a company of free trappers led by Bill Williams —famous in those days—and for many years thereafter led the wild, adventurous, and independent life of the mountain man. With the coming of the railroads and the settlement of the country that life ended, but in 1907, at the age of eighty-five, he still lived among the mountains of Montana, and still made his annual trapping trips, keeping up the habits that he had practised for sixty-five years.

"Uncle" Bill Hamilton, as he was long and affectionately known, was one of Montana's first citizens, and the residents of that State were proud of his long experience, his wide knowledge of the life of the early days, and his extraordinary skill as a sign talker. A good mountain man is, of course, a keen observer, but Hamilton possessed also a retentive memory which enabled him in his later years to make valuable contri-

butions to the history of the early West, which have
been recorded in the proceedings of the Montana Historical Society, in his book *My Sixty Years on the
Plains*, published in 1905, and in the present account,
which was published in *Forest and Stream* in the spring
of 1907.

It was in the year 1855 that Governor I. I. Stephens,
called by the Indians "The Short Man," made, at the
mouth of the Judith River, the first treaty with the
Indians of northern Montana. The object of this
treaty was to bring about a general peace among the
different tribes, which had long been at war with one
another. Like many efforts of this kind, the treaty
had no lasting effect.

This story deals with another attempt to put an end
to intertribal wars made ten years later, in 1865, by
General Francis Meagher and other commissioners.
William T. Hamilton was sent out to try to induce the
various tribes to come into Fort Benton and attend
this council. Some of the tribes were brought in and
a treaty was made, but it did not last long. The account which follows is crowded with the lore of the
plains—information as to the way in which in old times
people travelled through a hostile country. Those
who read it with attention, will learn much about
the ways of Indians and the ways of those who fought
Indians.

This is Bill Hamilton's story of the Council at Fort
Benton:

WILLIAM T. HAMILTON

The Territory of Montana was organized in 1864. Green Clay Smith was appointed its first governor, and General Francis Meagher became acting governor with supervision over all Indians.

From 1863 to 1865 a chronic state of warfare existed between all the Indian tribes in the Territory. In the course of this warfare, miners and freighters had sustained serious losses in stock, and many miners and cattle-herders had been killed by the Indians. There was no protection for life and property. At the mouth of the Judith River, fifty miles east of Benton, was stationed one company of soldiers, but they were infantry and could render no protection against mounted Indians.

In 1864 I sold my place at Missoula, and moved to Benton—the head of navigation for the Missouri River steam-boats, which carried all the supplies of every description needed by the rapidly increasing population, which was rushing into the Territory attracted by fabulous reports which were constantly being circulated of the discovery of rich placer and quartz mines.

When I arrived at Benton it was almost impossible to get anything to eat, and I determined that I would start a hotel. I built a log house, hired a cook, and a negro for a waiter, gave fifty dollars for an old stove, bought and borrowed all the cups, knives, forks, and tin plates that I could get from the Fur Company employees, and opened my hotel at one dollar per meal.

I bought some beef steers and slaughtered one on the river bank. Two whiskey barrels on end, with three slabs on them, set up by the hotel, formed the counter of a butcher shop, the first one opened in Chouteau County, Montana Territory. I sold beef at twenty cents and twenty-five cents per pound, disposing of from one to five beeves daily to boats and freighters. Presently I was obliged to hire a butcher and a herder.

In the spring of 1865 the governor appointed me sheriff of Chouteau County, which was about as large as the State of New York. I was also appointed deputy United States marshal. At this time the population was a mixed and motley combination. There were some trappers and free traders, good men; but the remainder were Fur Company employees, in all about forty-five men. There were some half-breeds, but none of them could be trusted except one, Joe Kipp. The Northwest Fur Company had bought out the old Fur Company and had put I. G. Baker in charge. Carroll and Steele, former clerks of the old company, had opened a store in Benton, and T. C. Power afterward opened one.

Through the Territorial delegate, the United States Government was asked to protect the inhabitants of the Territory against Indians, and the following occurrences were a part of the effort to secure such protection. A commission of three persons was appointed to consider this subject. It consisted of Acting Governor Meagher, Judge Munson, and E. W. Carpenter. They arrived at Benton early in September, and after holding a council determined that the Piegans, Bloods, Blackfeet, Gros Ventres, and Crow Indians must be brought into Benton and there induced to make a permanent and lasting peace. Runners were sent out inviting the Blackfeet tribes to come in, but no one could be found who would undertake to hunt up and bring in the Crows and Gros Ventres.

At this season the country between the Missouri and Yellowstone Rivers was usually overrun by war parties of Sioux, Cheyennes, Arapahoes, and Blackfeet, making travel exceedingly dangerous for any one, even for an experienced prairie man.

While they were trying to find a man to make this trip, some one suggested to the commissioners that I was accustomed to travelling anywhere, and they might get me. They sent, asking me to call on them at the agency, which was then at Benton, and when I came, the governor said: "Sheriff, we want a man to go and get the Crow and Gros Ventres Indians to come to Benton and meet us in council. Will you go and get them for us? We are informed that you can and do travel anywhere on the plains."

"Yes, I do," I answered, "if I have special business of my own to attend to."

The governor said: "The government is anxious to bring about a general peace between these warring tribes, and also to put an end to hostilities against the white people. In a few days a steamboat load of goods will arrive, to be given as presents to all Indians who meet us in council. We want you to go and bring in these tribes."

"But," I said to him, "how can I go? I have to look after my eating house, the butcher shop, the duties of sheriff, and of marshal. I have two prisoners on hand and no jail in which to confine them."

But they kept on talking and persuading until I saw that, as the Western phrase has it, they were going to get me into a jack pot. To cut it short, they prevailed on me to undertake the mission to bring in the two tribes.

I appointed a deputy to look after my business, and informed the commissioners that I must have a certain Piegan Indian as companion, and asked them to send a runner to Little Dog, the chief, with a paper, asking him to send Eagle Eye to Benton as soon as possible. In two days Eagle Eye was there. I had christened him Jack. I had once saved his life. He was a cool and brave man, and would die for me if called on to do so. He had been with me on two former trips.

I was at the agency when Jack arrived, and when I told him what was wanted of him, he gave a warwhoop that startled the commissioners. I owned two of the fastest horses in the country, and got two good horses for Jack. I selected one pack-horse, a fast one which would follow like a dog. I took some tobacco and some food with which to feast the Indians, calculating to put about seventy-five pounds on the pack-horse.

Brief digression may be interesting, and perhaps useful. I had a pair of Spanish panniers made of canvas or leather fastened together and hung over the pack-saddle. At the bottom of the off-side pannier was a four-inch strap ending in a buckle. On the nigh-side pannier a strap was fastened at the bottom, and these straps were buckled together under the horse's belly. This held both panniers down close to the horse's body. The panniers can be made of any size, according to the amount one wishes to pack. Mine would carry one hundred pounds of assorted goods. In case of emergency, the animal being saddled, you can place the panniers on the saddle, cinch, mount, and be off in twenty seconds.

On my best horse I kept day and night an Indian pad-saddle as a substitute for a riding-saddle. Its weight was ten pounds; the horse wore a hackamore for a bridle, and the reins were tied to the horse's mane. This was a useful precaution in case of being surprised or jumped by Indians and not having time to saddle. Such an occurrence may take place notwithstanding all your alertness. My other horse I rode with a California saddle. Jack was similarly fitted out, except that he had two Indian pads. I had bought from Judge E. R. Munson the first Henry rifle that ever came into the Territory, paying him one hundred and six dollars in gold-dust. I had two .45 calibre Colt's revolvers. Jack had a Sharp's rifle, using paper caps that I had given to him some time before. I got him two .45

calibre Remington revolvers. He had also his bow and arrows.

On the second day after Jack's arrival we packed up at the agency, a number of persons being present. The commissioners could not understand why we were so heavily armed, since we were going on a peaceful message for the government. Their questions and manifest ignorance of Indians brought a smile to the faces of many of those present, as if a war party would care what business we were engaged in, or, if they did care, would stop to ask. After a while we shook hands with our friends and started. Many of them said, "Look out, Bill, this is likely to be your last trip," but I felt that, being armed as we were, no small party would get the "age" on us.

Jack had told me that a Piegan war party which had returned a few days before had informed him that the Crows had been camped at Medicine Springs between the Moccasin Mountains, that being about ninety miles from Benton as the crow flies, but had moved their village some days before. He also told me there were three Blackfeet war parties out after Crows and Gros Ventres. We should have to look out for them. With this information as to where to pick up the trail, it would be easy for us to locate the Crow village, unless we met hostile war parties. For about half the distance to the Medicine Springs the country is very broken.

We forded the Missouri River and struck across a

rolling country to Arrow Creek, thirty miles from Benton, and reached the creek about sixteen miles east of Rattling Buttes. These buttes, at the east end of the Highwood Mountains, were in a dangerous country. It was a famous resort for war parties, and game of all kinds was abundant. Here we stood guard turn about. Because you see no Indians nor signs of any, it does not follow that none are in the neighborhood. In a hostile or semi-hostile country never trust to appearances, but be as much on the alert as if you knew the enemy was in close proximity. Have everything ready for action either to defend your position or to retreat.

The next morning before daylight we built a fire out of dry willows and made coffee. Our bill of fare was pemican and crackers. We had discovered a few buffalo feeding over a ridge near camp, and I asked Jack to try to get one with an arrow. It was too dangerous to use a gun to kill this game. If any Indians were within hearing, the report would have brought them to us in force, and might have caused us annoyance. Many a party has come to grief from the lack of such knowledge. Jack went off, and in a short time returned with the tongue, the hump, and one *dépouille*, which we used as a substitute for bread. By this time I had the stock ready to start.

After viewing the surrounding country from a high knoll and observing no signs of danger, we started. We had to pass over a broken country between Arrow

Creek and Wolf Creek, a distance of some eighteen miles. As we passed over a high ridge far over to our right, perhaps seven miles, we discovered about one hundred buffalo on a stampede. We left the ridge and approached a hill that had some trees upon it, and from this point looked over the country in order to learn, if possible, what had caused the buffalo to "raise," for buffalo seldom stampede unless they are frightened by somebody in the vicinity. We discovered nothing, and at length went on to Wolf Creek, where, on the south side of the stream, we came across foot-tracks where seven men had been walking. Jack declared that they were Blackfeet. They had passed along that morning. Evidently they had tried to find the Crow village, but had missed it. I told Jack that this war party would go to Deep Creek, and would run off some miners' horses, and would also take in a miner if the opportunity offered. Afterward we learned that some war party about this time did kill a miner and run off a number of horses.

We passed on, travelling in draws and hollows as much as possible, until we reached Willow Creek. The antelope and a few buffalo were feeding quietly; a sure sign that no Indians were about, and that there had been none before our arrival. The grass was good, and we camped and cooked our tongue, enjoying a feast fit for the gods of old, as mountain men have it.

We did not travel fast or far, but kept our horses in prime condition, so that, if in case of any emergency

we were forced to make fast time, we could get away
and keep from being made bald-headed.

We were not disturbed during the night, and the
next morning were off at daylight.   The game still fed
about us undisturbed.   We crossed Plum Creek (Judith
River) and discovered several pony tracks some days
old.   We concluded that the riders were Crows.

At length we got to the Medicine Springs between
the Moccasin Mountains.   The Crow village had been
there, but had gone.   We followed their trail until
dark, and camped at the east end of the Judith Mountains.   The next morning Jack went to the top of a
high butte, called Black Butte, and swept the surrounding prairie with a powerful field-glass, but discovered no
sign of village smokes.   Now began the dangerous part
of our trip.   A comparatively open country lay before
us.   To follow the lodge-pole trail was dangerous, yet
that was our only means of finding the Crow village.
All Indian war parties are likely to follow the village
trail of those they are after.   Jack said that there were
two more Blackfeet war parties out besides the one
that had gone up Wolf Creek, but these parties we did
not fear, because they were on foot.   The result might
be different if we came in contact with either Sioux,
Cheyennes, or Arapahoes, who always go to war
mounted, and in force.   We could easily stand off
eight or twelve Indians, but fifty or one hundred is a
different matter.   Nevertheless, we had to take the
risk.

Before starting we put everything in prime order. If some persons had been present I think they would have believed that we were preparing for a desperate fight or a desperate retreat.

From our camp in the Judith Mountains the big bend of the Musselshell River and the Bull Mountains were fifty miles to the southeast. There we expected to find the Crow village, unless prevented by hostile war parties.

We travelled on at a five-mile gait, carefully watching the trail for fresh tracks, either of men or horses. If either should be discovered, we would have to act according to circumstances. In front of us and on either flank a few scattered buffalo and antelope were feeding quietly.

About 2 P. M. we reached Flat Willow Creek, just above where Box Elder Creek flows into it. Jack mounted his best horse and made a circle three-quarters of a mile in diameter, to see if he could discover any Indian signs. I went to the crest of a high ridge, and with my glasses thoroughly swept the surrounding country without seeing any sign of a village smoke, then returned to where I had left the horses. When Jack returned I could see by his look that he had discovered something that troubled him. When I asked him what he had found he pointed up the creek and said: "South of that butte are the pony tracks of a mounted party of twenty-five going toward the south end of the Bull Mountains." If this party was hostile, it was the scouting party from some larger one, or it might be a scouting party of Crows. We had no means of knowing which. In any case, we had to do one thing first of all, and that was to let our animals refresh themselves. One of us kept a good lookout, while the other unsaddled one horse at a time, gave him a bath from the stream, dried, and resaddled him; repeating this until all the horses had had their bath. Such treatment refreshes a horse more than anything that you can do for him. All mountain men and many Indian tribes understand the secret.

We were now in the most dangerous part of the country from the Pan Handle of Texas to the British line. As an expert scout would say, "you must see all around you; must have eyes in every part of your head."

Dick, my best horse, was possessed of almost human intelligence. I had trained him to come to me on a run at a whistle, as almost any horse can be trained with a little patience. I mounted Dick, leaving Jack with the outfit. I went up the stream and picked up the trail that he had described and followed it. As Jack had said, it led toward the south end of Bull Mountains. When I reached a ridge on which were some trees, a plateau lay before me about one mile in extent and ending in a broken country with scattering trees. I could see that the trail led directly through a cluster of pines. I got into a draw, or low place, which ran down toward the Musselshell River and followed it down, hoping or expecting to come across the trail of the village. I followed the draw until within half a mile of the river, and then rode back across the country to Jack, without discovering anything.

Flat Willow Creek rises in the southeast end of the Big Snowy Mountains. A large war-party could rendezvous there and send out small scouting parties, learn if any enemies were in the vicinity, return, and report. To a war party all human beings are considered enemies, except the members of their own party.

I asked Jack what he thought of this party, whose trail he had found. The trail was not over a day old. He replied it was either a scouting war party, or a scouting party sent out by the Crow chief to find out if any enemies were in the country. I had come to this same conclusion, for in years past I had been out with many such parties on different occasions. At all events, if this party were enemies of the Crows, they had not as yet struck either the village or the lodge-pole trail, where the village had passed along. One thing was noticeable in this section. It was in the centre of the buffalo grazing ground at this season of the year, and yet as far as a powerful glass could view the surrounding country no buffalo were to be seen; though there was abundant sign where they had been not many days before. On the other hand, we could discover no signs where a run had been made. If anybody had been chasing the buffalo many carcasses would be in evidence on every side. A few antelope were to be seen, but they were shy and constantly on the watch, a sure sign that Indians had passed over the country.

It would be very instructive to writers of Indian lore if they could travel with an expert scout or with an Indian war party and observe their actions—their caution and the care taken to avoid being seen by their enemies and to circumvent them. They learn by the actions of animals and by the flight of birds if enemies are near, or of the people who have passed through, or who may yet be hidden in, some section of the country. Jack was an expert in observations of this kind. Not the flight of a bird escaped his eagle eye.

We remained here about two and a half hours. The horses had eaten, and were refreshed and in prime condition. When we started, we followed the trail and crossed the creek, the trail leading down the creek on the south side to the forks of the Musselshell River. Here the Crow village had remained only one night. They had made a long drive the day they got to this camp. Jack said that the Crows were frightened and were getting out of the country. It had been several days since they were in this camp. As it was sundown when we reached there, we camped, and the night passed without our being disturbed. Breakfast was over before daylight next morning. We expected that the trail would follow up the river, but instead of that it went southeast, toward the divide of the Yellowstone River, and when we reached the divide the trail turned east. Jack was well acquainted with this section of the country, having been here with Piegan war parties many times. The east end of the Bull Mountains was now some five miles south of us. Like the Big Snowies, this is a great rendezvous for war parties. We followed the trail, and about one o'clock in the day Jack turned north half a mile to a spring of water of which he knew at the head of the draw.

That night we remained there, keeping a careful lookout. Nothing happened in the night, and by daylight we were off again. Jack announced that he thought that the Crows would be camped either on upper or lower Porcupine Creek. As we went along we saw a few buffalo and antelope feeding quietly, good evidence that they had not been disturbed recently. As Jack was the most expert trailer, I placed him in the lead, directing him to keep his eye on the trail, while I would keep a general lookout over the country for any sign of danger.

We had travelled some five miles when, like a flash, Jack dismounted. He followed on the trail on foot for a short distance, and returning held up five fingers and made the sign for the Blackfeet Indian. They had come up from the Musselshell River. We looked at the tracks carefully and found them fresh. The ground was sandy in places, and where an Indian's foot had been, we discovered grains of sand still active, unsettled, dropping down from the sides of the track, a sure sign that they had been made recently. The same sign holds good with horse tracks, and this sign can be read by

any person with a quick eye.   Let him put his foot on
some sand and then carefully and patiently watch how
long it takes for the sand to become inactive.   All such
signs are carefully studied by mountaineers and Indians.   It was plain enough to us.   We went on, keeping a sharp lookout.   Some three-quarters of a mile
before us, we could see some timbered buttes, and the
trail led directly toward these trees.   There was a pos-
sibility that those five Indians might be there, and we
put our tools in condition for instant use.   We got
within three hundred yards of the buttes, wheeled to
the right, and putting our horses on a run, passed between two small hills and got beyond the first butte.
Nothing was discovered.   When we reached the trail,
Jack dismounted, looked at it carefully, followed it a
short distance and returned, saying: "The Indians are
running here."   In front of us were other buttes with
trees on them, and we were now satisfied that the
Blackfeet had discovered us and were at this moment
planning a coup by which they could take us without
loss to themselves.   To avoid being ambushed, we bore
to the left, keeping a long rifle shot from the timber
and a keen lookout.   We had passed perhaps one
hundred and fifty yards beyond the first butte, when
two rifle shots were fired, the bullets going wide of the
mark.   We wheeled to the left, rode behind a small
knoll and dismounted.   Before we got there, three more
shots were fired, the bullets coming unpleasantly close,
but doing no harm.

We had no sooner dismounted than five Indians charged us with a yell, for they made sure they had us. Our outfit was a tempting bait for them. There were five good horses, to say nothing of arms and other property. If they had succeeded in taking us in, they could have returned to their people as great warriors, and would have been allowed to paint their spouses' faces to their hearts' content, and these would have been envied by all the other women in the village, who would not have been permitted to take part in the scalp dance that would follow.

We let the Indians come within sixty yards, and then we showed ourselves and ducked. The Indians, fool-like, all fired; and, before they could reload or draw bows and arrows, the Sharp and the Henry got to work, and in less time than it takes to write this, five Black-feet were on their way to their happy hunting-ground. We got five Hudson's Bay flintlock guns, bows and arrows, and other plunder. Jack scalped two of the Indians. I took a fancy war bonnet.

When we got back, Jack told the circumstances to his friends in the Piegan camp. They blamed us for killing these people, saying that as we were mounted we should have run away. If we had run, the Black-feet would have been on our trail like a wolf on the trail of a wounded deer. They are hard to shake free from or to throw off the trail. Jack justified our acts, saying that they fired upon and charged us. If they had succeeded in getting us they would have scalped us both, they knowing him to be a Piegan. He added that any Indian, whether Blackfoot, Blood, or Piegan that shot at him and missed, must expect to be scalped. He was asked if he were not afraid that some of the friends of those we had put to sleep would revenge themselves by putting him to sleep. I could not but admire Jack when he answered them, his eyes sparkling like fire: "No! if any one or more want to try that, they all know when and where to find me." As it was, we would not be annoyed any more by this war party.

Jack told me that West Porcupine Creek took its rise a short distance from here. Passing by this timbered country, we came to one that was open, where a few buffalo were in sight. Here the trail bore to the right, going south, and followed a ridge. Jack said that this ridge lay between East and West Porcupine Creeks. We travelled some twelve miles and, when we passed over a ridge, discovered the smoke of a village on the lower or easternmost stream. It seemed to be about eight miles distant. We moved toward it at a lively gait, but when we were about a mile from the village, we could discern a great commotion beyond or south of it. Horsemen were galloping back and forth in every direction as if in a sham battle. Jack said that he heard shots and that he believed a fight was on. We pushed ahead and got to the village, and found, sure enough, that the Sioux had attacked it, trying to run off the Crow ponies. They had been discovered by the young Crow herders and the alarm was given; and, since Indians always keep their best horses close to the village, the warriors soon mounted and rushed out to protect their herds. Nothing is more disastrous to a camp than to lose its horses, and they will fight as desperately for them as for their families.

Bull Goes Hunting, the chief, met us, and, as he did so, put his hand over his mouth, signifying his astonishment at seeing us. He was an old acquaintance, a friend, and we went to his lodge. I left Jack and our outfit in the care of the chief, while I mounted Dick to go out and see the fight. Jack wished to go, but I would not allow it, for he might do some desperate act, such as to charge through the Sioux and might go under. At this time, he was too valuable a man to lose. A few young warriors went with me, and we soon got to the battlefield. The first man we met was Spotted Horse, a war chief. There were not over two hundred Sioux, and fully three hundred Crows. We joined in the half fight half runaway that was going on; though they had been fighting some time, not over six on either side had been placed *hors de combat*. A few were wounded, and a few ponies put out of action. Neither of the opposing forces showed any generalship.

Without underrating the Indian, or overrating the paleface, I may say that I have been with white men on the plains where forty of them would have made short work of either of these contending forces. By some poetical writers, the Indian is credited with possessing Spartan bravery; but, with a few exceptions, the reverse is true. There are but few mountain men who cannot outgeneral an Indian.

After a while the Crow chiefs got together for a council, and the result was more like the work of school-boys than of warriors and chiefs. I sat in the council. They spoke in their own tongue, half of which I understood. They also made signs for every word spoken, and each sign was as a, b, c, to me, as of course they knew. They wished me to understand every word that they spoke. They asked my opinion of the fight and what they should do. I advised them to call off their warriors, to form three equal bodies of men, and to charge the Sioux on both flanks and at the front at the same time. Then the fight would end, and the Sioux would retreat. The Indians gave a grunt and said nothing.

We all joined again in what one might call playful fighting. I could see that the Sioux were growing dis-couraged, but a desultory fighting continued for a short time, when some fifty of the bravest Crow warriors charged the right flank of the Sioux and emptied a few saddles, but were checked by a stand made by a few Sioux. This stand was made in order to give some of their wounded an opportunity to leave the field. As the Sioux were better mounted than the Crows, they outstripped us on the retreat. We followed them about a mile, forcing them to abandon some thirty tired ponies, which the Crows captured. They scalped and mutilated a few Sioux and collected all the plunder on the field. All the wounded Sioux had retired before the fight was over. Indians will remove the slain to keep the enemies from scalping them. Whites do the same.

We returned to the village. The chiefs now asked my object in coming to their village. We were now sitting in the lodge, where our things were, and I got out the large envelope containing my letter. It was sealed with wax, and had an eagle stamped on it as large as a dollar. All this show had a moral effect on the Indians, and when they saw it they believed that I was a messenger from the Great Father. After smoking the medicine-pipe, as is customary before a council, I interpreted the contents of the letter in condensed form, the substance of which I have already given. I urged the Crows to go to Benton, telling them that it would be to their advantage to do so. They would receive many presents, and besides would make peace with their ancient enemies. They listened to me attentively, and then gave reply in the negative, saying that their ponies' feet were getting tender and the animals thin in flesh, that there were no buffalo between where we were and Fort Benton, and that they must remain where they were in order to secure meat for their families. All this was common sense from their point of view, and left me no ground for argument. A Crow party had recently been to Fort Union, and had been informed by the traders there that the next moon some white chiefs would be there to meet the Crows in council. This proved to be the fact, as we afterward learned. The Crows could go to Fort Union by easy stages and be among buffalo all the way, provided their enemies did not run the game out of the country.

Jack gave the Crows the two scalps, the guns, and other things that he had taken, and they gave him a good mule and complimented him on being a great warrior. We told them that another Blackfeet war party was out, said to be looking for Crows, but that we did not know where they were. We got the women to cut some bunch-grass for our stock, in order that they might be in good condition to make an early start next morning. During the night Jack and I stood guard turn about, and many young Crows did the same. By daylight we had breakfasted. The chiefs had assembled to see us off, and I asked them if they knew where we might find the Gros Ventres. They replied that we would find them either south or east of, and near to, the Bear Paw Mountains. I told them that we should try to get them to go to Benton if we could do so. It was amusing to Jack and to me to listen to the chiefs as they gave us advice about travelling, just as if neither of us had had any experience. Though it was not needed, we took their advice in good part. We paid the women for the grass and started.

When we left the village, the war-dance was in progress in one part, and in another persons who had lost relations were mutilating themselves, cutting off their fingers or puncturing their legs and heads with the point of a knife, making the blood flow freely, and, as they did this, wailing and mourning the loss of friends and relatives in the fight. Jack, whose horses were good to lead, had saddled his mule. When we started on the back track, we kept east of our old trail. We apprehended little danger of meeting Sioux, Cheyennes, or Arapahoes, and we did not at all regard the other Blackfeet war parties.

We made a bee-line for the mouth of the Musselshell River, and got there at 9 A. M. next day, for Jack knew every foot of the country. No Indian signs were visible. We collected some dry poles, bound them together with willow twigs, put all our property on the raft, tied riatas to the end of it, and, mounting, drove the stock across the river, keeping hold of the ends of the ropes. The horses were good swimmers, and we soon had the raft across. After the horses had been rubbed down, saddled, and packed, we mounted and were off. Not many minutes were occupied in accomplishing the crossing. We had no time to waste, for the Indians might be upon us at any moment.

We now made a bee-line for the Little Rocky Mountains, and when we came to a creek called Poshett,[1] which rises on the south side of the Rockies, we began to see carcasses of the buffalo in different places. The meat had been taken off, and a careful inspection showed that the buffalo had not been slain more than

[1] Fourchette Creek, southeast of Little Rocky Mountains.

five or six days. As we followed up the creek there were more signs that a run had recently been made.

We had travelled fast that day, and when we reached a cluster of box-elder trees, with good grass, we determined to remain there that night, unless some hostiles should come and veto our intention. Before unpacking we looked over the surrounding country for signs of village smoke, and, discovering nothing, we cooked, feasted, and kept our live-stock on the best of grass, all the while keeping a good lookout.

We had breakfast before daylight next morning, packed up, and were off. Following up the creek, we struck a lodge-pole trail going east, between the two Little Rockies. After it had passed the buttes, the trail bore to the left, going north, and now we saw fresh pony-tracks, a sure sign that the village was not far off. Before us lay a plateau, and beyond that was Beaver Creek, where we found the Gros Ventres village. We had been discovered before we got near it, being met outside the village by Famasi, the head chief, an old acquaintance, who escorted us to his lodge.

After feasting and smoking, a council of all the chiefs was held, and the object of our visit was stated to them. They consulted among themselves for some time, the result of the council being that they agreed to go to Benton, and they asked me when they would be wanted there. I told them that the commissioners were now waiting for them, and that they had better start the village for Benton to-morrow, for it would take them two and a half or three days to get there. It was sixty miles as the crow flies to Benton, but I expected to be there the following night. I told the chief that he had better send two or three of his men with us, and he agreed to do so.

I got six women to cut an abundance of grass for our stock. They also built a small corral for us. Before daylight the Indians turned out their ponies to graze, and by daylight breakfast was over, the lodges were down, and the women were getting everything ready for packing. The ponies were now brought in. Bear Wolf and Star Robe, two sub-chiefs, were selected to accompany us. Here Jack traded his mule for eight fine garnished robes. He wanted me to take seven of them, but I selected four. He packed the robes on one of his horses, and by seven o'clock we started, taking the best and most direct route to Benton, passing on the south side of the Bear Paw Mountains. We nooned at Eagle Creek, about half-way. Small bands of buffalo were seen, and we killed two fat ones. Selecting the choicest parts, we feasted as no mortals ever feasted, unless they have feasted on fat cow buffalo.

Our camp was about one and a half miles from the mountains. Star Robe, with my glass, was looking the mountain over, and when he returned to camp he said that seven Indians were coming down the stream afoot. Jack said: "Blackfeet! I will stop them from coming here!" He stripped down to his breech-clout, mounted his best horse, and took the ridge. I had Dick

ready for emergency, in case something should happen
to Jack.   About half a mile up the stream Jack halted.
Some two hundred yards beyond him the seven
Indians came up on the ridge.   I was watching every
move made.   One of the Indians approached Jack.
After a short time he returned to the other Indian,
and they all went back to the mountain.   Jack informed us that he had told the Indians not to come
nigh us, as they would get shot, but to go to Benton,
where all the Indians were going to meet the white
chiefs in council.

Those Indians did go to Benton, and Jack, knowing
them, introduced me to them.   They laughed at the
idea of the two of us being able to put all of them to
sleep; that nettled Jack, and he asked me to show them
what I could do with my "medicine gun," as he called
my Henry rifle.   At this place the Missouri River is
about two hundred and fifty yards wide, and on the
farther, or south, side near the water there stood a
stone about one foot in diameter.   There were about
one hundred and fifty Indians present at the time.
I had practised at that rock more than once.   I fired
seven shots at it in rapid succession, and each shot
would have hit an Indian.   All the Indians put their
hands over their mouths—a sign of astonishment.
They wished to examine the rifle, but I refused to let
them touch it, let alone examine it.   I was determined to keep them mystified about the Henry rifle
as long as I could.   I was offered four times the price

I paid for it—one hundred and six dollars, as already stated.

When I reported to the commissioners, they were somewhat disappointed that the Crows were not coming to the council. I notified the commissioners that the Gros Ventres would be here in two days, and that two of their chiefs had come here with us. The commissioners requested me to take care of these chiefs until the village arrived. I did so, charging the commissioners one dollar a meal for each Indian, the same price that I charged the white men; but I ought to have had two dollars, as one of these Indians could get away with as much grub as two white men.

Some northern Indians were now beginning to come in. Three days after our return the steamboat got to Benton. Two days after the arrival of that boat fully thirty-five hundred Indians were in camp on Benton Bottom. The Piegans and the Bloods had about three hundred and fifty lodges. Father-of-all-Children,[1] the Blackfeet chief, had fifty lodges, but doubled up; that is to say, two families in one lodge. The total number of Indians, big and little, was about four thousand, and more parties were constantly arriving, swelling the number. The other Blackfeet Indians were too far away to attend the council, and besides that, they had no right to be there to receive presents from the United States, as

[1] *Mĕn ĕs tō' kōs*, literally, All are his children, but commonly spoken of as Father of all children.

they belonged to Canada. The people from the north pitched their lodges mostly on the upper end of the Bottom, but the Gros Ventres pitched theirs on the lower end, some three hundred yards east of the old fort. Formerly they had been friends with the Piegans and the Bloods, but for the last four years they had been at war, and there was the bitterest hatred between them. Hence this wide separation of their lodges. The council-chamber had been put in order. The American flag was handsomely displayed, with other decorations. The steamboat had been unloaded and the goods stored. This was about the 20th of September, 1865.

As stated in the earlier part of this narrative, I had been appointed deputy marshal, though I knew nothing about the duties of the office. I asked General Meagher what was expected of me as marshal, and he replied: "Keep order, see that the chiefs are seated in their allotted places, and that the interpreters are ordered to bring all chiefs and principal warriors to the council."

At the appointed time, all had come except the Gros Ventres. Tunica, the interpreter, returned from the camp, saying that the Gros Ventres chiefs were afraid to come. The commissioners commanded me, as sergeant-at-arms, to bring the chiefs and headmen of the tribe to the council. I was armed at all points. Dick was saddled, and I went to the village. I got six of the leading chiefs, who wanted to bring their arms

with them, but I gave them to understand that this
would not be permitted by the white chiefs in council,
that no one could enter the council-chamber armed,
except myself. I gave them assurance that no harm
would come to them in council, and soon returned with
the chiefs, and placed them on the left of the Piegans.
They had been acquainted with each other before the
war, and had been good friends.

It was one P. M. when the clerk produced a roll of
closely written sheets of paper. It looked to me to be
two quires, the treaty which came from the Indian Com-
missioner at Washington. The clerk began reading it
by sections, and then waited to have it interpreted. The
Piegans, Bloods, and Blackfeet needed but one interpreter, but the Gros Ventres had to have their own interpreter. It took fifteen to twenty minutes to get
through with one sentence, and even then neither interpreter nor Indians understood one-tenth of its meaning. I saw that it would take forty days to get through
if a change was not brought about. Little Dog, the
Piegan chief, told his interpreter to inform the commissioners that the council would be adjourned until next
day in order to consult on the mode of procedure to
be used thereafter and the language to be employed in
carrying through a treaty with a wild, untamed lot of
Indians, ninety per cent of whom had no desire to mix
with or deal with any whites, except to trade for certain commodities which they stood in need of. The
commissioners knew as little of how to proceed to make

those Indians understand their meaning as an Apache would know of Latin.

My eating-house now did a rushing business, for that evening I was asked to give supper to all the chiefs. It would have been amusing to any one with a knowledge of Indian character to see the warriors who, when they heard I was going to give all the chiefs their supper, came to me and claimed to be chiefs. We did feed perhaps a dozen leading warriors besides the chiefs. I notified the cook to be prepared to feed about forty Indians. We had plenty to eat, but no fancy dishes. The cook was well up in his business.

After supper, the commissioners called the interpreter and me to council with them, for they saw that some change must be made in the proceedings. We told them that they must condense, must leave out "party of the first part," "party of the second part," "for and in consideration of, etc.," and must state in as few words as possible what they desired of the Indians. The clerk got to work, and in half an hour had the forty closely written sheets of paper condensed to less than one, which contained the meaning of the whole.

At nine o'clock next morning the council met again, all the chiefs being in their seats. The Small Robe band of Piegans claimed the land on the south side of the Missouri River as far as Musselshell River. They ceded in the treaty all their rights to this territory. Other Piegans and the Blood Indians claimed territory along the summit of the Rocky Mountains south to the Little Blackfoot River, and thence southeast to the Missouri River. In the treaty they ceded all the territory from the mouth of the Marias River up the Marias to the Teton River, following the middle of the stream to its source, for a stipulated sum to be given them for twenty years. The Gros Ventres had no land to cede. The Blackfeet also had no land to cede, and according to the views of many they had no business in this treaty, because they lived in, and claimed to belong to, what they called Red Coat Land, namely, that belonging to King George. Some of them wore King George's medals, and showed that they felt proud of them. All the country east of the Teton River was set apart for a Piegan and Blood reserve. The treaty was concluded by five P. M. All the Indians understood what was wanted of them, and the preliminaries were thus shortened by at least thirty-nine days. The treaty was not satisfactory to all the Indians, but they had to abide by it. Without the influence of some of the mountaineers—who never received any credit for the part they took in bringing it about—that treaty would not have been made at that time.

The next day began the distributing of the goods. It would take the pen of a Mark Twain to describe the scenes that took place. Two days were required to get through this distribution, and the goods that remained and were to be issued to half-breeds were put in my charge, for distribution when the breeds had all arrived.

A DISTRIBUTION OF GOODS TO THE GROS VENTRES

The next morning the commissioners paid me out of the Indian goods for feeding the Indians and for my trip across the country, and I had Jack paid for his time, also from the goods. The commissioners then left for Helena with Agent Gad. E. Upson. He knew as much about an Indian as I did about the inhabitants of Jupiter.

About ten A. M., one hour after the commissioners had left, Little Dog, chief of the South Piegans, came into town and found us. This man was one of the noblest and bravest chiefs living at that day. He was a friend to the whites, and had killed four of the under chiefs of his tribe for warring against the whites. He could muster about two hundred and fifty warriors. When he found me, he told me that the North Piegans, under Mountain Chief, the Bloods, and the Blackfeet, had secured some whiskey and were getting ugly and singing their war-songs. Little Dog advised the whites to remain in their houses. He believed that these northern people would attack the Gros Ventres camp, and might also shoot at the whites. Some Indian women had warned us of the situation just before Little Dog came in. Now the agent had a twelve-pound brass cannon. We put this in a "doby" building which was used as a warehouse, and through the wall knocked a hole about twelve inches in diameter for the muzzle, as well as several port-holes for rifles. There was no one present who knew much about cannons, but we loaded the piece with six pounds of powder rammed tight, twenty pounds of one-ounce balls, and some smaller bullets, for we were determined to have it double-shotted. J. V. Cochran, who lives in Billings, Montana, had charge of the cannon. He was, and is, as game as a war eagle, and if called upon, would have fired the cannon if it had burst in a thousand pieces.

We had rifle-pits dug at different points of vantage, and there were forty-five white men to defend them. At the fort, the Northwest Fur Company had twelve men, all of them in the fort, with the gates locked. No assistance could be expected from them.

I mounted Dick and, with Little Dog and Jack, paid a visit to the Gros Ventres. They had already been warned, had their lodges pitched in a circle, their ponies corralled, and rifle-pits dug all around the village. All the warriors were stripped to the breech-clout, and many of them were painted as demons are supposed to paint. Famasi and Star Robe, the chiefs, met us outside. Little Dog informed them that he would try to prevent the hostiles from attacking them, and advised them not to shoot first if the hostiles came. He declared that he and his people would be their friends, and bidding them good-by, we returned. After looking over the ground and seeing that everything was in order for defence in the town, I went with Little Dog and Jack to the village of the South Piegans. The young men were busy putting their arms in order for action, for they expected a fight. It must be remembered that at this time bad blood existed between many of the North Piegans and the South Piegans, and though things were outwardly peaceful enough, a war between them could easily have been precipitated. Leaving the South Piegans, I rode around to the other villages and notified all the chiefs that they must control their young men, must not permit them to commit any overt act, and must keep them away from the Gros Ventres village, or half of their warriors would be killed. Jack confirmed my assertion, adding much more to it. The chiefs used their utmost endeavor to control their young men, and they partially succeeded with many.

The day after the Indians left the boys joked me about forty-five men going to kill half of fifteen hundred warriors, saying: "Bill had more gall than the devil, and could out-bluff six."

About eleven o'clock five hundred naked warriors in their war regalia, painted and mounted on their best ponies, which were also painted, went down the bottom toward the Gros Ventres village, yelling and uttering their war-cries. The ground fairly trembled under the horses' feet. Every one expected that the fight was on. Little Dog had sixty warriors at the upper end of the town. I remained with him, and we carefully watched the proceedings below, expecting every moment to hear shots. The Indians rode around the Gros Ventres camp, some two hundred yards distant from it. If one shot had been fired by either party, a bloody fight would have followed, as those Indians who were now held back by their chiefs would then have joined their friends. The whites could not have left the town to give assistance to the Gros Ventres, nor could the Gros Ventres leave their village to help the whites. I think that if it had come to the point, Little Dog would have joined the whites. It was believed by many experienced Indian men present that our visit to the Gros Ventres village prevented what might have been a massacre, or at least would have been a hard fight. There were many hot-headed and brave young Gros Ventres, and it may have been that our warning kept them from some rash acts.

Little Dog notified all the hostile bands that if they attacked the whites they would have him to fight. They were all of them afraid of him, and I know that his stand had a moral effect.

The hostiles rode around the Gros Ventres village many times, yelling, calling names, and sending forth challenges to the Gros Ventres to come out and fight; but the Gros Ventres remained quiet in their rifle-pits. I learned afterward that it was all their chiefs could do to keep their young men from accepting the hostiles' challenges to fight. After a great deal of this verbal defiance, the hostiles rode back to their camp on a run, firing off their guns in the air. When opposite the town they halted and formed a half circle and began to sing their war-songs. After the songs a few approached within two hundred yards of the agency building, calling the whites dogs and women, names which were understood. The interpreters were directed to tell the Indians to stop their talk or we would kill them, and presently they rode back to their company, gave a yell of defiance, and left for their villages.

This lull gave us all an opportunity to eat dinner. I took Little Dog, Jack, and three other chiefs with me to dinner, and just as we had finished eating a fearful yell was heard. The chiefs jumped up and mounted quickly, making signs to the whites to remain in the houses. I mounted Dick and went with the chiefs, though many of the men called out to me: "Don't go, sheriff." I had decided what I should do in case of a fight. If the hostiles attacked the town, and Little Dog attacked the hostiles, I would remain with him, for there I would be of more benefit to the town than I would be in the building. If, on the other hand, Little Dog failed to act, I could return to the town.

The yell was given by some one thousand two hundred painted savages, each of whom had tied from five to twenty yards of calico to his horse's tail and started out on a run all over the bottom. Calico of many colors was flying in all directions, and each Indian was trying to make his pony step on the calico tied to the horse next in advance. They were yelling and firing off their guns in every direction. It was a wild orgy, such as neither I nor any one else had

ever beheld, and we had witnessed many a wild
scene. It was something for a Rembrandt or a Remington to paint; the first scene of the kind, and, I
believe, the last, ever seen in the United States.

[A scene somewhat similar to the one described took
place in southern Nebraska in the year 1867 when the
Cheyennes ditched a freight train on the railroad then
being constructed across the continent. The Indians
who took part in the wrecking of this train have told
me how the freight cars were broken open, the goods
taken from them and scattered over the prairie, and
how the young men in sport knotted the ends of
bolts of calico to their horses' tails and then galloped wildly in all directions, the cloth streaming behind them in the wind.]

That night the Gros Ventres, like the Arabs, silently
moved their village, without being discovered by their
enemies. The next morning all the Indians except
Little Dog's band left for the north, to go to their own
country. Before they left two war parties had been
organized to raid upon the miners and ranchmen in
different sections of the Territory. Such was the result of this great treaty.

Before they moved out a few of us visited the Indian
villages. As many Indians were dissatisfied with the
treaty, they looked on us with distrust, and hatred was
plainly visible in their faces and their actions. We
assumed the authority to notify the chiefs that they
must control their young men and keep them from steal-

ing from the whites, or war on them by the whites would continue. In part the treaty was successful. As a whole it was a failure, for a chronic state of warfare continued for years.

INDEX

INDEX

367